Introduction to
Microeconomics

Introduction to Microeconomics

DAVID LAIDLER

University of Western Ontario

SECOND EDITION

Philip Allan

First published 1974 by

PHILIP ALLAN PUBLISHERS LIMITED
MARKET PLACE
DEDDINGTON
OXFORD OX5 4SE

First published 1974
Reprinted 1976, 1977, 1979
Second edition 1981
Reprinted 1982
Reprinted 1985

British Library Cataloguing in Publication Data

Laidler, David E W
    Introduction to microeconomics. – 2nd ed.
    1. Microeconomics
    I. Title
    350   HB171.5

    ISBN 0-86003-003-4
    ISBN 0-86003-131-4 Pbk

Set by MHL Typesetting Limited, Coventry
Printed in Great Britain at The Camelot Press Limited, Southampton

Contents

viii

Preface

PREFACE TO SECOND EDITION

The primary purpose of this second edition of *Introduction to Microeconomics,* like that of the first, is to provide an account of the subject that will be accessible to second year undergraduates taking a single honours degree in economics. The book is still intended to be read slowly and carefully, but in this edition I have reorganised the presentation of the subject matter in order to make it more accessible. There is a little more illustrative material than before, and much more important, chapters are now divided into short, explicitly labelled sections so that readers will have much less trouble finding their way around this edition than they did the first. Moreover, I have added some straightforward numerical exercises to the study questions. A good deal of new material has been incorporated in this edition, particularly on the theory of the firm and those mistakes that I know about in the first edition have been removed.

My colleague James Melvin helped me get certain details of the treatment of returns to scale right this time, and Charles Stuart, now at the University of Lund, offered much helpful advice on the treatment of bilateral monopoly. I am grateful to both of them, as I am to John McInerney of the University of Reading, Michael Sumner of the University of Salford, and Ian Walker of the University of Manchester, who read earlier drafts of this edition and provided a great deal of helpful advice as to how it could be improved. Most of their advice was gratefully accepted and taken, but considerations of space prevented me from following all their suggestions. Thus I alone am to blame for any errors and omissions that the reader might find in this second edition. Finally, I am grateful to Laurie Bland, Terry Caverhill, and Monica Malkus, all of whom coped ably with various stages of the typing of the manuscript.

DAVID LAIDLER
February 1981

PREFACE TO FIRST EDITION

This book is intended primarily to be used by second year undergraduates taking single honours degrees in economics. It pre-supposes that the reader has already had an introductory course with a significant content of elementary microeconomic analysis. The mathematical techniques used are virtually all geometric. However, the student who has had an elementary mathematics course dealing with basic calculus, and hence with such matters as the inter-relationship between functions and their derivatives, the geometric representations of these inter-relationships, as well as with the basic mathematics of constrained maximisation will find the going a lot easier than the reader who has had no exposure to mathematics since GCE ordinary level.

I have not aimed this book specifically at the future specialist in economic theory. Rather, I have tried to present, in one volume, enough microeconomic analysis so that the student who has mastered it will have a background adequate to permit him to take third year applied courses without further specialist study in microeconomics *per se*. Nevertheless, I hope that the future specialist in theory will also find that reading the following pages is helpful. There is probably enough material to keep a second year student busy, but teachers who wish to use it in third year courses are likely to find it a little thin. However, suitably supplemented with references to journal articles and other books, it could be used at the third year level. The suggestions for further reading attached to the text are primarily intended for use at this level, and they often extend, rather than repeat, the subject matter which I have specifically treated. This is particularly so in the case of the theory of the firm, where I have confined my exposition to dealing with the single product neo-classical profit maximising enterprise. Industrial organisation is now so frequently taught as a subject in its own right at the undergraduate level that it seemed wise to avoid producing, in a couple of chapters on alternative theories of the firm, an inevitably inadequate duplication of the subject matter of a fully fledged course in the area. The same may be said of the analysis of labour markets, for here I have left questions of human capital, trade union behaviour and such to be dealt with in a specialist course in labour economics.

Microeconomics is at least as much a way of thinking about problems as it is a coherent body of substantive hypotheses and one does not learn how to think along certain lines without actually doing so. Some microeconomics can be learned by reading about it, but the area can only be mastered by actually doing microeconomic analysis for oneself. With this in mind, I have attempted to pitch my exposition at a level which will force the average reader to work quite hard at mastering the arguments presented. I have also set study questions which sometimes extend the analysis covered in the text rather than call for its mere reproduction. In short, I hope that the reader will find himself involved in a process of 'learning by doing' as he works his way through.

I began writing this book while on a term's leave at Brown University in Providence, Rhode Island, and owe a considerable debt to some of my colleagues there. George Borts, James Hanson, John Kennan, and Mark Shupak all had their brains picked more often than they realised, while I owe special thanks to Allan Feldman who read and commented on an early version of Part I. At Manchester, John McInerney and Michael Sumner read and commented copiously on a first draft of the whole book, placing me considerably in their debt by so doing. Mrs Coral Parrett and Mrs Vicky Whelan coped most patiently with the tedious process of typing and retyping the manuscript, while Mrs Marjorie Watts drafted the many diagrams. I am extremely grateful to all three. I would dearly like to implicate everyone I have named in any errors and omissions that the reader might find in the analysis that follows; I can find no sound reason for doing so and am forced, therefore, to accept sole responsibility.

D.L.
February 1974

1
Introduction

Started book beginning of June 1986

Scarcity and Economics

Economics is about scarcity. The word 'scarcity' is used here in a special sense: it refers to a state of affairs in which, given the wants of a society at any particular moment, the means available to satisfy them are not sufficient. If all desires cannot be totally satisfied, then choices have to be made as to which of them are going to be satisfied, and to what extent. To say that economics is about scarcity then is also to say that it is about choice. There is no suggestion here that the scope of the subject is confined to purely material matters, such as the production and distribution of those goods and services that happen to make up such statistical magnitudes as the gross national product. Economics is relevant here to be sure, but its scope is potentially much wider. Any social or private situation which involves a choice of some sort has an economic aspect.

At any time the individuals making up a particular society will desire a wide variety of items – food, clothing, housing, holidays, recreation, access to countryside and seashore, to music, to art, to sporting events, to educational facilities and so on – but the means available to provide all these are

1

limited. The population is of a given size, and possesses a particular mix of skills; a certain given level of technology and mix of capital equipment are available (to say nothing of given amounts of open space and seashore). Thus not everyone can have all that he desires of everything. For any one individual to have more of one thing, he must either have less of another thing, or someone else must have less of something.

The scope of the scarcity problem as it faces society is enormous and complex. Given available resources it must somehow be decided how they are to be used, which goods are to be produced and in what amounts. It must also be decided how the resulting output is to be distributed among the individuals that make up society. Moreover, though at one moment it makes sense to treat resources as given, these can be changed over time both in quality and quantity by devoting part of current output to this end. The provision of productive resources for the future, then, is yet another one of the competing ends to which current production can be devoted. In addition, there is the problem of so organising matters that, at any time, the scarce resources that are available do not lie idle but do, in fact, get used. Thus, questions about the allocation of resources, the distribution of income, economic growth, and the maintenance of full employment are all economic problems, for they all arise from the fact of scarcity. If all wants could be satisfied simultaneously, it would not matter how resources were used, how income was distributed, how the balance was struck between the satisfaction of present and future wants or the extent to which particular resources were utilised.

Different societies organise themselves in different ways to cope with these problems. Capitalist societies invest individuals with property rights in particular productive resources and then allow them to use those resources as they see fit. From the interaction of individual decisions a social solution to the scarcity problem emerges, a solution not in the sense that the problem vanishes, but in the sense that a particular level and pattern of output and resource use emerges, along with a particular distribution of income. A socialist economy deals with the same problem by investing the state rather than individuals with property rights in resources and then attempting to formulate a coherent and consistent plan for their use. Again a solution to the problem is achieved.

It is not only at the social level that scarcity exists and choices have to be made. Individual economic agents face the problem too. Such agents may be individuals, families, capitalist firms, co-operative enterprises or government departments, but all are faced with choices about the use of the scarce resources available to them. An individual or a family must allocate its time between work and leisure, while bearing in mind that the income realised from work is available for the purchase of the various goods and services which it may want to consume. A firm, be it a capitalist enterprise concerned only with its own profits, or some kind of socialist co-operative consciously seeking to contribute to the achievement of socially determined goals, does not have an inexhaustible supply of inputs available to it, nor will it be able to engage in the production of every conceivable output. Somehow it must be decided what goods are to be produced by the enterprise and at what scale, utilising what inputs with what technical processes. A government department in charge of, shall we say, providing education, does not have inexhaustible funds at its disposal. Somehow the resources available to it must be divided between nursery schools, primary education, secondary education and higher education.

The problems facing individual agents are particular manifestations of the general social problem. The responses of individual agents are interdependent and contribute to the solution of the scarcity problem at the social level. In any planned economy there is still a large area of choice left open to individuals; perhaps the most difficult problem facing any planning bureau is to provide the incentives and instructions to individual agents that will ensure that the choices which they then make will be consistent with the overall plan laid down for the use of the resources available to society. In a capitalist economy the related problem arises as to whether the means by which individuals' choices are linked together and impinge upon each other, the system of contracts and market transactions, are such as to ensure that the plans of all individuals are compatible with one another and with the overall availability of resources.

An Outline of the Book

Quite clearly it is impossible to come to grips with questions such as these without knowing a great deal about the behaviour of individual agents. If one wishes to argue that capitalism results in a satisfactory state of affairs - having, of course, carefully explained what is meant by that deceptively simple word 'satisfactory' in the first place — one must know how individuals behave. But individual behaviour is not just a problem for the apologist for capitalism. As has already been argued, to devise a plan for a socialist economy that will actually work requires that individual agents, whether as workers or consumers, must be persuaded to behave in a manner compatible with that plan. Thus, a knowledge of how individual agents react to particular instructions or incentives must be basic to any kind of planning exercise. Microeconomics is particularly concerned with the behaviour of individual economic agents. Much of this book is concerned with their behaviour towards problems as they arise in capitalist economies, and the author makes no apology for that since this book is intended for readers who live in that kind of economic system. Nevertheless, a good deal of the analysis that follows is of much broader application, as the reader will easily discern for himself.

First, we are going to deal with the behaviour of the individual consumer as he faces his own version of the scarcity problem — how to allocate a given income between the various goods available to him. We are going to see how he reacts to changes in his income and the prices of those goods and see what we may say about the way such changes affect his economic wellbeing. Moreover, the same analysis developed to deal with current expenditure decisions can be modified to deal with the question of the determinants of saving behaviour, and choices involving hours of work. These problems will also be discussed, as will certain aspects of choice when the outcomes of particular courses of action are uncertain. We shall outline a new approach to consumer theory which pays particular attention to the complexity of so many modern goods and services and to the existence of differences between different brands of what are basically the same good.

Second, we shall examine the question of production, in particular in a capitalist economy. We shall mainly deal with the theory of the profit maximising firm and the principles governing the choices it makes about levels of output, levels of factor utilisation and pricing in the markets for both factors and outputs. We shall also touch upon the analysis of a firm that pursues a goal other than profit, the maximisation of sales revenue, and as the reader will discover the analysis here has a great deal in common with the theory of the profit maximising firm. The latter is worth close attention, not because it is the only available approach to the problem, but because it is perhaps the most fully developed analysis of the behaviour of business enterprises and also because it provides a set of predictions about behaviour with which the predictions of other approaches may be compared.

Third, we shall discuss the problems of coordinating the choices of firms and consumers in a brief account of general equilibrium analysis. We shall outline the conditions which must hold if the behaviour of firms and households are to be consistent with one another and with the overall resource constraint on the economy. We will pose the question of whether we can say anything about the desirability of the resulting solution to the scarcity problem, being careful to note those conditions which might hold in an abstract model of capitalist market economy but are unlikely to hold in any actual economy. The problems here are complex and we can only note them at this stage. First, because individuals own resources and obtain their incomes by selling the use of those resources, a particular income distribution is implied by any solution to the allocation problem: does this influence the judgments that we may make about the desirability of a particular allocative scheme? Second, what about the allocation of resources towards satisfying those wants which are not always brought into the range of ordinary market transactions — access to the recreational facilities afforded by a river, for example? How does a capitalist economy deal, or fail to deal, with such problems? The discussion of these and related issues takes up the final section of this book.

Part I
Elements of the Theory of Consumer Behaviour

2
The Basic Theory of Consumer Choice

Introduction

Economics is about scarcity, about social situations which require that choices be made. The theory of consumer behaviour deals with the way in which scarcity impinges upon the individual consumer and hence deals with the way in which such an individual makes choices. This consumer need not, of course, be an individual person. He may be, but the theory is of potentially broader application. Families and households also make collective consumption choices on behalf of their members. The theory as we shall present it takes the consumer unit as given. It therefore presents us with an important instance of how other social sciences, such as sociology and social psychology which deal, in part, with the way in which people organise themselves into household and other units, could complement economics.

The theory of consumer choice has many applications. It enables us to deal with the selection of consumption patterns at a particular time and the allocation of consumption over time, and hence with saving. The individual supplying labour can be thought of as choosing the amount of leisure time available to him, so the same theory is relevant there as it is when we come to consider behaviour in the face of risk. Moreover, in constructing a theory to deal with problems such as these, we are forced to think carefully about and to define precisely such much abused terms as 'real income' and the 'cost of living', so that our theory gives us many valuable insights into matters of potentially considerable practical importance. We shall deal with all these matters, and more, in the chapters that follow, but first we must build up a language of analysis, a general framework in terms of which all these apparently diverse matters can be reduced to their common elements. Three factors are involved in constructing the elementary theory of consumer choice. First, we must consider the items which the consumer finds desirable, the *objects of choice*. Second, since the desirability of an object does not necessarily imply that it is available to be chosen, we must consider any limitations that might be placed on the alternatives available to the consumer, the *constraints upon his choice*. Finally, because choice necessarily involves a process of selection among alternatives, we must consider the way in which the consumer ranks the alternatives available to him, his *tastes* or *preferences*.

The Objects of Choice and the Budget Constraint

The objects of the consumer's choice are goods and services. In the most general case we may consider patterns of consumption at each particular moment in time and over time. To keep things simple we will now confine ourselves to the choice facing an individual at a particular time, ignoring for the moment the problem of allocating consumption over time. We will also simplify the world by assuming that it contains only two goods, X and Y. This abstraction from a world with many goods to one with two is not quite so restrictive as might appear at first sight, for it is always possible to think of X as being one particular good and Y as being a composite bundle of all other goods.

Now consider figure 2.1. On the horizontal axis we measure quantities of X per unit of time, let us say per week, and on the vertical axis quantities of Y per week. Any point in the area bounded by these two axes may be interpreted as a pattern of consumption involving a particular mixture of X and Y per week. Thus the point on the X-axis at 5 X

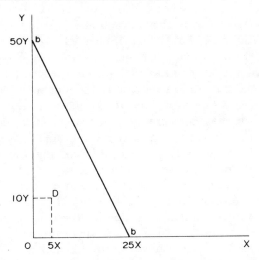

Figure 2.1 Each point of the diagram represents a bundle of goods. The point D represents a bundle made up of $5X$ and $10Y$. The line bb is a budget constraint drawn on the assumption that a consumer has an income of £50 and faces prices for X and Y of £2 and £1 respectively. The budget constraint divides those bundles of goods that the consumer can obtain, given his income and their prices, from those that he cannot.

represents a consumption pattern of $5\,X$ and no Y per week, the point D represents consumption of $5\,X$, $10\,Y$ per week, and so on. In short, the objects of choice in this particular simplification of the theory of consumer choice are consumption patterns measured in terms of bundles of goods per week and each such bundle is represented by a particular point on a diagram such as figure 2.1.

Now, in principle, we may extend the axes of figure 2.1 indefinitely and hence encompass any conceivable bundle of X and Y, but this does not mean that the consumer is in fact able to select any bundle of X and Y which he finds desirable. Goods and services are generally not free and what a consumer can get at a particular moment is limited by the purchasing power then at his disposal. Suppose, for simplicity, that his only source of purchasing power was his present income. This may be expressed as a certain sum of money per week and it puts an upper limit on his consumption. We may represent this in figure 2.1 in the following way.

X and Y are goods that have prices and it is reasonable enough to suppose that these prices may be taken as constant as far as the individual consumer is concerned. Suppose that the price of X is £2 per unit and that of Y £1 per unit. Suppose also that the consumer's income is £50 per week. Then it is obvious that, if he devotes all of his income to the consumption of X, he may consume not more than 25 units of X per week; alternatively he may consume 50 units of Y per week. However, there is nothing to stop him mixing X and Y in his consumption pattern. We can calculate how much he spends on any particular quantity (less than 25) of X, and this sum subtracted from income gives the amount left over to be spent on Y. This amount divided by the price of Y tells us the maximum amount of Y that can be bought, given the quantity of X. If we carry out this calculation for every quantity of X between 0 and 25 and link up the resulting bundles of goods we derive the line bb in figure 2.1 which represents the consumer's so-called *budget constraint*. This line separates all those consumption bundles that our consumer can afford to buy from those that he cannot afford. Given the prices we have assumed, it is clear that for every unit of X given up, two units of Y may be substituted. Hence the slope of this constraint is obviously the inverse of the ratio of the prices we have assumed. If X costs £2 and Y £1, then the ratio of the price of Y to the price of X is 1/2 and the rate at which Y may be substituted for X is 2/1.

The Consumer's Tastes

We make two basic assumptions about our consumer's tastes. First, we assume he is able to compare any two bundles of goods. He can decide whether he prefers bundle 1 or 2 or is indifferent between them. Second, we assume that he makes these comparisons in a consistent fashion. By that we mean that if in comparing bundles 1 and 2 he finds 1 to be preferable, and if in comparing 2 with a third bundle he prefers 2, then on comparing 1 and 3 he will decide that he prefers 1.

This assumption that he has consistent preferences is all that economists imply when they speak of the consumer being 'rational'. However, in constructing the elementary theory of choice, it is usual to make certain subsidiary assumptions in addition to the basic one of consistent preferences. First, having already assumed that the objects of choice are desirable, it is but a small step to the proposition that, when compared with D (the point in figure 2.1 representing $5X$ and $10Y$) any bundle that has either more X and no less Y or more Y and no less X will be preferred. In terms of figure 2.2 this means that any point in the shaded area above and to the right of D will be preferred to D, and that D will be preferred to any point in the area below and to the left.

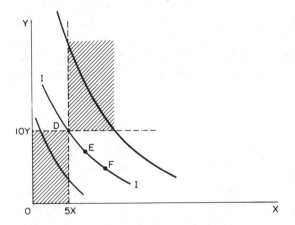

Figure 2.2 The indifference map. Any point in the area above and to the right of D represents a bundle of goods preferred to D; D is preferred to any point below and to its left. Thus the indifference curve $I\,I$ passing through D must have a negative slope. It is generally assumed that such curves are convex to the origin.

It follows from this that if D is one of a set of bundles of goods between which the consumer is indifferent, such bundles must lie in the areas below and to the right of D and above and to the left of D. It is usual to go further than this and argue that all such points must lie on a continuous negatively sloped line, an *indifference curve* such as the line II in figure 2.2, a curve that is convex towards the origin. A smooth convex curve is by no means the only formulation of an indifference curve compatible with the assumption of rationality, but it is both intuitively plausible and, as we shall see below, productive of sensible predictions about behaviour. This particular shape involves what is called a *diminishing marginal rate of substitution* between the goods. This shape implies that the more X there is relative to Y in the bundle to begin with, the more X is required to compensate the consumer for the loss of a given amount of Y. Thus, in figure 2.2 the movement from E to F involves the same loss of Y as that from D to E, but requires a larger gain in X to keep our consumer on the same indifference curve. The *marginal rate of substitution* of X for Y is the ratio of the amount of X needed to compensate for a small (in the limit infinitesimal) loss of Y to that loss of Y. It is given by the slope of the indifference curve, which is negative, becoming more negative (i.e. *diminishing*) as we move down the curve from left to right.

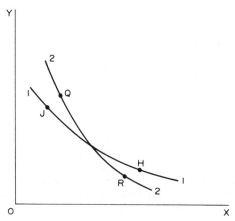

Figure 2.3 Indifference curves that cross are incompatible with the assumption that consumers order bundles of goods consistently.

Now II is a particular indifference curve. We may think of the consumption of any bundle of goods on it as yielding a particular level of satisfaction, or *utility*, to the consumer. However there are indifference curves passing through every point on figure 2.2, each one negatively sloped and each one convex to the origin. Those which pass through points above and to the right of *D* link up bundles of goods that yield higher levels of satisfaction than those on *II*; those below and to the left yield lower levels of satisfaction. Such curves can never cross one another, for this would violate the rationality assumption. Consider figure 2.3 in which two indifference curves have been drawn to cross and consider their interpretation. The consumer is indifferent between points *H* and *J* on curve 1 and between *R* and *Q* on curve 2. However, bundle *H* has more of both *X* and *Y* than does *R* and hence must be preferred to it; for exactly the same reason, point *Q* must be preferred to *J*. There is clearly an inconsistency here that violates the rationality assumption, and it obviously arises because the curves cross one another.

The Solution to the Choice Problem

We now have all the ingredients necessary for the solution of the consumer's choice problem. We have defined the objects of choice. These are bundles of goods, *consumption patterns,* made up of various quantities of *X* and *Y*. We have also derived the constraint upon the consumer's choice. His money income combined with the prices of *X* and *Y* have enabled us to draw a line, a *budget constraint,* that separates those bundles of *X* and *Y* that are attainable from those that are not. Finally, we have characterised the consumer's tastes in an *indifference map* showing how his satisfaction (*utility*) varies with (*is a function of*) his consumption pattern. This *utility function* has two basic properties. Each indifference curve is convex to the origin, and as we move upwards and to the right the indifference curves represent higher and higher levels of satisfaction. In figure 2.4 we bring these three ingredients together, and the solution to the consumer's choice problem immediately appears.

The consumer wishes to do as well as he can for himself, to select that consumption pattern out of all those available to him that will yield the highest possible level of satisfaction — he wishes to *maximise his utility.* In terms of figure 2.4

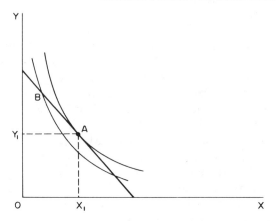

Figure 2.4 *A* is the bundle of goods which, of all those available, yields the consumer the highest level of satisfaction. This maximum satisfaction bundle occurs where an indifference curve is tangent to the budget constraint.

this involves selecting a consumption pattern on as high an indifference curve as possible. Clearly that pattern is given by the point *A* with the consumer getting X_1 of X per week and Y_1 of Y.

Consider the properties of this solution which we call a situation of *equilibrium* for the consumer because there are no forces that would make him move away from *A*. First, the point *A* lies *on* the budget constraint, not inside it. This happens because we have assumed that, when compared to any particular bundle of goods, a bundle with more of one good and no less of another is preferred. For any consumption pattern within the budget constraint, there is at least one on the constraint with just this property. Does this then mean that the analysis of consumer choice rules out saving? It does not, for, as we shall see below, it is possible to characterise saving as an act of devoting current income to future consumption. For our analysis, we made the simplifying assumption that we would not for the time being consider the choice of consumption patterns over time. Hence we have ruled out saving here for the sake of simplicity, not predicted that it cannot take place.

The second point to note about the solution depicted in

figure 2.4 is that at A an indifference curve is just tangent to the budget constraint. As the reader will discover, such tangency solutions continuously occur in geometric representations of economic theory. The slope of the budget constraint tells us, as we saw above, the rate at which our consumer is permitted to substitute X for Y by the structure of prices. For every amount of Y he gives up he gets some amount of X. The slope is equal to the ratio of the price of Y to that of X. The slope of an indifference curve at any particular point tells us the rate at which he would have to substitute X for Y in order to maintain himself at a given level of satisfaction, or to enjoy a constant level of utility. This slope is, of course, the marginal rate of substitution of X for Y. Thus we may charcterise a point of tangency between an indifference curve and a budget constraint as a situation in which the marginal rate of substitution of X for Y is just equal to the ratio of the price of Y to the price of X.

That A is indeed a point of maximum satisfaction, or maximum utility, can be seen in another way. Consider the point B in figure 2.4. Suppose the consumer found himself at this point for some reason. His income and the set of prices facing him would enable him to get more X for a particular sacrifice of Y than is necessary to keep him on the indifference curve that passes through B. Thus, by substituting X for Y along the budget constraint he can move on to higher and higher indifference curves; until, that is, he comes to A. As he moves from B towards A, Y becomes progressively more valuable to him relative to X and the rate at which he is willing to give up Y in return for X falls. At A the rate at which he is willing to give up Y to get X coincides with the rate at which the price structure permits him to do so. Any movement to the right of A would involve having to give up more Y than is required by the maintenance of a particular level of utility, so further substitution will not be made.

To sum up then, the utility maximising choice involves selecting the bundle of goods where the budget constraint and the indifference curve touch tangentially. At this point both have the same slope and we can say that the rate at which the consumer is willing to substitute X for Y to maintain constant utility is equal to the ratio of the price of Y to that of X.

3/6/86

Income-Consumption and Price-Consumption Relationships

Finding an equilibrium consumption bundle is the starting point of the theory of consumer choice; it is not its end point. We wish to use this analysis to derive predictions about behaviour. We wish to be able to say how the composition of the bundle of goods an individual chooses will change when the observable variables that underlie the budget constraint change in value. There are three such variables: the consumer's income, the price of X and the price of Y.

A different level of income, with the prices of X and Y remaining the same, does not imply a different slope for the budget constraint. This slope tells us the rate at which X may be substituted for Y and, as we have seen, depends only upon the ratio of the two prices. However, a different level of income does involve a different location for the budget constraint. The higher the income, the further up and to the right does the budget constraint lie, for the more bundles of goods can the consumer afford.

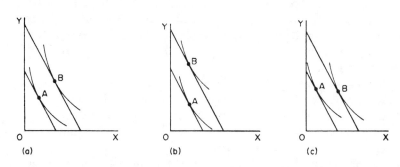

Figure 2.5 As the consumer's income increases he moves from A to B. In panel (a) this movement involves an increase in the consumption of both goods: they are both normal. In panel (b) consumption of X falls: it is an inferior good, but Y is normal. In panel (c), X is normal and Y is inferior.

There is very little that can be said in general about the consequences for consumption of different levels of income. At higher levels of income the chosen consumption pattern may include more of both X and Y, more X and less Y, or more Y and less X. Any one of these solutions is compatible with an indifference map of the general form we have been assuming, as is apparent from figure 2.5. All we can do is give labels to the possibilities. Thus, if the quantity of a good consumed falls as income increases, we call that good an *inferior* good. If it rises, we call it a *normal* (or sometimes a *superior*) good. There is no reason why a good must always be in one category or another. We can easily conceive of a good being normal at low levels of income and becoming inferior at higher levels. In figure 2.6 we consider a variety of income levels in combination with a particular indifference map, and, linking up the points of tangency along what is called an *income consumption curve*, depict just such a case for the commodity X.

Now the analysis carried out so far has been of the behaviour of a consumer at a particular time and figure 2.6 shows what consumption patterns would be selected at different levels of income *at that time*. This is *not* necessarily the same

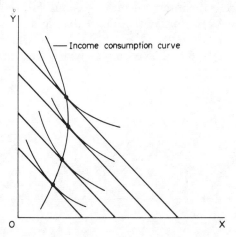

Figure 2.6 An income consumption curve. As it is drawn, Y is everywhere normal. X is normal at low levels of income, but becomes inferior at high levels.

thing as indicating how his consumption pattern will change *over time* as his income changes *over time.* However, it is precisely the ability to make predictions about such changes that we seek from economic theory. If we are willing to assume that tastes remain stable over time, in other words that the indifference map does not change, and that there are no factors involved *in the movement* from one preferred consumption pattern to another that influence the consumption pattern being aimed at — and we will meet cases below where this particular assumption is inappropriate — we may treat the income consumption curve as telling us how the consumer's consumption pattern will respond to changes in income over time.

In addition to the income consumption curve, we may derive *price consumption curves,* one for variations in the price of X and the other for variations in the price of Y. Since the analysis is the same for each we need only explicitly consider varying the price of X while holding the price of Y and money income constant. Clearly, when the price of X varies the point at which the budget constraint cuts the Y-axis is unchanged, since this represents the amount of Y that can be bought when all income is devoted to its purchase. What does change is the intercept on the X-axis and the slope of the constraint. As the price of X increases, less X can be bought for the same money and so the point at which the budget constraint cuts the X-axis moves nearer the origin and the

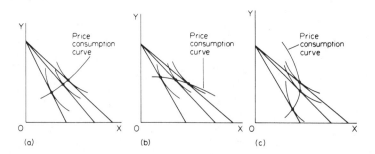

Figure 2.7 As the price of X falls the consumer moves along a price consumption curve. X and Y are complements in panel (a) and substitutes in panel (b), while X becomes a 'Giffen' good in panel (c).

slope becomes steeper. At the same time, the slope of the budget constraint is given by the ratio of prices of X to that of Y. Raising the price of X increases this ratio and hence the slope of the constraint.

For every price of X there is a preferred consumption bundle and the points representing these may be linked up into a price consumption curve. Figure 2.7 shows three possible situations, all compatible with our assumptions. There is again, little to be said about the shape of the curve, but note that the possibility depicted in panel (c), where over a certain range the quantity of X consumed actually falls as the price of X falls, is more an analytic curiosity than a practically relevant case. It is known as the *Giffen case* after the economist who first noticed the possibility of such behaviour. In panel (b) we have the quantity of Y consumed falling as the price of X declines, while in panel (a) we have a case in which the quantity of both X and Y consumed rises as the price of X declines. In the first of these cases X and Y are termed *substitutes* and in the second *complements*, for obvious reasons.*

The Income Effect and the Substitution Effect

The shape of the price consumption curve for a given level of income and given price of Y obviously depends upon the precise form of the indifference map, and the same can be said of the shape of the income consumption curve at a giveri set of relative prices. This apparently innocuous observation leads us directly to the next step of our analysis, for it points to the *interdependence of the effects of income changes and price changes upon consumption*. Consider figure 2.8 with

---

* As the student who reads on will discover, the possibility of complementarity can only arise in a two-good world such as we have here, because of an income effect. If we abstract from the income effect, then with normally shaped indifference curves, in a two-good world, the goods in question can only be substitutes. Possibilities for complementarity that do not hinge on an income effect do re-emerge however when there are more than two goods.

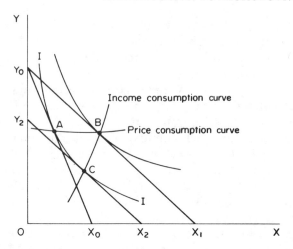

Figure 2.8 A movement along a price consumption curve from A to B may be broken down into a substitution effect around an indifference curve (from A to C) and income effect along an income consumption curve (from C to B).

the consumer initially in equilibrium at A on a budget constraint given by the line joining X_0 and Y_0. Now let the price of X fall so that the budget constraint pivots on the Y-axis and becomes $Y_0 X_1$; the consumption pattern moves to B.

This is, of course, a movement along a price consumption curve. However, B is also a point on an income consumption curve and there is another point on that same income consumption curve at C where a budget constraint, $Y_2 X_2$, having the same slope as $Y_0 X_1$ is tangent to the indifference curve II. This is the indifference curve on which A also lies. The movement along the price consumption curve from A to B may be looked upon as being made up of a movement around a particular indifference curve from A to C and one along an income consumption curve from C to B. The first component of this change is termed the *substitution effect* and the second the *income effect*.

It should be obvious that the substitution effect of a fall in the price of X always involves a movement round an indifference curve to a point below and to the right of A. A *negative* price change leads to a *positive* change in quantity demanded as far as the substitution effect is concerned and this effect is thus said to be *negative* in sign. This must always be the case so long as indifference curves are convex to the origin. The further to the right we move on any given curve, the more shallowly sloped it is. When the price of X falls, we find the point to which the substitution effect takes us by moving to a point at which the indifference curve on which the initial equilibrium bundle is located slopes more shallowly. This must be below and to the right of this initial bundle.

The sign of the income effect depends upon whether or not X is a normal good. If it is, then the *positive* change in income implicit in the fall in the price of X will lead to a *positive* change in the quantity of X demanded. Thus the income effect will be *positive*. This will accentuate the tendency, already implicit in the substitution effect, for the quantity of X demanded to increase as its price falls. If, on the other hand, X is an inferior good, the income effect will be *negative* and will tend to offset the substitution effect since it will work in the opposite direction. Though there is no necessity that this must happen, it is logically possible that a negative income effect could more than offset a negative substitution effect and lead to a fall in the quantity of X demanded as its price falls. This would give us the backward bending price consumption curve of figure 2.7(c), the Giffen good case. We can now see that a Giffen good *must* be an inferior good, but there is of course no necessity that an inferior good be a Giffen good.

The Engel Curve and the Demand Curve

Now from the foregoing analysis we may derive the *Engel curve* and the *demand curve* for X. The Engel curve shows the relationship between a consumer's income and the quantity of a good that he buys. Figure 2.9 gives an example of the derivation of such a curve, and should be self explanatory. The slope of the Engel curve at any point is known as the *marginal propensity to consume X* and measures, for a small change (in the limiting case an infinitesimal change) in income, the ratio of the resulting change in the consumption of the

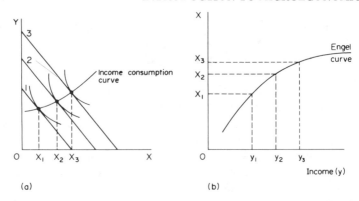

Figure 2.9 Increases are income (from y_1 to y_2 to y_3) shift out the budget constraint in panel (a) (from 1 to 2 to 3). From the income consumption curve we read off the associated levels of consumption of X (X_1, X_2, and X_3). We plot these against income in panel (b) to generate the Engel curve.

good to that change in income. We may also define the *average propensity to consume* the good as the ratio of the quantity of it bought at any particular level of income to that level of income, or equivalently, given the good's price, as the proportion of income devoted to buying it. The ratio of the marginal propensity to consume the good to the average propensity to consume it is defined as the *income elasticity of demand* for the good, and measures the proportional change in the consumption of the good as a ratio to the *proportional* change in income that causes the variation.

Some extremely simple algebra makes this obvious enough. Let us use the symbol y for income and the symbol δ to mean a 'small change in'*. It should be clear that the marginal propensity to consume can be written algebraically as $\delta X/\delta y$. Equally clearly, the average propensity to consume X is X/y.

---

* The reader will notice that we are here using a lower case y to stand for income and upper case Y to stand for all other goods. So long as we are dealing with the demand for X, holding the price of all other goods constant, the level of money income and the maximum amount of all other goods that can be bought with money income — the point at which the budget constraint cuts the Y vertical axis — move in perfect harmony with each other. The two differ only in units of measurement. Indeed, it is possible to define arbitrarily the

The ratio of the marginal propensity to consume X to the average propensity may then be rearranged as follows to give the ratio of a proportional change in the quantity of X demanded to a proportional change in income, the income elasticity of demand for X:

$$\frac{\delta X/\delta y}{X/y} = \frac{\delta X}{X} \bigg/ \frac{\delta y}{y}$$

Obviously an inferior good, for which the marginal propensity to consume is negative, also has a negative income elasticity of demand, while one for which the marginal propensity to consume is positive, but lower than the average propensity to consume, has an income elasticity of demand betwen 0 and 1. The proportion of income spent on such a good falls as income increases. Exactly the opposite holds true for a good whose income elasticity of demand is greater than unity.

The demand curve which relates the quantity of X demanded to the price of X is just as easily derived; this is done in figure 2.10 for the usual case of a non-Giffen good so that the curve is negatively sloped. Here too there is an elasticity concept to be explained. The inverse slope of the curve, $\delta X/\delta P$, divided by the ratio of quantity demanded to price, X/P gives us the *price elasticity of demand* for the good. This measures the ratio of a proportional change in the quantity demanded of the good to the proportional change in price that brought it about. In symbols we have

$$\frac{\delta X/\delta P}{X/P} = \frac{\delta X}{X} \bigg/ \frac{\delta P}{P}$$

The price elasticity of demand is negative, because the demand curve is downward sloping, i.e. $\delta X/\delta P$ is negative.

---

units in terms of which quantities of all other goods are measured so that one unit of money income buys one unit of all other goods. The reader will find that a good deal of the literature on demand theory uses the symbol Y to stand interchangeably for both money income and quantities of other goods. I have used upper and lower cases of the letter here to distinguish between the two concepts while at the same time reminding the reader that variations in the two quantities are intimately related to one another.

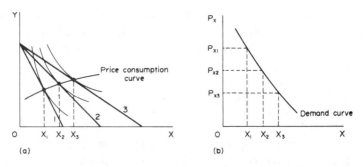

Figure 2.10 As the price of X falls (from P_{x1} to P_{x2} to P_{x3}) the budget constraint in panel (a) shifts (from 1 to 2 to 3). From the price consumption curve we read off the associated quantities of X demanded (X_1, X_2 and X_3) and plot these against the price of X in panel (b), thus generating a demand curve. Here we hold money income and the price of Y constant.

However, we often neglect the sign of this parameter in discussing it and talk in terms of its absolute value. There is a relationship between the magnitude of the price elasticity and the volume of expenditure on a good. If the absolute value of the price elasticity of demand for a good is equal to one, then expenditure on the good does not change as its price changes. The effect on expenditure of a lower price is just offset by the higher quantity bought. If the absolute value is greater than one, then the increase in quantity bought more than offsets the influence of the fall in price and expenditure increases, while the opposite holds true when elasticity is less than one.

Finally, it should be noted that there is a third elasticity concept in demand theory: the *cross elasticity of demand*. This measures the responsiveness of the quantity of X demanded to changes in the price of Y (or *vice versa*). Thus, the cross elasticity of demand for X with respect to P_Y, the price of Y, is given by,

$$\frac{\delta X/\delta P_Y}{X/P_Y} = \frac{\delta X}{X} \bigg/ \frac{\delta P_Y}{P_Y}$$

The sign of this elasticity will be positive if the goods are substitutes and negative if they are complements, as the reader may readily verify for himself by considering the direction of consumption changes in response to price changes in the two different cases.

Concluding Comment

This chapter has largely been devoted to setting out a framework of analysis and defining concepts. These concepts will turn up time and time again throughout this book and the reader will see that mastering them has not been an end in itself but simply a necessary precondition for apply micro-economic analysis to what it is hoped he will find interesting and relevant problems. We will not use every idea developed in this chapter in each of the chapters that follows, but all of them will be used again somewhere.

5/6/86

3
Further Analysis of the Demand Curve and Some Applications

Introduction

This chapter is devoted to that most common of all analytic devices, the demand curve, and in particular to questions involving what we mean when we derive a demand curve 'holding the consumer's income constant'. These questions will lead us to deal with notions such as real income and the cost of living. As the reader will see, the analysis, presented in the preceding chapter, of income and substitution effects, provides the main foundation for our discussion of these matters.

Factors Causing Shifts of the Curve

The demand curve derived towards the end of the previous chapter shows the relationship between the quantity of X demanded and the price of X, given the price of Y and given the consumer's money income. It follows immediately that any change in either of the latter two variables will cause the whole curve to shift. In figure 3.1, A represents a particular equilibrium at a particular level of income and set of prices. Associated with A is a particular point on the demand curve for X.

Suppose income increased by a certain proportion. The

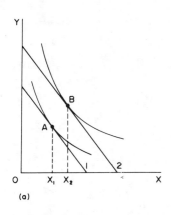
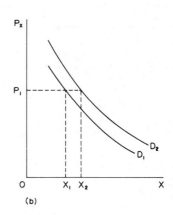

(a)   (b)

Figure 3.1 For a given price of Y and a given price of X (P_1), an increase
in income shifts the budget constraint out from 1 to 2 in panel (a). The
consumer's equilibrium shifts from A to B and if X is a normal good,
the quantity of it demanded at P_1 increases (from X_1 to X_2). This
experiment could be repeated for any price of X and hence panel (b)
shows the whole demand curve shifting to the right from D_1 to D_2.

consumer's equilibrium would shift to B. The indifference
map is drawn so that X and Y are normal goods and so, at
the higher income level, the consumer buys more X. Thus,
with no change in the price of X the quantity demanded has
increased. We can carry out this analysis for any point of the
demand curve for X, and thereby show that, for a normal
good, an increase in income shifts the demand curve to the
right. The reader should himself carry out the analysis that
would show that an increase in income shifts the demand
curve for an inferior good to the left.

Now let us analyse the effect of a change in the price of Y.
In figure 3.2 the indifference map is drawn in such a way that
X and Y are substitutes. Thus, if we again start at A, we see
that a fall in the price of Y shifts the consumer to a new
equilibrium at which, with the same level of money income
and the same price of X, less X is purchased. Once more this
analysis could be carried out for each point on the demand
curve for X and we can say that a fall in the price of Y, where
Y is a substitute for X, causes the demand curve for X to shift
to the left. Clearly, were X and Y complements, the shift

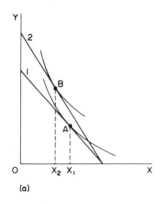
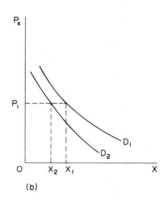

Figure 3.2 For a given level of money income and price of X (P_1), a fall in the price of Y shifts the budget constraint from 1 to 2 in panel (a). The consumer's equilibrium shifts from A to B and if X and Y are substitutes, the quantity of X demanded falls from X_1 to X_2. This experiment could be repeated for any price of X; hence in panel (b) the whole demand curve for X shifts to the left from D_1 to D_2.

would instead be to the right as the reader should demonstrate for himself.

Money Income and Real Income

Consider the following variation on the type of exercise we have just been carrying out. Suppose that there was a drop in the price of Y by a certain percentage, followed by a fall of the same percentage in the price of X. The combined effect of these two changes would be exactly the same as that of an increase of equal proportion in income if the two prices were constant. This is yet another example of the interconnectedness of price and income effects in demand theory, and it should prompt us to look more closely at the nature of the demand curve with which we have so far been dealing, particularly with regard to the income concept that underlies it.

The demand curve in question is derived holding *money income* and the price of Y constant. As we move along the curve to lower and lower prices of X, we are also, in terms of an indifference curve diagram, moving to higher and higher levels of utility, to higher and higher levels of what we might call *real income*. Apparently, in order to make an individual better off, all that we need to do is lower the price of one good to him. Does it follow, therefore, that we could increase the living standards of the whole community by cutting the price of one good? If we simply subsidised X, could we make everyone better off? It would be appealing indeed were it possible, but there is a certain lack of plausibility about the proposal, at least in an economy operating in the region of full employment of a more or less given stock of factors of production with given technology. Yet careless use of our demand curve would suggest that the trick could be carried off.

The problem here involves the things which have been held constant in deriving the demand curve. For one individual it is possible to hold the price of Y and his money income constant, lower the price of X and observe him move along his demand curve for X. However, if the price of X was lowered to the whole community this movement along the demand curve would only represent the first stage in the story, not the end of it. The industry producing X would have to expand, and given full employment it could only do so by attracting resources from the production of Y. Thus, the expansion in the demand for X would have to be accompanied by a contraction in the supply of Y, a consequent increase in Y's price and a *shift* of the demand curve for X.

All this amounts to saying that, in a fully employed economy, for consumers viewed as a group, it is real income that is fixed, not money income, and the price of all goods save one; it is impossible to analyse the effects of changing the price of one good by a tax or subsidy using a demand curve whose underlying assumptions imply that real income can vary. The 'other things equal' assumptions we made are inconsistent with the problem being analysed. However, it is up to us to decide what things we hold constant in our analysis. There is nothing sacred about holding the price of Y and money income constant and varying the price of X. We can instead, even when dealing with an individual, hold his real income constant, or at least we can once we have given precise meaning to the phrase 'constant real income'.

Constant Real Income and the Compensating Variation in Money Income

We have already used a real income concept in our analysis of the income and substitution effects in the previous chapter. We there referred to the substitution effect as a movement along a given indifference curve and the income effect as a movement to a higher curve. It is reasonable to think of constant real income as meaning, for an individual, the ability to gain a particular constant level of satisfaction from consumption. A demand curve holding *real* income and the price of *Y*

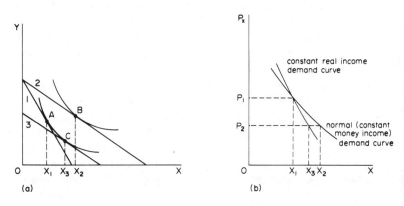

(a)   (b)

Figure 3.3 In panel (a), holding the price of *Y* and money income constant, a fall in the price of *X* from P_1 to P_2 shifts the budget constraint from 1 to 2, and the quantity of *X* demanded increases from X_1 to X_2. In panel (b) this shift is shown as a movement along a 'constant money income' demand curve. The substitution effect of this price change involves moving from constraint 1 to constraint 3, a change in consumption pattern from *A* to *C* and an increase in the demand for *X* from X_1 to X_3. This change is shown as a shift along a constant real income demand curve in panel (b). Because *X* is here depicted as a normal good, the income effect of the price change is positive. The constant real income demand curve relies on the substitution effect alone and hence, if *X* is a normal good, is steeper than the constant money income demand curve that also contains an income effect. If *X* were an inferior good, the constant real income curve would be the shallower of the two.

constant may then be derived. Starting from A in figure 3.3(a), let us lower the price of X, and at the same time vary money income by just enough to keep a budget constraint having the slope implied by the new price ratio in tangency with the original indifference curve (i.e. constraint 3). The required cut in money income just compensates the consumer for the income effect of the fall in the price of X and so the relevant cut in money income is called a *compensating variation*. The resulting demand curve is plotted in figure 3.3(b) and clearly, has *only* a substitution effect underlying it and hence *must* be negatively sloped. Equally obviously an increase in the consumption of X must be combined with a fall in the consumption of Y. When real income is held constant, X must be a substitute for all other goods taken together (though this does not rule out the possibility of X being complementary to some subset of goods in the overall bundle labelled Y). Now the movement from A to C in figure 3.3(a) was accomplished by a compensated fall in the price of X. It could equally have been the result of an equiproportional compensated rise in the price of Y, as is shown in figure 3.4. When

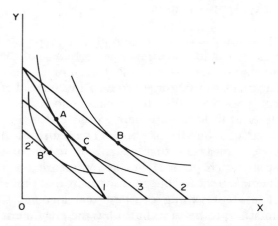

Figure 3.4 The substitution effect from A to C may be a component of the effect of one of two price changes: a fall in the price of X shifting the budget constraint to 2 and the equilibrium consumption bundle to B; or an equiproportional rise in the price of Y shifting the constraint to $2'$ and the equilibrium consumption bundle to B'. Recall here that the slope of the budget constraint depends only on the ratio of the prices of X and Y.

real income is held constant the change in the quantity of X demanded as a result of a change in its price is exactly the same as it is to an equiproportional but opposite change in the price of Y.

This is all very well as far as it goes. We can carry out the compensating variations in income in figures 3.3 and 3.4 and consider only substitution effects because we have already drawn an indifference map. We know how much we must shift the budget constraint in order to restore our consumer to his initial level of real income because we can see the point at which a budget constraint having the slope implied by the new prices is tangent to the old indifference curve. But if we were dealing with an actual consumer we could not do this. We could not 'see' his indifference map and therefore could not know how big a change in his money income was needed to keep him at the same level of utility and so compensate him for the effects on his real income of a particular price change.

6/6/86

The Slutsky Approximation

Our lack of knowledge about the precise shape of the indifference curve would undermine the usefulness of the analysis under discussion were we not able to get around this particular stumbling block by using an approximation. Instead of defining real income as the ability to purchase goods yielding a particular level of utility, let us define it instead as the ability to buy a particular bundle of goods. Thus, instead of treating any budget constraint that is tangent to the indifference curve upon which point A lies as representing a given level of real income, treat any budget constraint that passes through point A as representing constant real income. This is an approximation, to be sure, but it has the great merit of being a usable approximation, for, given any price for X and Y, it is clearly a routine piece of arithmetic to calculate the level of money income that will just permit the bundle of goods represented by A to be purchased.

The ability to attain a constant level of utility notion of real income is sometimes referred to as *Hicks real income* and

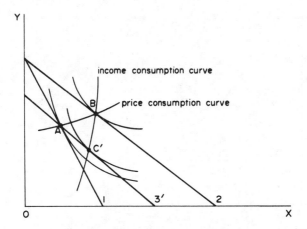

Figure 3.5 An alternative way of analysing the income and substitution effects of a price fall when 'constant real income' is defined to mean the ability to purchase a given bundle of goods rather than to achieve a given level of satisfaction. Constraint $3'$ passes through A. The substitution effect is from A to C' and the income effect from C' to B.

the ability to purchase a given bundle of goods concept as *Slutsky real income* after the two pioneers of modern choice theory who utilised these concepts in their analysis. In chapter 2 we analysed what we may now term the Hicks substitution and income effects. In figure 3.5 we show their Slutsky equivalents.

Clearly, the Slutsky substitution effect puts the consumer on a higher indifference curve than the one from which he starts, and does therefore involve some increase in Hicks real income. It should be noted that this is so whether we deal with a price fall or a price increase, though only the former case is explicitly analysed in figure 3.5. The Slutsky substitution effect is nevertheless unambiguously negative, even for an inferior good. This follows from the smooth convexity of the indifference curves. There can be no point to the left of A on budget constraint $3'$ that is not on a lower indifference curve than the one passing through A. Similarly, there must be points to the right of A that are on higher indifference curves. Therefore, the consumer will move to the right of A, hence

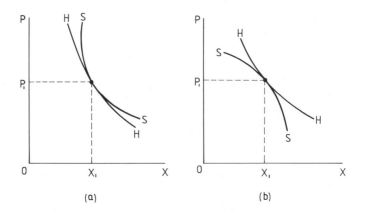

Figure 3.6 (a) If X is a normal good, then the Slutsky constant real income demand curve SS passing through $P_1 X_1$ is tangent to the Hicks constant real income curve passing through the same point from above and to the right. (b) If X is an inferior good, the tangency in question is from below and to the left.

increasing his consumption of X and decreasing his consumption of Y, when the price of X and hence the slope of the budget constraint fall.

The fact that a Slutsky substitution effect encompasses a small increase in Hicks real income means that we can say something about the slope of the demand curve derived holding Slutsky real income constant as compared to that of the Hicks constant real income demand curve. Consider figure 3.6. If we begin at a particular price P_1 and quantity X_1, then, whether we lower or raise the price of X, holding Slutsky real income constant will put the consumer on a higher indifference curve than the one from which he starts. Thus, where the Slutsky constant real income demand curve that passes through $P_1 X_1$ lies, relative to the Hicks constant real income curve that passes through the same point, will depend upon the sign of the income effect. If X is a normal good, the Slutsky curve will be tangent to the Hicks curve from above and to the right, and if X is an inferior good, from below and to the left, as the reader should easily be able to satisfy himself.

A market demand curve that is derived by holding individuals' real incomes constant will more easily enable us to
predict the consequences for the quantity of X demanded of
lowering its price by subsidy — or raising its price by tax —
than will one derived from the more orthodox constant
money income demand curve. The prediction will still be an
approximation, however, because constant real income in the
sense of a group of individuals each enjoying a given level of
utility is not the same thing as constant real income in the
sense of an economy producing output at a given level of
productive capacity. It was the existence of an overall constraint on production that gave rise to the difficulty that led
us into the foregoing analysis in the first place. However, the
ability of consumers to consume a given bundle of goods is
obviously not unrelated to an economy's ability to produce a
particular composition of output; hence our assertion that a
constant real income demand curve, and perhaps particularly
if it is real income in the Slutsky sense that is held constant,
is likely to be a useful tool in such circumstances.

Constant Real Income and the Equivalent Variation in Money Income

The analysis so far has been based on the breakdown of the
response of a consumer to a price change into an income and
substitution effect, the income effect in question being
measured in terms of a compensating variation in money
income. The response may be broken down in another way.
Consider figure 3.7. Again we start at point A, and let the
price of X fall. However, instead of noting that the point B
lies on an income consumption curve that must pass through
the indifference curve upon which A lies, we may with equal
justice note that A must lie on an income consumption curve
that passes through the indifference curve upon which point
B lies. The income consumption curve in question would do
so at a point such as C''. We can, therefore, break down the
movement from A to B as an income effect taking us from
A to C'' and a substitution effect taking us from C'' to B.
The income effect with which we are dealing here is the

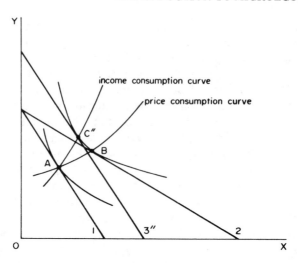

Figure 3.7 An alternative way of analysing the income and substitution effects of a fall in the price of X. The constraint moves from 1 to 2 and the equilibrium bundle from A to B. We shift the budget constraint at initial prices from 1 to 3″. This gives an 'equivalent' gain in real income, measured in terms of satisfaction, to that bestowed by the price fall. The substitution effect is then measured as C″ to B, while the income effect goes from A to C″.

result of what is known as an *equivalent variation* in income. It gets this name because the shift of the budget constraint from 1 to 3″ has an effect on real income *equivalent* to that of the price change whose effects are being analysed. It will not, in general, be quantitatively of the same order of magnitude as the income effect that we get from the compensating variation, and hence the size of the substitution effect will be different also. We will take up this point in more detail in the next chapter.

We may of course construct a Slutsky approximation to the Hicksian analysis contained in figure 3.7; this is done in figure 3.8. As with the Hicks analysis there is no need for the income and substitution effects involved here to be of the same size as those produced from an analysis using a compensating variation, but this ought not to worry the reader. When analysing the substitution effect with a compensating variation, we are dealing with the responsiveness of the demand for X to

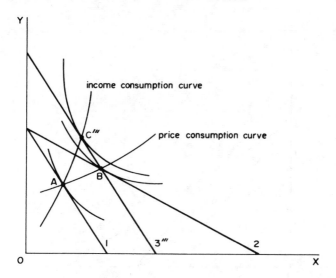

Figure 3.8 Income and substitution effects of a price fall analysed in terms of an equivalent variation when real income is defined as the ability to purchase a given bundle of goods. Constraint $3'''$ goes through B. Thus C''' to B is the substitution effect and A to C''' the income effect of a price fall shifting constraint 1 to 2.

changes in its own price, with real income held constant at the level given by the ability to purchase bundle of goods A (or to maintain that level of utility yielded by A in the Hicks case). When dealing with the equivalent variation, it is the responsiveness of the demand for X to changes in its price at a different higher level of real income that is at stake. There is no reason why the responsiveness of the demand for a good to changes in its own price should be independent of the level of real income, and all that we are observing here is the lack of such independence.

The 'Standard of Living' and the 'Cost of Living'

The compensating variation and the equivalent variation, measured according to Hicks or Slutsky, are alternative measures of the amount by which a consumer's real income

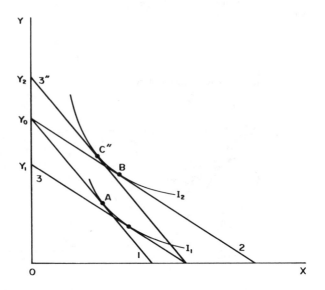

Figure 3.9 When the price of X falls and the budget constraint shifts from 1 to 2, the consumer's 'cost of living' falls. We may measure this fall in units of money by seeing how much his money income must be altered to carry out the compensating variation or the equivalent variation. The first is the amount of income needed to buy $Y_0 - Y_1$ units of Y, the second the amount needed to buy $Y_2 - Y_0$ units.

changes as a result of a price change; they are alternative ways of measuring the extent to which the purchasing power of a given money income changes when a particular price changes; or to put the same point a third way, they measure the extent to which the 'cost of living' changes as a result of a change in the price of a particular good. The foregoing analysis, abstract as it is, is therefore of considerable practical relevance. It underlies most attempts to measure variations in that elusive concept the price level, and is extremely useful in showing just why the concept is such a difficult one to capture. The price level, or cost of living, refers to the money outlay necessary for a consumer to maintain a given standard of living. A natural interpretation of the phrase 'standard of living' is surely a given level of utility, consumption along a particular indifference curve. Figure 3.9 shows yet again the consequences for consumption of changing the price of one good. The consumer has shifted from A to B. How has his cost of living changed? How has the money outlay necessary to maintain a given standard of living been affected by this price change?

There is no unique answer to this question. It all depends upon which standard of living is the given one, which indifference curve we wish to keep the individual on. Suppose it is the curve upon which A lies. Then the cost of living to our consumer has fallen by the amount by which it is possible to reduce his income after the fall in the price of X and still keep him on that original indifference curve. His cost of living has fallen by the amount of the Hicks compensating variation which shifts constraint 2 to 3.

Suppose instead, and there is no reason to prefer one to the other, that we decided to take the level of utility at B as the one whose cost of acquisition we were trying to measure. Then the individual's cost of living has fallen by the amount by which it would have been necessary to increase his money income in order to let him enjoy that standard of consumption at the original set of prices, to shift constraint 1 to 3″, that is to say by the Hicksian equivalent variation.

There is, as we have seen, no reason why these two measures should be the same. There is, after all, no reason why the effects of a given price change on the cost of maintaining two different standards of living should be the same. In short, the very concept of the cost of living is ambiguous. We must specify the standard of living required before we can measure changes in the cost of maintaining it. Moreover, the extent of such changes for a given change in prices depends upon the shape of the indifference map and hence is specific to a particular individual. There is no such thing as a general cost of living. How a particular set of price changes affects the living standards of particular individuals with given money incomes depends very much upon their tastes, and tastes differ between individuals.

7/6/86

Measuring Changes in the Cost of Living

The problem of measuring price level changes is even more difficult than the above argument would indicate, for in-

difference curves are not observable. There is no way of
assessing quantitatively the variations in money income
necessary to maintain a given level of utility at different
sets of prices. This is why the Slutsky method of analysing
the income and substitution effects is important. Instead of
asking questions about the cost of maintaining a given level
of utility it enables us to ask questions about the cost of
obtaining a particular bundle of goods. It should go without
saying that our measure of how a particular price change
affects the price level will depend upon the bundle of goods
we choose to consider.

Suppose we chose bundle of goods A as appropriate; then,
as is apparent from figure 3.10, we would have to measure
the Slutsky compensating variation if we wished to assess
the effect on the cost of living of a fall in the price of X. The
amount to which we could reduce money income after the

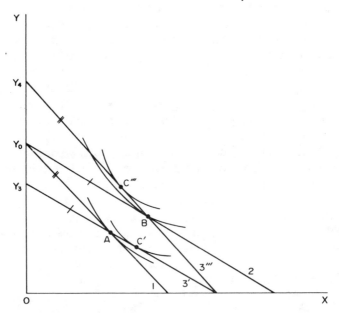

Figure 3.10 The price of X falls, shifting the constraint from 1 to 2.
The change in the cost of living may be measured by the Slutsky compensating variation that shifts 2 to $3'$, or the equivalent variation that
shifts 1 to $3'''$. The amounts of income involved would respectively
purchase $Y_0 - Y_3$ and $Y_4 - Y_0$ of Y.

fall in the price of X would be calculated by multiplying original money income by the ratio of the cost of obtaining bundle A at the new set of prices, to that of obtaining it at the old set. This ratio is of course a price index, in fact the well-known Laspèyres or *base period* weighted index. Alternatively, we could use bundle B as the one whose cost of acquisition we were concerned with. The level of income resulting from carrying out the Slutsky equivalent variation would be given by the original level of money income multiplied by the ratio of the money income necessary to obtain bundle B at the old prices, to that necessary at the new prices. This ratio is the *inverse* of another well-known price index, the Paasche or *current period* weighted index. The formulae for these two index numbers are:

$$\text{Laspèyres} = (P_{X1}.X_0 + P_{Y1}.Y_0)/(P_{X0}.X_0 + P_{Y0}.Y_0)$$

$$\text{Paasche} = (P_{X1}.X_1 + P_{Y1}Y_1)/(P_{X0}X_1 + P_{Y0}.Y_1)$$

where the subscript 0 refers to the base period, the time before the price change, and subscript 1 to the current period, the time after the price change.

These formulae will already be familiar to most readers, as will the fact that the two indices usually give different answers to questions about the cost of living. In fact, they answer questions about what has happened to the cost of acquiring particular and different bundles of goods, not a particular unambiguously defined level of utility. To all the difficulties in the cost of living concept we noted in the context of Hicks' analysis of income effects, we have added an extra problem here by substituting a given bundle of goods for a given level of utility. Whether any index of the price of a particular bundle of goods is relevant to measuring the cost of living for an individual depends very much upon the relationship between that bundle of goods and the consumption pattern of the individual. The implications of this for using allegedly general cost of living indices to measure changes in the purchasing power of the incomes of particular groups with such diverse consumption patterns as, for example, the rich, the old, students, poor families with young children, etc., should be obvious.

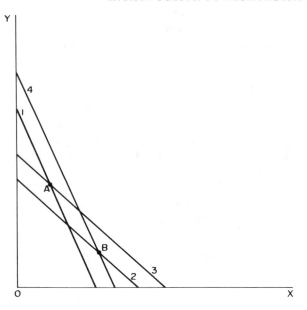

Figure 3.11 The price of X falls and that of Y rises shifting the budget constraint from 1 to 2. The consumer is observed to shift from consumption pattern A to B. In terms of the Laspèyres index his cost of living has risen, since a compensating increase in income from constraint 2 to 3 would be needed to enable him to buy A at the new prices. According to the Paasche index the cost of living has fallen, since bundle B could only have been obtained at the original prices by increasing income from constraint 1 to 4.

Both the price indices would give qualitatively the same result in terms of figure 3.10, both would show that the cost of living had fallen, but this need not always happen. In figure 3.11 we start off again at A, but now permit the price of X to fall and that of Y to rise simultaneously with the net effect of a shift to B. Has the cost of living risen or fallen? The cost of obtaining bundle A is higher in the second period than in the first, so according to the Laspèyres index a positive compensating variation is required. The cost of living has increased. But initially it would have also required a higher level of income to obtain B than it does after the price changes. From the point of view of the Paasche index and the equivalent variation, the cost of living has fallen.

If we knew about the shape of the indifference map we would not face this particular ambiguity, for it would be possible to tell whether point A or B lay on the higher indifference curve. This kind of problem arises from the use of bundles of goods as approximations to given levels of utility and *may* be encountered whenever two situations are compared in which some prices are lower and others higher.

Comparisons of living costs across national boundaries, for example, often give rise to such ambiguities. Suppose that, in figure 3.11, budget constraint 1 was interpreted as reflecting prices in Britain, and constraint 2 as reflecting American prices. Our analysis tells us that we cannot say whether the cost of living is higher in one country or the other. We can, however, conclude that the cost of a British consumption pattern is lower in Britain than in America, and that the cost of an American pattern is lower in America. It is not surprising that such a state of affairs is possible, but willingness to accept this proposition involves acceptance of the fact that international comparisons of such inherently vague notions as the cost of living and the standard of living are capable of yielding ambiguous and sometimes contradictory results that must be handled with the greatest care.

4

Consumer's Surplus and Marshallian Consumer Theory

Introduction

The income effects with which we have dealt in the last chapter measure the change in satisfaction, or utility, that an individual experiences as a result of a change in the price of a particular good. We have seen that, when the price of a good falls, the individual moves onto a higher indifference curve, and that the increase in utility that he experiences as a result of this is equal to that which he would have gained had he received instead an 'equivalent' variation in his money income. We have also seen that an alternative measure of the same gain is the amount by which his money income may be diminished after the price fall in order to leave him just as well off as he was initially, i.e. the 'compensating' variation in his money income. The changes in utility which we are discussing here are often referred to as changes in *consumer's surplus*. The term is an old-fashioned one, but the concept involved is vital in understanding the response of consumers to discriminatory pricing, as it is in understanding what is involved in the application of *cost—benefit analysis* to decision making. In this chapter, we will first of all elucidate the concept in question, and then show how a particular version of consumer theory enables that concept to be analysed in a remarkably simple way.

The Concept of Consumer's Surplus

It is a trivial implication of indifference curve analysis that, if we start the consumer out of equilibrium and permit him to substitute X for Y until he reaches his preferred bundle of goods, this act of substitution makes him better off. He gains more from increasing his consumption of X than he gives up in reducing his consumption of Y. If we start from a situation where no X at all is consumed, as at B in figure 4.1, where Y_0 is consumed, and move out to A, then the consumer moves from a lower indifference curve to a higher indifference curve. The increase in utility involved here is the consumer's surplus from consuming X; it is the maximum gain to be made from being able to trade X for Y at the price ratio underlying the budget constraint, and it is clearly tempting to look for a means of measuring this gain in terms of money.

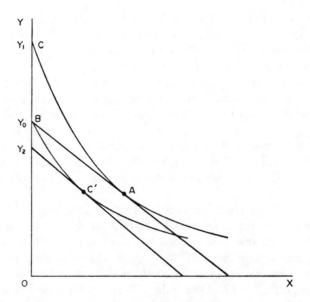

Figure 4.1 The amount of income needed to buy $Y_1 - Y_0$ of Y gives the consumer a gain in utility equivalent to the one he gets from moving from B to A, since he is indifferent between A and C. The amount necessary to buy $Y_0 - Y_2$ just compensates him for his ability to consume X since he is indifferent between points B and C'.

There are several ways of getting such a measure in terms of figure 4.1, but we will discuss only two of them. Suppose we began with our consumer facing the price of X that is implicit in the budget constraint of figure 4.1, and suppose that he was consuming bundle of goods A. Now suppose that we prohibited him from consuming X. We could ask the following question: by how much would we have to increase his income in order that he did not lose by this prohibition? Clearly, we would have to raise his income by enough to enable him to move from point B to point C, to increase his consumption of Y by $Y_1 - Y_0$. If we know the price of Y, the computation of the amount of income involved here is just a matter of arithmetic. The change in income involved is just enough to *compensate* the consumer for the loss of the ability to consume X. It is one measure of the gain that accrues to him from being able to consume X at the going price.

On the other hand, we could think in terms of offering him a choice between being forbidden to consume X or accepting a reduction in income. We could then ask how large a reduction in income would leave him just as badly off as the prohibition on the consumption of X. Obviously his income could be reduced until he ended up consuming at C', for here he would obtain just that level of utility attainable at B. The change in income here is again easily calculated; it is the amount that would enable him to purchase $Y_0 - Y_2$ of Y. It is in fact the variation in income that has an *equivalent* effect on his utility to a prohibition on consuming X at the going price.

In short, we have here yet another application of the ideas of compensating and equivalent variation to measuring gains and losses in real income, and there is no reason why the two measures should yield the same answers to the question 'how much does the consumer gain from being able to consume X at the going price?'. One tells us how much it would take to compensate him if he was prohibited from consuming X and the other tells us how big a change in income would be equivalent in its effects to such a prohibition. These sound like the same thing at first, perhaps, but they are not, as must be evident from the preceding discussion. Moreover, the reader should note that, as always, which measure is called the 'compensating' and which the 'equivalent' variation depends upon the starting point for the experiment. In the above discussion we have started from point A. If we start instead from point B, as we do in the caption to figure 4.1, the labels attached to these measures are reversed.

But why should the concept of the total gain from consuming a good be important? An example will help here. Suppose a government agency was trying to decide whether or not to provide a particular service, for example the operation of a bridge over a river. If the benefits to society of having the bridge outweighed the costs, we might all agree that it should be built. Suppose that a toll was to be charged. Would it be the case that toll revenue could be regarded as measuring the benefits consumers obtained from the bridge, so that, if such revenue did not cover the cost of operating the bridge it should not be built? Consider figure 4.2 and suppose that X_1 represents the bridge crossings per week made by a particular

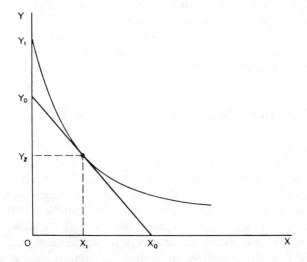

Figure 4.2 The consumer pays as much income as would purchase $Y_0 - Y_2$ units of Y in order to obtain his X_1 units of X. However, consuming X_1 units of X yields him the same gain in utility as he would have had from consuming $Y_1 - Y_2$ units of Y. The amount of income necessary to buy this amount of Y is therefore one measure of the total benefit that he gets from consuming X.

consumer at a particular toll per crossing. The actual revenue received from this consumer would be given by whatever sum of money would buy $Y_0 - Y_2$ of Y at going prices, but the *net* benefit to him of making bridge crossings could be measured by whatever sum of money would buy $Y_1 - Y_0$ of Y. That is to say that the total benefit to this consumer from operating the bridge is the revenue that can be raised from him *plus* his consumer's surplus. In terms of figure 4.2, $Y_1 - Y_2$ is one measure of this total benefit. This example should suffice for the moment to establish that the concept of consumer's surplus is worth attention. The analysis embodied in figures 4.1 and 4.2 tells us how it might be measured, but, unfortunately, only in principle. We can only find such distances as $Y_1 - Y_0$ and $Y_1 - Y_2$ if we know the shape of the indifference map. Again we are in need of some quantifiable approximation if the analysis is to be of practical value. It is to the development of one such approximation that we devote the rest of this chapter, an approximation that has the great advantage of utilising the shape and location of the demand curve as its analytic basis. In order to carry out this task we must return to consider the very foundations of our analysis of consumer choice, paying particular attention to the nature of the utility function.

Ordinal and Cardinal Utility

Up to now we have not said a great deal about the indifference map. We have simply noted that higher indifference curves represent higher levels of utility; we have not found it necessary to specify how much higher. We have been dealing with an *ordinal* utility function, that is, a function that tells us the *order* in which a consumer ranks bundles of goods but tells us nothing at all about the intensity of his likes or dislikes for particular consumption patterns. We can only use relative terms such as 'better' and 'worse', 'preferred' and 'not preferred' in this context. It is possible, however, at least in principle, to conceive of a *cardinal* utility function which, in addition to telling us about how bundles of goods are ordered, tells us about the intensity of likes and dislikes, measuring satisfaction, or utility, in precise units. To argue by analogy for a moment, in the measurement of length, an ordinal scale would tell us only that some distances were longer or shorter (or the same length) than others. A cardinal scale would be set up in units of yards, feet and inches and would tell us how long each distance was and hence *how much* longer (or shorter) than any other. So long as we deal with questions about choice under conditions of certainty, the ordinal utility assumption suffices as a basis for consumer theory but, as we shall see later, a cardinal utility function is extremely useful in dealing with choice in conditions of risk; indeed the existence of such a function is implicit in the possibility of such a choice.

Marshallian Consumer Theory

Alfred Marshall's demand theory, which predates the analysis we have dealt with so far, uses cardinal utility and enables us to develop a measure of consumer's surplus that is a usable approximation to the quantities analysed here and earlier. In order to analyse the demand for a particular good X in Marshallian terms, we make three key assumptions. First, we assume that the total utility gained from consuming any quantity of X is independent of the quantity of Y consumed, and *vice versa*. Second, we assume that the marginal utility of Y is constant, i.e. that the utility gained from consuming Y rises in strict proportion to the quantity of Y so that equal increments of Y yield equal increments of utility. Finally, we assume that the marginal utility of X diminishes as consumption of X increases, i.e. that equal increments in X yield successively smaller increments in utility.

These assumptions are difficult to take literally, to be sure, and we will see what they imply about the nature of the indifference map in a few pages; but for the moment let us pursue their other implications. In figure 4.3 we measure on the vertical axis utility per unit of X (in terms of some arbitrary unit of measurement such as 'utils') and on the horizontal axis the quantity of X consumed per unit of time. We then plot the relationship between the marginal utility of X per

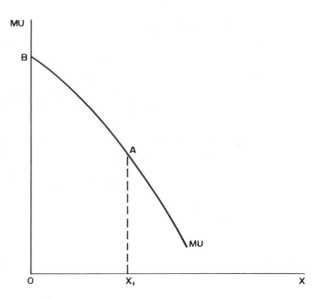

Figure 4.3 The marginal utility of X declines as the quantity of X consumed increases. The area $OBAX_1$ measures the total utility of consuming X_1 units of X.

unit of X and the quantity of it consumed. The area under this curve between the vertical axis and one unit of X measures the utility per unit of time gained from consuming the first unit, the area under the curve between 1 and 2 units of X measures that gained from consuming the second, and so on. Hence the total utility per unit of time gained from consuming any particular quantity of X per unit of time is found by adding up all these areas. Thus, for X_1 units, for example, this addition yields the area $OBAX_1$ as a measure of the total utility derived from consuming X_1 units of X.

Now X has a price. For each unit of X bought a certain quantity of Y must be given up because money income is given up. This means that a certain amount of utility from consuming Y must be forgone for each unit of X consumed and, since the marginal utility of Y is constant, the amount of utility sacrificed is constant per unit of X obtained. The 'price' to the consumer in terms of utility forgone per unit of X consumed is constant and may be represented by a straight

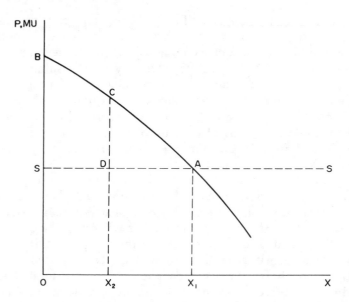

Figure 4.4 If OS measures the amount of utility that must be forgone per unit of X consumed, then utility is maximised by consuming X_1 units of X. The consumer's surplus from so doing is given by the area SBA.

line such as SS on figure 4.4. The area under the marginal utility curve of X is the total utility gained from consuming it and, by exactly similar reasoning, the area under the line SS is the total cost in terms of utility of acquiring it. The net gain from consuming a particular quantity of X is then the difference in these two areas. For example at X_2 units of X, this net gain is given by the area $BCDS$.

The utility maximising consumer obviously wishes to maximise this net gain. Equally obviously, in terms of figure 4.4, this will involve him consuming X_1 units of X at which point the marginal gain from consuming it is just equal to its price in terms of utility forgone. The total net gain from consumption of X is, in this case, given by the area SBA and is the consumer's surplus accruing from the consumption of X measured in utils. It is trivially easy to translate this measure in unobservable utils into one in terms of money. With a given price for

Y, and a given marginal utility of Y, we can freely translate utils into units of money. There is a strictly proportional relationship between every pound spent on Y, the volume of Y acquired, and the utility yielded by the consumption of the Y purchased. Thus, the 'price' in terms of utility forgone of X may be transformed into a price measured in pounds and pence. Similarly, the marginal utility of X may be measured in terms of the sum of money that would have to be devoted to the purchase of Y in order to yield an equivalent flow of utility.

Thus, we may substitute monetary units for utility units on the vertical axis of figure 4.4; the price of X then becomes a money price, and the assumption of utility maximisation ensures that the marginal utility curve will relate the quantity of X demanded to its price. Hence the marginal utility curve becomes a demand curve. Consumer's surplus may be measured as the area under the demand curve for X, minus total expenditure on X: thus we have our monetary measure of consumer's surplus in terms of observable phenomena. We also

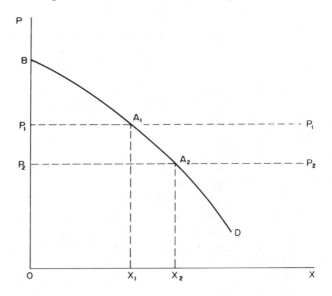

Figure 4.5 The gain in consumer's surplus as a result of the price of X falling from P_1 to P_2 is given by $P_1 A_1 A_2 P_2$.

have monetary measures of the change in utility that arises from changes in the price of X. Thus, if the price of X falls from P_1 to P_2 in figure 4.5, consumption increases from X_1 to X_2 and the money value of the gain in utility is given by the area $P_1 A_1 A_2 P_2$.

Now the measure of consumer's surplus in figure 4.4 is apparently unambiguous, and in figure 4.5 the measure of the change in consumer's surplus, which is just another name for the effect on real income that arises from a price change, is also unambiguous. Our careful distinction between compensating and equivalent variations seems to have vanished in the process of producing these measures of consumer's surplus in terms of areas under the demand curve for X. Let us now see how this has come about.

9/6/86

Marshallian Analysis in Terms of Indifference Curves

The nature of the approximations into which our search for an easily quantifiable measure of consumer's surplus has led us, and the reason why the distinction between compensating and equivalent variations has vanished, are easily seen if we translate Marshallian analysis into the language of indifference curves.

In terms of such analysis, to postulate cardinal utility means that we can label each of our indifference curves by the level of utility associated with it. The assumption that the marginal utility of Y is constant means that successive increments in Y, if the quantity of X is constant, lead to equal increments in utility, while the independence of the marginal utilities of X and Y means that these equal increments in utility are the same regardless of the quantity of X being consumed. In figure 4.6 these assumptions are translated into an indifference map. They involve the indifference curves being equally spaced along *any* line drawn perpendicular to the X-axis; this can only happen if each curve has the same slope where it cuts such a perpendicular. This obviously means that there is a zero income elasticity of demand for X. The quantity of it bought would depend only on the slope and not on the location of the budget constraint. Hence, when prices change,

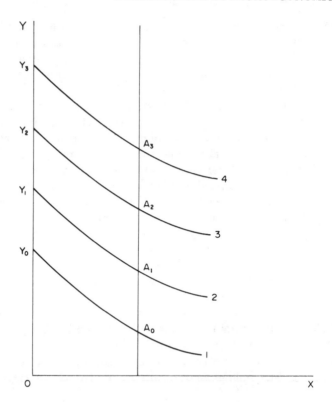

Figure 4.6 The indifference map implicit in Marshallian utility theory. Up any line perpendicular to the X-axis (including the Y-axis itself) the indifference curves are parallel to each other. Thus the slope of each curve is the same at Y_0, Y_1, Y_2 and Y_3, and for example at A_0, A_1, A_2 and A_3. At any quantity of X, successive equal increments in the amount of Y yield equal increments in utility from 1 to 2, 2 to 3, etc. The curves become more shallow as we move to the right; hence successive equal increments in the amount of X consumed for any given quantity of Y yield successively smaller increases in utility.

there is no income effect on the demand for X, only on the demand for Y.

The measure of consumer's surplus which we have dealt with in this chapter and the measures of effects on real income of price changes which we dealt with in Chapter 3 all involve measuring the vertical distance between pairs of indifference curves. Measures based on equivalent and compensating variations could differ because we imposed no requirement that the vertical distance between given indifference curves be the same at every point. The Marshallian assumptions, however, do impose this requirement and hence, in terms of indifference curve analysis, different measures yield the same answer.

As we have seen, these same assumptions imply that various areas under the demand curve for a good may be used to measure overall levels of, and changes in, consumer's surplus. Such measurements are quite commonly used in applications of demand theory to concrete problems, but they are approximations to the much more slippery, and ambiguous, quantities analysed earlier. As the reader might expect, the closer to zero the income elasticity of demand for X, and the smaller the effect on income of whatever change is under analysis, then the better is the approximation and the more accurate will be the predictions based upon its use.

The Impossibility of Comparing Utility between Persons

The problems in measuring consumer's surplus which we have discussed in this and the preceding chapter have all been concerned with the ambiguity of this concept when analysing the individual consumer's situation. We may produce an apparently unambiguous monetary measure of an individual's satisfaction from consuming a particular good if we make all the special assumptions set out in this chapter. It must be noted, however, that even making these assumptions there is no basis in economic theory for adding these measures of satisfaction over individuals to produce some global measure of the gain to the community from consuming a particular good. Even if we are willing to postulate the existence of a cardinal utility function for each member of the community, there is no basis for comparing these functions between people and hence no way of adding them up. A pound's worth of satisfaction to one man and a pound's worth of satisfaction to another may or may not be the same amount of satisfaction. There is no way of knowing. Thus, though getting a measure of consumer's surplus is one of the major problems in cost—

benefit analysis, it is by no means the only one. Equally important is finding a means of comparing consumer's surplus between individuals when, as is inevitably the case, the benefits (and costs) that must be measured accrue to different individuals. This section of the book has nothing to say on this score.

Thus, to return to our bridge-building example, we now know much more than we did about the extent to which the benefits to individuals from having the services of a bridge might be measured, but we have learned nothing about how to sum these individual benefits in order to get a global measure of 'the benefit to the community' of the bridge. The problem here is one involving the distribution of economic benefits between individuals, and it is raised now only to warn the reader that it has not yet been treated in this book. We shall deal with it in a more general framework in Part VI when we take up problems involving the interaction of individuals in the economic system. For the moment, we will continue our analysis of the behaviour of the individual consumer.

15/6/86

Review chapter
before proceeding.

✓ Reviewed (1st occasion)
17/6/86

✓ Reviewed (2nd occasion)
21/9/86

Part II
Further
Applications
and Extensions
of Consumer
Theory

5
The Individual's Supply of Labour

Introduction

In this chapter we apply the theory of choice to aspects of the supply of a productive service — labour. In particular, we consider the choice of an individual member of the labour force as to how many hours work per week he will undertake. As always, we need to know about three factors in order to set the problem up in manageable form — the objects of choice, the constraints upon choice, and the tastes which govern the choice. Once these are properly defined, subsequent analysis is straightforward.

The Nature of the Choice Problem

Consider first the objects of choice. At first glance one might think of each member of the labour force being faced with a choice between work and leisure, but a moment's reflection makes it apparent that only one item is in fact being chosen. When hours to be worked have been selected, the number of hours available for leisure are already determined and *vice versa*. In mentioning work and leisure we are specifying only *one* of the objects of choice, and in our analysis it is convenient to deal explicitly with leisure and hence implicitly with work. As our individual gives up leisure, he receives wage

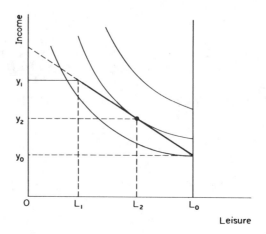

Figure 5.1 The choice between combinations of income and leisure. Note that hours worked may be measured moving to the left from L_0. If we read the diagram from right to left in this way, it depicts the choice of the best available combination of a 'good' (income), and a 'bad' (work). The individual here chooses to work $L_0 - L_2$ hours for a wage income of $y_2 - y_0$.

payments in recompense for his efforts. He gains income — the ability to purchase consumption goods — and the objects of choice for him are therefore income and leisure.

We measure income along the vertical axis of figure 5.1 and leisure along the horizontal axis. Now let us consider the constraint upon the individual's choice. First of all there is the obvious physical constraint that limits the number of hours of leisure available in a week to the number of hours that there are in the week. This point is given by L_0 on the horizontal axis of figure 5.1.

Working is only one source of income, there is no reason why any person cannot also receive unearned income. Such income receipts are common indeed in a modern economy in which the state provides a number of services to individuals. Free education for children, health insurance — the benefits of which are unrelated to contributions — and so forth, are all part of income, but receipt of them does not depend in any way upon hours worked. More traditional forms of un-earned income accruing from ownership of wealth belong here as well. Thus, there is no reason to suppose in general that the level of income associated with not working, i.e. with L_0 hours of leisure per week, is zero. In figure 5.1 it is assumed to be y_0 and the budget constraint is drawn vertically up to this level of income. Beyond this point, however, more income can only be obtained by working and hence by sacrificing leisure.

Each hour worked increases income by the hourly wage that the individual can command. Hence the slope of the budget constraint above point $L_0 y_0$ is given by the wage rate, with a negative sign of course, showing the rate at which income can be substituted for leisure. It is clearly not possible to continue the constraint to cut the vertical axis, since no individual can work every hour of the week without some 'leisure' time being devoted to eating and sleeping. Thus there is a cut-off at some minimum amount of leisure L_1 and an associated maximum income level of y_1. Thus, the constraint on the choice we are analysing is characterised as a kinked relationship such as shown in figure 5.1. The continuity of the constraint over the range $L_0 y_0 - L_1 y_1$ does imply that the individual may choose the length of his own work week. This is obviously too simple for direct application to modern labour market institutions. Despite this degree of simplification, however, the analysis is of some interest.

As to the individual's tastes, if income and leisure are both goods in the sense that more of one of them without sacrifice of the other increases satisfaction, then we are safe in characterising them by a conventional indifference map. One may object to this on the grounds that perhaps the first few hours work a week may actually be a pleasant alternative to the boredom implicit in complete idleness and prefer indifference curves that actually become upward sloping at high levels of leisure as in figure 5.2. But because this extra complication adds nothing to the analysis that follows, we ignore it from now on. This is not to say, though, that the assumption underlying it lacks plausibility.

The formal solution to the choice problem portrayed in figure 5.1 is obvious enough. Our worker will consume L_2 hours of leisure per week at the going wage, hence working $L_0 - L_2$ hours for an income of y_2.

or average amount per hour

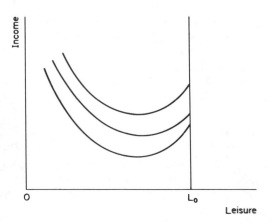

Figure 5.2 The indifference map implicit in the assumption that, after a certain point, leisure becomes a 'bad'. Moving to the left from L_0 the individual would be willing to pay for permission to work for the first few hours.

7/6/86

Variations in the Wage Rate

We are now in a position to see how the individual's supply of man hours changes in response to changes in the constraints under which he operates. First let us derive his supply curve of effort as a function of the wage rate. As the wage rate rises the mid-sector of the budget constraint becomes steeper, pivoting on point $y_0 L_0$, as in figure 5.3(a). The 'price' of income falls, and, provided only that it is a normal good — hardly a proviso to argue about — the amount of it demanded rises as our individual moves from A to B. However, we are mainly interested in what happens to the demand for leisure and hence the supply of hours worked. To put the matter in the language of consumer theory, this is a cross effect rather than an own price effect. If income and leisure are substitutes, then hours worked will increase with the wage rate, but if they are complements, hours worked will actually fall. The former case, with its upward sloping supply curve of hours worked is shown in figure 5.3; the latter with a backward bending supply curve is shown in figure 5.4.

Now if there were only a substitution effect to consider here there would be no problem. A fall in the price of income

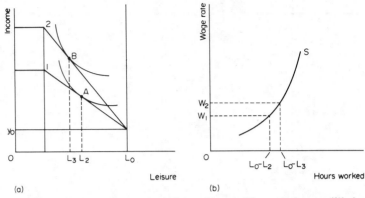

(a)   (b)

Figure 5.3 The wage rate rises from W_1 to W_2 and the equilibrium moves from A to B. More income is demanded but less leisure. If income and leisure are indeed substitutes, the supply curve of labour slopes upwards as shown in panel (b).

would be synonymous with a rise in the price of leisure. It is because there is an income effect at work that we run into ambiguity. We examine this matter more closely in figure 5.5. After the wage rate rises, we carry out a Slutsky compensating variation on our individual's budget constraint by lowering his unearned income until he is on constraint 3. Clearly, his

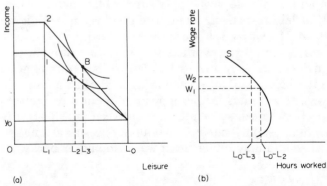

(a)   (b)

Figure 5.4 The wage rate rises from W_1 to W_2 and the equilibrium moves from A to B. More income is demanded, but in this case the indifference map is drawn so that income and leisure are complements. Thus we get the backward bending supply curve of labour depicted in panel (b).

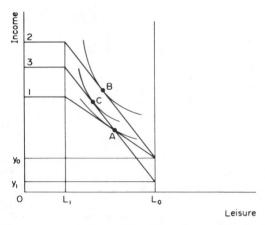

Figure 5.5 The movement from A to B involves a substitution effect from A to C and an 'income effect' from C to B. The compensating variation to get from constraint 2 to 3 may be thought of as involving a cut in unearned income from y_0 to y_1.

overall response to the rise in his wage rate can be broken down into a movement from A to C, a substitution effect, and a movement from C to B, an income effect. If leisure were an inferior good, there would be no ambiguity in the individual's response: the negative income effect and the negative substitution effect would reinforce one another to produce an upward sloping supply curve of labour. However, to think of leisure as being an inferior good is implausible, to say the least. If it was such a good, we would expect to observe the longest hours being worked for wages by those whose unearned incomes were highest! If leisure is a normal good though, the income effect on hours worked of an increase in the wage rate operates in the opposite direction to the substitution effect and may or may not outweigh it. This is why an individual's supply curve of labour services as a function of the wage rate may either be upward sloping or backward bending.

Overtime Payments

We may look at overtime payment arrangements in the light

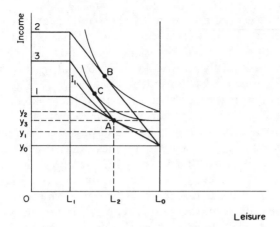

Figure 5.6 If the wage rate rises, the individual moves from A to B with a gain in utility equal to that yielded by an increase of $y_2 - y_1$ in unearned income. Such a movement as that from A to B may or may not involve an increase in hours worked. If the new wage rate is introduced as an overtime only rate, we have a pure substitution effect from A to C, an unambiguous increase in hours worked, but the gain in utility is here only equivalent to $y_3 - y_1$.

of the foregoing analysis. They are a form of price discrimination, by which we mean that a different price is paid for different units of the same good, and they can prevent the supply curve of labour from bending backwards. Consider figure 5.6 and suppose that our typical individual, at the going wage rate on constraint 1, was supplying $L_0 - L_2$ hours of work. Now suppose that his employer wished to induce him to work longer hours. One course of action would be to offer the same old wage rate for all hours worked up to $L_0 - L_2$ and a higher rate thereafter.

In terms of figure 5.6, the effect of this is to kink the budget constraint at A, making it more steeply sloped above and to the left of this point (constraint 3). But if A was initially an equilibrium point, there must exist a point on a higher indifference curve, such as C, which also lies on the more steeply sloped segment of the constraint, the movement to which is motivated by a pure Slutsky substitution effect.

The price discrimination involved here clearly reduces the real income of the wage earner relative to what it would have been had he received the same wage rate for every hour worked, as is easily shown. In figure 5.6, at the original wage rate, the individual is on indifference curve I_1, and hence at a level of utility exactly equivalent to that which he would have attained with an unearned income of y_1. The difference between this and y_0 measures the surplus that accrues to him from working at the wage rate in question. Were the wage rate simply to go up so that his new budget constraint was given by 2, then this change would be equivalent to an increase of $y_2 - y_1$ in unearned income. However, if the new rate is an overtime-only rate, the gain is reduced. It is equivalent to an increase in unearned income of only $y_3 - y_1$. It is perhaps small wonder, therefore, that the length of the basic working week is so often a bone of contention in wage negotiations between unions and employers.

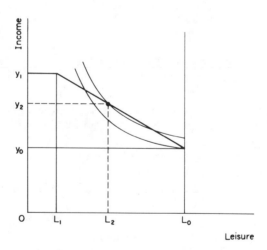

Figure 5.7 If the length of the working week is fixed by the employer along with the wage offered, the individual is faced with a choice between two income leisure combinations: L_0, y_0 and L_2, y_2. As this figure is drawn, the latter is on the higher indifference curve and he will choose to work.

The Effect of Fixing the Length of the Working Week

Now the reader will no doubt have been somewhat concerned that our analysis so far has dealt with an individual who is able to choose the length of his working week to the very minute. In fact, of course, the length of the basic working week tends to appear to him as institutionally determined. The effect of this is to present the individual with an all or nothing choice. He may work $L_0 - L_2$ hours at the going rate or none at all. Such a choice is depicted in figure 5.7. Our individual will work if the point L_2, y_2 lies on a higher indifference curve than the point L_0, y_0, otherwise not. If

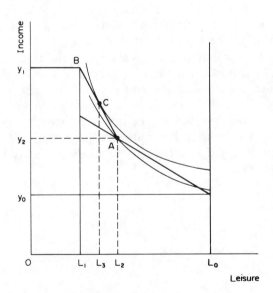

Figure 5.8 If the individual is permitted a free choice of overtime hours beyond $L_0 - L_2$ at an increased wage rate, his constraint is given by the point L_0, y_0, and any point along the line AB linking L_2, y_2 and L_1, y_1. As the indifference map is drawn here, he moves to point C and works $L_3 - L_2$ overtime hours. Note though, that if the indifference curve passing through A had been drawn to slope more steeply than the continuous section AB of the constraint, our individual would have refused to work overtime.

the length of the basic working week is given at a fixed wage, but there is flexibility in the worker's choice of overtime hours, then we may be back with the analysis of marginal choices. Figure 5.8 deals with this case.

Concluding Comment

There are other variations on the foregoing analysis that we could carry out. Furthermore it should be noted that the concept of the 'utility of income' used throughout the discussion is a summary measure of the utility that can be had from the goods that income will buy. Though the analysis of this chapter has treated the income—leisure choice as if it is made without explicit consideration of the allocation of income among consumption goods, this is a simplifying assumption rather than one that is generally valid. A fuller analysis of these matters, which is beyond the technical scope of this book, would have leisure, income, and the allocation of income among consumption goods all chosen simultaneously. Nevertheless, it is to be hoped sufficient has now been done to show the reader that the theory of consumer behaviour may readily be applied to problems involving the labour market and is indeed quite a flexible analytic device in this context.

6
Allocation of Consumption over Time

Introduction

We now apply the theory of consumer choice to the allocation of consumption over time. First, we shall deal with a situation in which the individual may lend and borrow on the capital market and set out the analysis that underlies much modern work on saving decisions and the consumption function. Then we shall extend the framework to permit the individual the opportunity of transforming goods currently available to him into future goods by way of production. This extension of the basic analysis is the foundation for a great deal of work on investment theory.

The basic postulate of the theory is that it is consumption that yields satisfaction. The objects of choice in all the analysis that follows are consumption now and in the future. Obviously a full characterisation of this choice problem would have us considering the time path of consumption over an individual's planning horizon, a horizon which might well be as long as his lifetime. However, we make the drastic simplification of dividing the planning period into two discrete chunks, the current period and the next period, t and $t + 1$, and consider the allocation of consumption between them.

The Framework of Choice Without Production

To begin with, we will rule out the possibility that our individual is able to engage in production on his own account.

If we make this simplifying assumption, we may characterise his choice problem in figure 6.1. There, we plot consumption in period t on the horizontal axis and consumption in period $t + 1$ on the vertical. The objects of choice in the analysis that follows are allocations of consumption between the two periods. The constraint upon choice is constructed as follows. We assume that the individual receives a particular amount of income, y_t, in time t and expects, as if with certainty, to receive a particular amount of income, y_{t+1}, in time $t + 1$ as well. There is no reason for us to treat these two amounts of income as equal, and in figure 6.1 we have made y_{t+1} greater than y_t. Now if our individual consumes all his income in each period, his consumption pattern will also be given by y_t, y_{t+1}, but he can, by borrowing or lending, reallocate consumption between periods. If we assume that the capital market is perfect, that the single rate of interest (r) at which he borrows and lends is completely uninfluenced by the amounts in which he does so, then the budget constraint, known in this case as the *market opportunity curve*, is a straight line having the slope $-(1 + r)$ and passing through y_t, y_{t+1}.

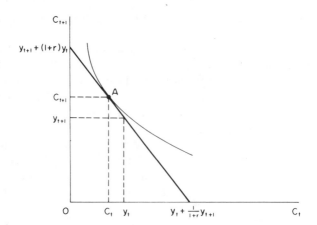

Figure 6.1 The level of saving is the result of a choice of consumption levels for now and the future. Given y_t of income now and the certainty of receiving y_{t+1} in the future and faced with an interest rate of r, the individual depicted saves $y_t - C_t$.

To see this, neglect questions about what might be biologically feasible and consider what would happen if the individual decided to undertake no consumption at all in the current period. He could then set aside all his current income to earn interest at rate r and in the next period have consumption equal to $y_{t+1} + (1 + r)y_t$. Alternatively, he might decide to carry out all his consumption for the two periods in the current period, devoting all of his next period's income to paying off the debts thereby incurred. At an interest rate of r, the maximum he could borrow against his future income would be equal to $y_{t+1}/(1 + r)$ and his maximum current consumption $y_t + [y_{t+1}/(1 + r)]$. For every pound saved out of current income, $1 + r$ pounds of future consumption is obtained, and for every pound of future income devoted to repaying debts, $1/(1 + r)$ pounds of current consumption can be obtained. Hence the market opportunity curve in figure 6.1.

A conventional indifference map describes tastes and completes the picture set out in figure 6.1, the slope of any indifference curve at any point defining the marginal rate of substitution between current and future goods.

22/6/86

Time Preference and the Solution to the Choice Problem

It is worth digressing for a moment to ask why, if the consumption goods available are identical in the two periods, the marginal rate of substitution between them should ever differ from -1, one unit of future goods for one unit of current goods. There are two distinct problems here. First, if the quantities of goods available in the two periods are not the same, there is no reason to suppose that an extra unit will be equally valued in both periods — one would expect an extra unit of goods to become relatively more highly prized the smaller was the bundle to which it was being added.

The foregoing argument just restates the reasons for expecting there to be a convex indifference map in any application of the theory of consumer behaviour. In this particular application we must also consider a second problem implicit in the fact that the goods in question are available at different times and for this reason alone are not the 'same' in every

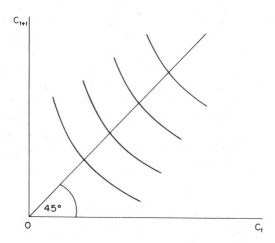

Figure 6.2 The marginal rate of substitution between present and future consumption is defined as $-(1 + \rho)$, where ρ is known as the 'rate of time preference.' The 'rate of time preference proper' is the rate of time preference where equal amounts of consumption are available in each period. If the rate of time preference proper is zero, then the indifference curves in this diagram will all cut a line drawn at $45°$ from the origin at right angles, since they will have a slope of -1 at that point.

respect. Neglect all other differences between bundles of goods, and consider situations in which equal quantities are available in each period. Consider, that is, bundles along a $45°$ line drawn through the origin of an intertemporal indifference map such as we have in figure 6.2. It is not obvious that the marginal rate of substitution between present and future consumption will be -1 here; indeed many arguments, that may be summarised in the word 'impatience', have been adduced for suggesting that present goods will be valued more highly on the margin when they are available in the same quantities as future goods.

Now the marginal rate of substitution between present and future goods is frequently referred to as being equal to $-(1 + \rho)$, where ρ is defined as the *rate of time preference*, i.e. the amount by which future goods are discounted on the margin relative to present goods for all reasons. The marginal rate of substitution between present and future goods *when equal quantities of them are available in each period* involves a particular value for ρ known as the *rate of time preference proper*, which measures the amount by which future goods are discounted on the margin simply by virtue of their being available in the future. A zero rate of time preference proper implies that the indifference curves all cut a 45° line drawn from the origin with a slope of -1.

In any event, the solution to our choice problem depicted in figure 6.1 occurs at A with a saving out of current income equal to $y_t - C_t$. This is a point at which, to adopt the terminology just introduced, the rate of interest and the rate of time preference are equal to one another. The solution has a number of characteristics worth noting.

For one thing, it tells us that current saving, and hence current consumption, depend not just upon current income but also upon future income and the rate of interest. If we use the word 'wealth' to describe the total purchasing power currently available to an individual (in this case current income plus the present value of future income) then the point at which the market opportunity curve of figure 6.1 cuts the horizontal axis clearly measures wealth, and we may equivalently say that current consumption depends upon wealth and the rate of interest; these two variables are sufficient to locate the budget constraint. The implications of this for analysis which uses a simple consumption function that makes consumption depend only on current income should be obvious.

Saving and the Rate of Interest

We may use the framework set out in figure 6.1 to answer questions about the effect on consumption, and hence on saving, of variations in the rate of interest, being careful to distinguish between the implications of *different values of the rate of interest considered as alternatives* on the one hand and the consequences of *changes in the interest rate* on the other. Consider figure 6.3, which is based on figure 6.1. If the individual's income pattern in the two periods is given by y_t, y_{t+1} and the rate of interest is equal to r_1, then the market

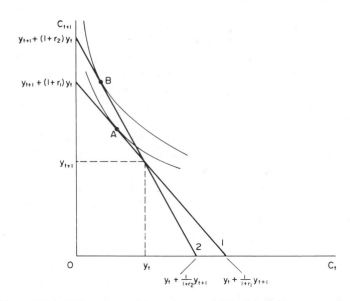

Figure 6.3 A higher rate of interest, r_2, shifts the market opportunity curve from 1 to 2, pivoting it at point y_t, y_{t+1} because this endowment of goods is available as a consumption bundle without borrowing or lending. At the higher rate of interest our individual will select point B rather than A.

opportunity curve is determined and we have equilibrium at A, just as in figure 6.1. If the rate of interest had been higher at r_2, the budget constraint would instead be given by the market opportunity line labelled 2. Clearly, our individual would, in this second case, select point B, given the nature of the indifference map. As we have drawn it, he would consume fewer current and more future goods at this higher rate of interest. In other words, at a higher rate of interest he saves more. Obviously, as we show in figure 6.4, preferences could equally easily have been such as to lead to a lower savings level at a higher interest rate; the influence of the rate of interest on the level of savings is therefore ambiguous.

We do not have to look too far for the source of this ambiguity. If we carry out a compensating variation in wealth to enable us to break down the difference between A and B into a substitution effect and an analogue to an income effect — call it a *windfall effect* — we get the constraint labelled 3 in

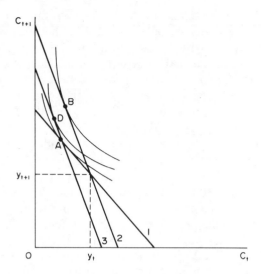

Figure 6.4 The movement from A to B at a higher interest rate may involve an increase or decrease in saving. The substitution effect, from A to D, unambiguously points to more saving but the 'windfall' effect from D to B may offset this tendency because it is reasonable to suppose that current consumption is a normal good.

figure 6.4. The substitution effect of a higher rate of interest from A to D clearly involves an increase in saving. It is the windfall effect from D to B that offsets this substitution effect more than completely when a higher interest rate leads to less saving. In figure 6.3 the windfall effect was not enough to offset the substitution effect. The windfall effect works against the substitution effect because the indifference map is drawn so that both current and future consumption are normal goods.

So far we have been careful to talk about the rate of interest being higher and lower, rather than rising and falling. What then does the foregoing analysis tell us about the effects of *changes* in the rate of interest on the savings rate? If savings are channelled into an institution such as a building society, in which the borrower pays a given rate of return, variations in which do not alter the capital value of savings to the lender, then the foregoing analysis is applicable without modification.

However, if lending takes the form of purchasing a bond — a promise to pay *a given sum of money* in the next period — then it requires a little further thought, for here variations in interest rate do affect the current capital value of savings.

Consider figure 6.5. Our individual starts out at y_t, y_{t+1} with the market rate of interest such that the budget constraint is given by 1. His preferred allocation of consumption is at A, just as in figures 6.1, 6.2 and 6.3. However, now let him buy a bond in order to accomplish this reallocation; he has moved to point A. In purchasing the bond he has given up $y_t - C_t$ of current income in return for a guaranteed receipt of $C_{t+1} - y_{t+1}$ in the next period. The issuer of the bond has promised him this volume of extra consumption. Thus, no matter what now happens to the rate of interest, our individual saver can still stay at A. Now suppose, after he has bought the bond, but still during the first time period, the rate of interest rises. He can now move away from A along a more steeply sloped budget constraint than the original one. Since

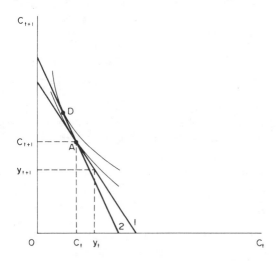

Figure 6.5 When an individual saves by buying a bond he ensures for himself the ability to consume at point A no matter what should subsequently happen to the rate of interest. Thus a rise in the interest rate pivots the market opportunity curve from 1 to 2 at A. The result is a pure substitution effect from A to D and an unambiguous increase in saving.

the constraint has pivoted at A, our individual is no longer in equilibrium there. He will move to D, buying another bond in the process on new, now more favourable, terms. His saving will unambiguously increase, for the change that we have been analysing here is clearly the outcome of a Slutsky substitution effect. Thus, in this case we can conclude that there is a positive relationship between the amount of saving and the rate of interest.

Intertemporal Choice with Production Opportunities

So far in this chapter we have considered the behaviour of an individual who is able to reallocate his consumption over time by borrowing or lending in a perfect capital market. However, instead of being limited to taking currently available resources and lending them out with a view to consuming the proceeds of the loan in the future, the individual may also have the opportunity of using those resources in a production process that yields output consumable in the future. Let us now analyse the factors that will determine whether, and to what extent, he will take advantage of access to such a production process, and, in doing so, develop the basis of what, in macro-economics, is known as 'neo-classical' investment theory.

In the analysis that follows, the objects of choice facing the individual remain the same as they were above, namely consumption in the present period, C_t, and consumption in the next period C_{t+1}. The criteria in terms of which the choice is made are also the same and are summarised in exactly the same indifference map as was used there. The availability of access to a productive process (or processes) as opposed to, or in addition to, a capital market does, however, change the constraint upon choice. In this respect, the analysis we are about to carry out, which is mainly due to Jack Hirshleifer, differs from that described above.

The Production Opportunity Curve and the Internal Rate of Return

It is convenient to begin by considering an individual who for

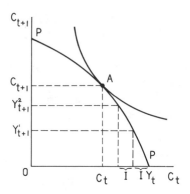

Figure 6.6 Intertemporal choice with production. *PP* is a production opportunity curve. Starting with an initial endowment of Y_t, successive equal investments of I in production yield diminishing increments in output. The utility maximising investment-production-consumption plan occurs at point A, where the rate of time preference equals the internal rate of return in production.

some reason has no access to a market in which he can borrow and lend and who can only transform currently available goods into goods available in the future by devoting them to production. A situation such as might face such an individual is described in figure 6.6. First, we assume for simplicity's sake, that our individual's entire endowment of consumption goods for the two periods is made available to him in time t. Hence, at the outset, he is at point Y_t on the horizontal axis in figure 6.6. Second, we assume that there are available to him a whole array of opportunities for transforming current goods into future goods by way of production, and that he is able to undertake as many, or as few, of these as he likes, and in any order. That is, we assume that his production opportunities are *divisible* and *independent*. A simple example of such a state of affairs would involve an individual whose endowment of goods came in the shape of corn, which he could either consume today, or plant in his field with a view to consuming the resulting crop. The assumption of divisible production opportunities would here mean he could plant just as much or as little corn as he chose, and the assumption of independence that he could plant his corn in any part, or parts, of his field that he chose without the yields being in any way affected.

This assumption of independence is important because there is no reason to suppose that all opportunities facing an individual will be equally productive; in terms of our primitive example, some parts of the field might be more fertile than others. However, if our individual may take up his production opportunities in any order, he can begin with the most productive one, move on to the next most productive one, and so on. The concave to the origin shape of the curve labelled *PP* in figure 6.6, which we may call a *production opportunity curve*, follows from the assumption that, production opportunities are undertaken in diminishing order of productivity. Thus, if, starting from point Y_t an amount of resources I is devoted to production, the resulting output will be Y_{t+1}^1. If another equal amount I is added to production, the resulting output overall will be Y_{t+1}^2. However, the *increment* in output in this second case will be smaller than the initial one, the increment in output resulting from a third equal increment of amount I to the resources devoted to production would be yet smaller again, and so on.

Let us consider the slope of the production opportunity curve a little more closely. As we move up it from right to left, resources are being withdrawn from current consumption and devoted to production. These *investments* yield a payoff in terms of consumption goods in the next period in amounts that may be read off the vertical axis, and this payoff may be thought of as having two components, the first just replacing the initial outlay, and the second representing a net return on the investment. Earlier in this chapter we showed that the slope of the market opportunity curve was $-(1 + r)$ where r is the market rate of interest, and defined the slope of a typical indifference curve as $-(1 + \rho)$ where ρ is the rate of time preference. By exact analogy with these arguments, we may define the slope of our production opportunity curve at any point as $-(1 + R)$ where R is the marginal rate of return on investment, or as it is usually called in the context of the analysis we are developing here, the *internal rate of return*.

The solution to the choice problem depicted in figure 6.6 is straightforward. As in the previous chapter, the objects of choice are consumption in time t and $t + 1$, and the indifference map is identical to that used there. Because we have assumed that our individual has no access to a capital market, but does face a set of production opportunities, the production opportunity locus becomes the relevant constraint upon his choice. The utility maximising solution to our individual's choice problem clearly lies at point A, where the production opportunity curve carries the individual onto, and is just tangent to, his highest attainable indifference curve. Here he consumes C_t of goods in the current period, and invests $Y_t - C_t$, thus producing for himself C_{t+1} of consumption goods for the next period. The reader might note that the fact that point A is one of tangency between an indifference curve and the production opportunity curve means that this equilibrium occurs where there is equality between the rate of time preference ρ, and the internal rate of return on investment R.

Access to a Perfect Capital Market

Now there is really nothing very startling about the analysis just presented. What we have said is that, given that he is excluded from borrowing and lending on the capital market, the amount that any individual will devote to productive investment will be determined by the tangency of an indifference curve to a production opportunity curve, and hence will depend upon his tastes. If we don't have specific information about his tastes, there doesn't seem to be anything very concrete that we can say about our individual's behaviour. As we shall now see, if we change the assumptions of our analysis to permit our individual to have access to a perfect capital market of the type which we analysed earlier in this chapter, in addition to having access to the kind of productive opportunities we have discussed so far, this conclusion changes radically. We find that we are able to make precise predictions about his investment decisions without having to know anything at all about his tastes beyond the usual assumption that they may be characterised by a convex to the origin indifference map.

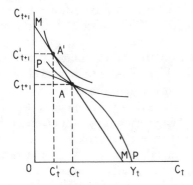

Figure 6.7 Intertemporal choice when access to a perfect capital market is made available after the individual has committed himself to investment—production plan A. The market rate of interest is assumed to be higher than the internal rate of return at A, so the individual re-arranges his consumption plan by further lending, moving to point A'.

To see why this is so, consider what would happen if we suddenly were to allow the individual whose choice behaviour we have been analysing to have access to a perfect capital market where he can borrow and lend at a given interest rate. Consider figure 6.7. Suppose that he had already decided to move up to point A, but had not yet done so, when access to the capital market was granted to him. By moving from point Y_t to point A he changes the endowment of goods available to him, and the first question he might ask when faced with these borrowing and lending opportunities is whether they enabled him to improve further upon point A. He can, after all, move to that point through his own production activities and then treat the resulting combination of present and future goods available to him as the starting point for any borrowing and lending activities. Suppose for the sake of argument that the rate of interest ruling in the capital market is higher than the internal rate of return on investment at A. Then, passing through point A is a market opportunity curve, MM, a straight line with a slope of $-(1 + r)$ which is by assumption steeper than that of the production opportunity locus at A. Clearly, if our individual insists on investing $Y_t - C_t$ of his resources in production, and hence on moving to point A on the production opportunity locus, he can now further improve matters by moving from point A up to the left along the market opportunity curve as far as point A', lending out an amount $C_t - C_t'$ on the capital market and earning in return $C_{t+1}' - C_{t+1}$. This yields him a higher level of satisfaction than that achieved by investment alone.

However, this is the best that he can do *only if* he is already tied to his original investment- -production decision at A when he gains access to the capital market. If he is not tied to that decision then he can, by revising his investment plans, achieve an even greater gain in utility than that depicted in figure 6.7. The reason for this is straightforward. Wherever our individual may choose to settle on his production opportunity curve, he may start his borrowing or lending activities in the capital market from that point. There is, that is to say, an attainable market opportunity curve passing through every point on the production opportunity curve. As we have drawn it, figure 6.7 depicts a state of affairs in which the market rate of interest is higher than the internal rate of return ruling at point A, so that there is a segment of the production opportunity curve below and to the right of A that lies outside of the market opportunity curve passing through that point. This means that our individual, by cutting back on his original investment plan and moving downwards to the right along his production opportunity curve, is able to put himself onto higher and higher market opportunity curves, and hence open up the possibility of achieving higher and higher levels of utility.

Now it is obvious that the further out to the right lies the market opportunity curve upon which our individual places himself, the higher is the level of utility that he can enjoy. Hence a utility maximising individual is going to plan his production activities in such a way as to put himself onto the highest possible market opportunity curve and that in turn will be the one that is just tangent to the production opportunity curve. This is the state of affairs depicted in figure 6.8. Here, as before, we start our individual with an initial endowment of Y_t and face him with production opportunities described by the curve PP. In the absence of access to the capital market, our individual chose that com-

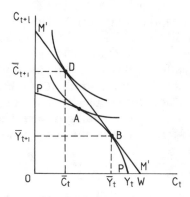

Figure 6.8 Intertemporal choice when all production opportunities are available, and access to a perfect capital market exists. The preferred investment production plan is now at point B, rather than A, and the utility maximising consumption plan is at point D. The choice of point B is independent of the individual's tastes and may be described as the result either of equating the internal rate of return in production to the market rate of interest, or of choosing the production plan with the highest present value, denoted by W, at the market rate of interest.

bination of present and future consumption denoted by point A as the solution to both his production and consumption plans; given that he has access to the capital market, he chooses instead point B as a solution to his production plan, investing $Y_t - \bar{Y}_t$ in order to produce $\bar{Y}_{t+1}$, and then moves along the market opportunity locus $M'M'$ to point D which denotes the utility maximising solution to his consumption plan. As the reader will see, this involves him lending out $\bar{Y}_t - \bar{C}_t$ on the capital market in order to obtain $\bar{C}_{t+1} - \bar{Y}_{t+1}$ as a return.

Now figure 6.8 shows that having access to a perfect capital market enables a maximising individual to separate his production and consumption decisions, but it shows more than that. A moment or two spent examining the diagram in question should convince the reader that, although the solution to his consumption plan — the choice of point C — certainly depends upon our individual's tastes as depicted in his indifference map, the solution to his production plan — the choice of point B — depends solely upon the shape of the production opportunity curve and the slope of the market opportunity curve and is completely independent of his tastes. That is to say, the individual's investment—production decision depends entirely upon factors that are given exogenously to him, these factors being the nature of the production opportunities available and the market rate of interest. Thus we can make statements about the rules that a utility maximising individual will follow in making investment—production decisions, without referring to the precise properties of his indifference map.

Rules for Selecting the Optimal Investment—Production Plan

We have seen that, in order to maximise his utility from consumption, our individual must first choose an investment—production plan that puts him on the highest attainable market opportunity locus. One way of characterising the outcome of this production choice involves noting that the highest attainable market opportunity curve is one whose intercept with the horizontal axis of a diagram such as figure 6.8 lies as far to the right as possible. As we showed earlier in this chapter, this horizontal intercept has an economic interpretation. It measures the maximum quantity of current consumption goods that our individual can command, i.e. the *present value* of his income stream, or his *wealth*. That is why it is labelled W. Thus the proposition that a utility maximising individual will choose his investment—production plan so as to get onto the highest market opportunity curve available to him may be rephrased to say that he will choose that plan which *yields him the highest present value*, which *maximises his wealth*, at the current rate of interest. The same proposition may be rephrased to say that he will choose a production plan at which the slopes of the production opportunity curve and the market opportunity curve are equal, at which *the internal rate of return in production is equal to the market rate of interest*. These two alternative ways of characterising the rule whereby a utility maximising individual will formulate his investment—production plans seem at first sight to be equivalent, and indeed in terms of the case considered in figure 6.8 they are. However, the first of them is in fact more general and yields the 'right' solution in a wider variety of cases than the second, as we shall now show.

The key characteristic of the situation depicted in figure 6.8 that makes the two decision rules seem equivalent is the assumption of *independence* among production opportunities that we made at the very outset. This assumption implies that our individual is able to take up the production opportunities available to him in any order, and so enables us to arrange them in order of decreasing productivity and hence construct a production opportunity curve everywhere concave to the origin. However there are many ways in which this assumption of independence may be violated, and figure 6.9 depicts two of them.

In panel (a) of that figure we show what would happen if there were some indivisibility in production opportunities such that the individual was forced to choose between two sets of productive opportunities and was unable to mix them together in any way. Such a state of affairs would arise in the context of our earlier example if for some reason our corn planting individual had to choose between two fields for his crop and, having chosen one of them to be planted, was excluded from any use of the other. If one field had some extremely fertile patches, and some not so fertile, its use might face our individual with a production opportunity curve such as $P'P'$, and if the other was of more even fertility, but with its best patches inferior to those of the first field and its worst patches better, the curve relevant to it would be the less concave one labelled $P''P''$. Our individual must now choose which production opportunity locus to be on, as well as where to locate on it. As the reader will see from inspecting figure 6.9(a), the rule 'maximise present value' does enable him to select both the better production opportunity locus, and the best point on it, while the rule 'equate the internal rate of return to the market rate of interest' enables him to find only the best point on each production opportunity curve but not to choose between them.

Panel (b) of figure 6.9 depicts a situation in which, although the individual faces but one set of production opportunities, he is not free to take them up in any order, but is in fact forced to undertake some rather low productivity opportun-

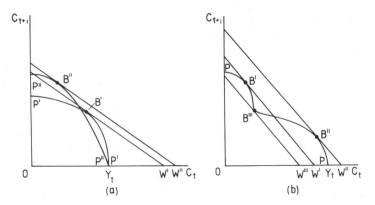

Figure 6.9 Two situations in which the rule 'equate the internal rate of return to the market rate of interest' will not necessarily find the best investment—production plan, but in which the rule 'maximise the present value of the plan at the market rate of interest' will do so:

(a) The production opportunity curves $P'P'$ and $P''P''$ are mutually exclusive. Points B' and B'' both satisfy the internal rate of return rule, but B'' has a higher present value, W'', than does B' whose present value at the market rate of interest is W'.

(b) The production opportunity curve PP has a convex section that results from a lack of independence among the production opportunities available. Here, the internal rate of return rule cannot distinguish between any of the three tangencies shown, though B''' whose present value is W''' is clearly a utility *minimising* rather than maximising plan. Application of the present value rule enables plan B'' whose present value is W'' to be identified as superior to B' whose present value is W'. The reader with some knowledge of calculus will recognise that the 'internal rate of return' rule corresponds to the application of first order conditions for a maximum, that the application of second order conditions would rule out B''' in panel (b), and that the application of the 'present value' rule involves the application of conditions capable of finding a global, as opposed to merely local, maximum.

ities (the flatter central section of the curve) before certain high productivity opportunities become available to him. Such a situation might arise in our example if for reasons of fertility maintenance a particular balance of production had to be adopted, so that, in order to go beyond a certain acreage of corn, it was first necessary to grow some less productive, but fertility restoring, crop such as grass if additional corn plantings were to be undertaken. Such a situation as we are here describing gives rise to a production opportunity curve that is convex rather than concave to the origin over that segment where lower productivity opportunities must be taken before those with high productivity. Again, simple inspection of the diagram will enable the reader to see that the 'maximise present value' rule will enable the individual to find the best investment–production plan, while the other rule will leave him with three possible plans. One of these (at point B''') is the *worst* he could select rather than the best, and the other two are the best available on their own particular concave segment of the curve. However, the rule 'equate the internal rate of return to the rate of interest' gives no guidance as to how the choice between the latter two should be made.

Capital Market Imperfection

The qualifications to our analysis that we have just discussed do not affect the basic conclusion established earlier that it is possible to discuss the factors affecting the choice of the best investment–production decision independently of the consumption decision, and hence to analyse investment decisions in terms of such objective factors as the market rate of interest and the nature of available productive opportunities. However, we did note that this conclusion was conditional upon the individual being faced with a perfect capital market, and it is now time to consider this important qualification in more depth. A perfect capital market is one in which the individual can borrow and lend, up to limits imposed only by the need to remain solvent, at a rate of interest which is given to him, and which is the same regardless of whether he is borrowing or lending and regardless of the scale at which he might be doing either. Only with capital market perfection can we draw the market opportunity curve as a straight line in the way that we have done throughout this chapter. If, as we shall now see, we drop this assumption, the independence of consumption and production decisions vanishes.

There are many types of capital market imperfection that we could introduce into our model, but to make the point it will suffice to deal only with one quite simple case. Let us therefore assume that the market interest rate that our indi-

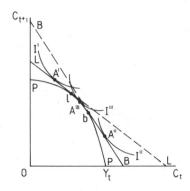

Figure 6.10 Intertemporal choice with production opportunities given by *PP*, but with access to an imperfect capital market where the borrowing rate of interest exceeds the lending rate. Here the optimal investment production plan for a would-be borrower will be point *b*, for a lender it will be point *l*, or for an individual who chooses neither to borrow nor lend it will be at a point such as A'''. I', I'', I''' are *alternative* indifference curves typical of these three possible cases, and A', A'' and A''', represent the corresponding alternative consumption plans. Thus, when the capital market is imperfect, the choice of an investment—production plan comes to depend upon the individual's tastes.

vidual faces differs, depending upon whether he is a borrower or a lender, and that it is higher in the former case. To keep the analysis simple, let us also assume that the rate of interest at which the individual lends, if he chooses to do so, does not vary with the amount involved, and that the borrowing rate that he faces is similarly constant (albeit at a higher level). Finally, and again purely for the sake of simplicity, let us assume that the production opportunities facing the individual are independent of one another so that he faces a production opportunity curve that is concave to the origin.

Figure 6.10 depicts the state of affairs implicit in these assumptions. Once more the individual starts with Y_t of resources and faces a production opportunity curve *PP*. However, instead of one market opportunity curve (or rather one set of market opportunity curves each passing through a different point on *PP*) he faces two. One set has a slope determined by the rate of interest at which he can borrow, and the other set has a slope fixed by the rate at which he can lend. *BB* represents the highest borrowing opportunity curve that he can reach, and it is tangent to the production opportunity curve at *b*, while *LL* is the highest lending market opportunity curve, being tangent to the production curve at *l*. Because the individual can only borrow at the rate of interest underlying *BB*, points above and to the left of *b* on that line are not available to him. By similar reasoning, his inability to borrow at the same low interest rate at which he can lend rules out all points on *LL* below and to the right of *l*. These unattainable segments are drawn as dotted lines, and the effective constraint upon our individual's choice is made up of the discontinuous line consisting of the lower (solid) part of *BB*, the segment *bl* of the production opportunity curve and the upper (solid) part of *LL*.

What production plan will this individual choose? If his indifference map is characterised by shallowly sloped curves such as I', then he will want to be a lender on the capital market and his production—investment decision will take him to point *l*. If the relevant indifference curves are steep, like I'', and he wishes to be a borrower, then his investment—production plan will have him choose point *b*. If they are of some intermediate slope like that of I''', and are tangent to the production opportunity curve somewhere in the segment *bl*, then a point such as A''' will characterise both his production and consumption plans, and he will be neither a borrower nor a lender in the capital market. In any event however, the investment—production decision that our individual makes depends upon the nature of his tastes in the cases we have analysed here in a way that it does not when the capital market is perfect.

Concluding Comments

We have by no means exhausted the microeconomic analysis of the allocation of consumption over time in this chapter. We have said nothing about the problems involved when there are durable goods; in this case the utility yielding act of consumption analysed in this chapter becomes separated from the act of consumer expenditure on a market purchase relevant for a macro theory of income determination. We have said nothing about how individuals might learn from each other so that their consumption patterns become interdependent.

In the field of production choices, we have said nothing about what happens when the individual is able to hire other productive services, for example labour, to cooperate in his production plans, or about what happens when he produces for market rather than his own consumption. Moreover, we have said nothing about how this analysis relates to those special types of investment in 'human' capital known as 'training' and/or education. Nevertheless we have done quite enough to show what a powerful tool our basic theory of consumer behaviour can be in this context. We have seen that a maximising individual will relate his consumption plans to his wealth rather than his income and that they will also vary in a predictable fashion with the rate of interest. This must mean that the simple relationship between consumption and income so frequently used in elementary macroeconomics is very much a first approximation to be defended only on the grounds of its simplicity. As far as investment decisions are concerned, we have seen how important is the assumption of a perfect capital market to the conclusion that they do not depend on individual's tastes. In enabling us to make these points, the analysis of this chapter is more than justified.

7
Choice in the Face of Risk

Introduction

The next topic we consider is not so much an application of our basic consumer theory as it is an extension of it. Up to now we have analysed choice-making behaviour on the assumption that the individual making the choices knows with certainty — or at least behaves as if he knows with certainty — the outcome of his choice. This is clearly an immense assumption and if we continue to make it we will be completely unable to analyse some important economic phenomena. For example, if the outcome of every choice was certain, there would be no role for insurance companies to play. After all, the basic service they provide is that of taking risks of behalf of their customers. Thus, we now go on to examine the question of choice in risky situations. Our first step will be to show that the ability to make consistent choices in conditions of risk implies the existence of a species of cardinal utility function; when this has been established, we will use this function to analyse further choice-making behaviour.

Risk, Probability and Cardinal Utility

Let us consider a situation which deals with as simple a choice involving risk as it is possible to conceive. Suppose we face an individual with the choice between receiving either the sum of £1 with certainty or a chance of winning £100 in a draw of some sort. Which alternative he chooses will depend upon the probability of winning the hundred pounds; a very small chance of winning will tend to make him select the certain alternative, while a very large chance of winning will tend to make him select the risky alternative. It is equally plausible that there is some value for the probability of winning £100 that just makes him indifferent between the certain and the risky alternatives. It is the consequences of assuming that such a probability does exist that we now examine.

If our choice maker is able to say that he is indifferent between one pound with certainty and winning one hundred pounds with a particular probability, then he is saying that the alternatives will yield him the same gain in satisfaction, the same increase in utility. The notion of one pound yielding a given increase in utility is relatively straightforward, but what do we mean by the utility associated with an uncertain situation?

To say that the probability of winning a particular draw is, for example, 0.2 implies that if the draw were repeated an indefinitely large number of times then two out of ten outcomes would be wins and eight out of ten would be losses. If it was a draw for a hundred pounds, then a hundred pounds would be obtained two times in ten, and nothing would be gained eight times in ten. Hence the utility of a gain of a hundred pounds would accrue to the person involved in the draw two times in ten. On average, 0.2 times the utility of one hundred pounds would be obtained per repetition (on the assumption that a zero gain yields zero utility). The assumption that we make about our individual's behaviour is that he treats the average utility that would be obtained from many repeated tries of the risky alternative as the gain in utility that he assigns to participating in it on any one occasion. This is an *ex ante* idea. Once the draw is made he either gets the utility of one hundred pounds or of nothing, and so it is only before the draw is made that the *ex ante* average or *expected* utility concept is relevant. We did not need to distinguish between *ex ante* and *ex post* utility levels in dealing with choice under conditions of certainty, for there the two were always the same. The consequences of making a particular choice were fully known before any choice was made. However, the distinction is obviously a vital one in dealing with situations involving risk.

If our choice maker is able to say that there is a particular probability of winning one hundred pounds that is to him exactly equivalent to receiving one pound with certainty, he is saying that the utility of one extra pound is equal to the expected utility of the risky alternative. Mathematically speaking, expected utilities are calculated by multiplying the utility of each possible outcome by the probability of its occurrence, and then adding these products together. This process yields a *probability weighted average of utilities*. In the particular case being analysed here, this expected utility is equal to the probability of winning one hundred pounds times the utility of a gain of one hundred pounds plus the probability of winning nothing times the utility of a zero gain. If we let $U(£1)$ be the utility of one extra pound and p_1 be the probability of winning one hundred pounds, then we have:

$$U(£1) = p_1 . \ U(£100) + (1 - p_1) \ U(0)$$

Now if it is possible to find a probability value that satisfies the above equation, it is presumably equally possible to find a value, call it p_2, that would make the utility of a chance at the draw equivalent to the utility of two extra pounds with certainty, and so on all the way up to one hundred pounds (at which point the value of p would clearly have to be equal to one).

We could write down a whole array of equations as follows:

$$U(£1) = p_1 . \ U(£100) + (1 - p_1) \ U(0)$$
$$U(£2) = p_2 . \ U(£100) + (1 - p_2) \ U(0)$$

$$. . . . .$$

$$. . . . .$$

$$U(£99) = p_{99} . \ U(£100) + (1 - p_{99}) \ U(0)$$
$$U(£100) = 1 . \ U(£100) + (0) \ U(0)$$

If there is no gain in utility attached to getting zero extra pounds, then $U(0)$ is equal to zero and these expressions can be rearranged to read

$$U(\pounds 1)\frac{1}{U(\pounds 100)} = p_1$$

$$U(\pounds 2)\frac{1}{U(\pounds 100)} = p_2$$

. . . .

$$U(\pounds 99)\frac{1}{U(\pounds 100)} = p_{99}$$

$$U(\pounds 100)\frac{1}{U(\pounds 100)} = 1$$

When we put it this way, it is clear that the probability indices on the right may be used as cardinal indicators of the utility of various sums of money. To be sure, everything is here being measured relative to the utility of gaining one hundred pounds with certainty; the analysis implies no absolute scale for measuring utility. We could equally well conceive of experiments that would measure the utility of gaining various sums of money relative to the utility of gaining two hundred or three hundred pounds or any other amount. We are in no position to say that one sum of money yields twice the utility of some other sum, for such a statement could only be made if we knew where to put zero on our utility scale; but we can say that the *difference* in the utilities yielded by two amounts of money is twice the difference in utilities of two other amounts.

The measurement of utility is thus rather like the measurement of temperature. A temperature which is twice the number of degrees of some other temperature on the Centigrade scale will not be twice the number of degrees on the Fahrenheit scale: 'twice as hot' doesn't mean anything. However, the relative size of differences between particular levels of heat is the same on the two scales. The difference between 30°C (86°F) and 20°C (68°F) is twice the difference between 10°C (50°F) and 5°C (41°F) no matter which scale is used. Utility and temperature are measurable in the same sort of way and to exactly the same extent.

Diminishing Marginal Utility and Expected Utility

Now the purpose of the foregoing analysis is to show that it is legitimate for us to draw a diagram such as figure 7.1 in which the utility accruing to an individual is related to his wealth. The units of measurement on the vertical axis are arbitrary, as is the location of the origin, but to exactly the same extent as if temperature were being measured there. This arbitrariness is irrelevant to the analysis that follows. The relationship is drawn on the assumption that successive equal increments of wealth yield diminishing increments in utility. It displays diminishing marginal utility of wealth. The consequences of making alternative assumptions will be considered later. We may use this utility of wealth function to analyse the nature of the choice facing an individual in a risky situation when he decides whether or not to insure against the risk in question. Suppose that he faced a fifty-fifty chance of losing

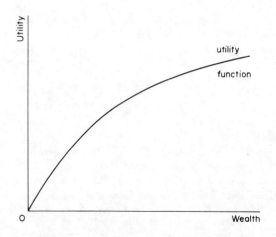

Figure 7.1 A utility function displaying diminishing marginal utility of wealth.

a certain amount of his wealth $(W_1 - W_0)$ within a particular time period. In terms of figure 7.2, given an initial level of wealth, W_1, he will end the period in question either at W_1 with an associated utility level of $U(W_1)$ or at W_0 with an associated utility level of $U(W_0)$. *Ex ante* he has a fifty percent chance of being in either situation. The expected value of his wealth therefore is $\frac{1}{2}W_0 + \frac{1}{2}W_1 = W_2$, but it is not wealth *per se* that is relevant to our individual but the utility that this wealth yields him. His expected utility in the risky situation is given by $\frac{1}{2}U(W_0) + \frac{1}{2}U(W_1)$. This measures the utility accruing to him as he views it *ex ante* at the beginning of the time period under consideration.

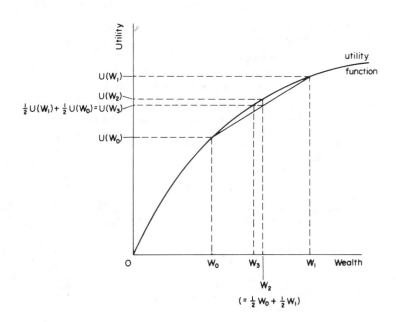

Figure 7.2 *Ex ante*, the individual faces a choice between a fifty-fifty chance of W_0 and W_1 and the certainty of W_2 which lies half-way between them. The expected wealth involved in the two alternatives is the same, but the expected utility of the certain alternative is higher by $U(W_2) - [\frac{1}{2}U(W_1) + \frac{1}{2}U(W_0)]$. A measure of the consumer's surplus gained by selecting the certain alternative by insuring is $W_2 - W_3$.

Insurance and Gambling

Now suppose that the individual can buy insurance against the risk that faces him. Suppose that, in return for a premium paid at the beginning of the period, some agent guarantees to reimburse him completely for any loss that he incurs during the period. For payment of a fee he can put himself in a situation of certainty. By reducing the level of wealth with which he begins the period by the amount of this fee he can guarantee that he will end the period with the same level of wealth. The utility of this alternative is clearly the utility of having W_1 minus the premium with certainty. Faced with the choice of insuring or not insuring, the individual will presumably choose the alternative that will yield him the highest level of *ex ante* utility. In terms of figure 7.2, so long as the insurance premium is less than $W_1 - W_3$ he would prefer to buy insurance. W_3 is the level of wealth which, if available with certainty, yields the same utility as a fifty-fifty chance of W_0 or W_1.

If we ignore the administrative costs of actually buying and selling insurance — we will return to these costs later — the maximum amount that this individual will pay for insurance is more than the minimum the agent providing insurance will accept by way of premium, always provided that the agent in question has a large number of customers, each facing similar, but independent risks. The minimum acceptable premium is one that will enable the insurer just to break even. If he is covering a large number of fifty-fifty risks, then half of his clients will have claims and a premium set at fifty percent of the loss on any one claim will just cover his outgoings. That is to say, *if we ignore any costs that the insurance agent incurs in running his business*, he will be able to offer his client what is usually called 'a fair bet'. A fair bet is one on which, were it to be repeated an indefinitely large number of times, both participants would expect, in the long run, to break even. The agent selling insurance to many people is in fact facing a large number of trials of the same situation, not over time, but over different clients at the same time. Provided that there is no connection between one client incurring a loss and another doing so as well, provided also that the risks taken by the insurance agent are *independent* to use a statistical term, he is enabled to offer his clients fair bets.

This implies in turn that the minimum premium that an insurer will charge will be such as to permit the insured to enjoy with certainty the level of wealth that, in the risky situation, was the expected value of his wealth. Because he may enjoy that wealth with certainty when insured, the individual now has a utility level of $U(W_2)$ and the difference between this and $\frac{1}{2}U(W_1) + \frac{1}{2}U(W_0)$, the utility when not insured, measures the gain to him of being in a situation of certainty; it is the consumer's surplus that arises from buying insurance at the minimum rate at which it can be provided. Another way of looking at the same point is to note that the difference between the minimum premium that is acceptable and the maximum premium that would be paid $(W_2 - W_3)$ measures the money value of this consumer's surplus and hence the scope available to a monopolistic seller of insurance to make a positive profit from dealing with this individual and to cover the administrative costs of the transaction.

Now the assumption of diminishing marginal utility of wealth is crucial to the foregoing analysis. As figure 7.3

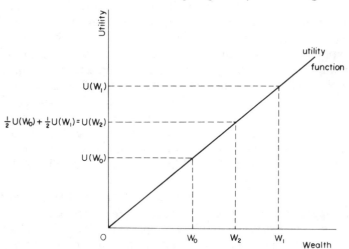

Figure 7.3 When the marginal utility of wealth is constant, not only the expected values of wealth involved in the certain and uncertain situations are the same, but also the expected utility. The alternatives here are a fifty-fifty chance of W_0 or W_1, or W_2 with certainty.

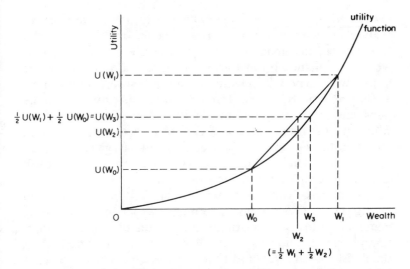

Figure 7.4 Increasing marginal utility of wealth makes the risky alternative preferable. Only the utility function distinguishes the analysis contained in this diagram from that depicted in figures 7.2 and 7.3. Here a gain of $W_1 - W_2$ would add more to utility than an equal sized loss $(W_2 - W_0)$ would subtract from it. Thus a fifty-fifty chance of such a gain or loss has a higher expected utility than the certainty of W_2. $W_3 - W_2$ measures the money value of the extent to which the uncertain alternative is preferred.

shows, a linear utility function — constant marginal utility of wealth — implies that the individual is indifferent between insuring and not insuring at the minimum premium that an insurer would offer, and would prefer not to insure at any higher premium. It is equally clear from figure 7.4 that increasing marginal utility of wealth will involve the individual in refusing insurance at any feasible premium. He will choose the risky alternative rather than the safe one and hence may be said to 'gamble'.

Insurance and Gambling: Further Analysis

If it is the case that increasing marginal utility of wealth implies gambling behaviour and decreasing marginal utility implies insuring, it would appear that an individual would always do one or the other. That is to say, a man who insures against large risks will also insure against small risks; a man who insures his house will insure against every other risk as well and will not fill in football coupons; a man who backs horses will carry only the minimum legal motorcar insurance. Such predictions are contrary to even casually observable facts and present something of a problem for the analysis which we have just described. One way of dealing with such awkward facts proposed by Friedman and Savage is to suggest that though, in general, the marginal utility of wealth diminishes overall, it may increase locally.

The shape of the utility function implicit here is displayed in figure 7.5. An individual might experience increasing marginal utility of wealth in the region of W_2 and hence gamble small amounts — this includes not insuring against small risks — and yet find that, for risks involving the possibility of large losses, the tendency of his utility function to display diminishing marginal utility of wealth was the dominant factor in his decision. The difficulty with this solution is that there seems to be no particular tendency for people at one particular level of wealth to gamble more on small amounts than do those who are better or worse off. It would be quite a coincidence if the workings of the economic system produced a distribution of wealth which gave each individual just that level of wealth at which its marginal utility was, to him, increasing. Virtually everyone, at every level of wealth, insures against some risks but not against others — hence gambling by default — nor does there appear to be any marked relationship between wealth and a propensity to engage in active gambling on the outcome of sporting events and games of chance.

Perhaps a more satisfactory approach to one aspect of this problem is to look more closely at the costs of running an insurance business. There obviously are administrative costs involved in selling insurance policies, and an insurance agent must cover these out of his premium income. Thus, he can, in fact, never quite offer a fair bet to a customer. He must charge a premium that takes some of the consumer's surplus that would accrue to his customer were a completely fair bet offered. Now as the reader ought to be able to satisfy himself

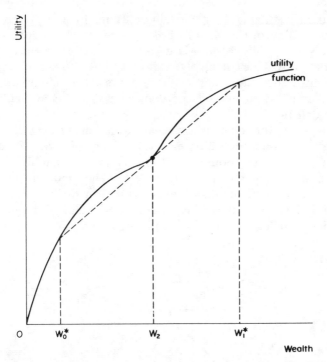

Figure 7.5 A utility function displaying successively decreasing, increasing and decreasing marginal utility of wealth. If an individual who has such a utility function is faced with the choice between W_2 with certainty and the fifty-fifty chance of W_0 and W_1, where the expected value of the uncertain outcome is W_0, then he will select the risky alternative so long as W_0 and W_1 fall within the bounds given by W_0^* W_1^*. He will prefer the certain alternatives if they lie outside these bounds. This is a special case of a general tendency of individuals with such a utility function to take risks when the variations in wealth involved are relatively small and to insure when the variations are relatively large.

easily enough, the smaller the loss which a particular consumer might face, the smaller the surplus accruing to him from buying insurance at a 'fair' premium. Thus, the less he will be willing to pay above that fair premium to cover the insurance agent's costs of handling the transaction. But there is no reason to suppose that these costs decline in any kind of simple proportion as the value of the loss against which insurance is being sought declines. It might easily take the same amount of time and trouble to deal with the paper work on a small policy as on a large one, and the same amount of work to assess the risk involved and calculate the fair premium. For insurance involving small amounts these administrative costs might well exceed the consumer's surplus available to cover them.

In short, for some risks the gain from having the insurance at a 'fair' premium is outweighed by the administrative costs. Hence, it is not bought and the consumer gambles. This possibility is illustrated in figure 7.6. The argument here is surely a plausible explanation of why individuals who insure against large risks nevertheless gamble by failing to buy cover against smaller ones. However, the argument does not explain

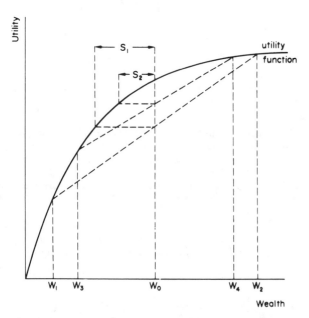

Figure 7.6 The gain from buying insurance at a fair premium against a 'large' risk: that of losing $W_2 - W_1$ with a fifty per cent probability is given by S_1. For a 'small' risk, that of losing $W_4 - W_3$ with a fifty per cent probability, the gain from insuring at a fair premium is S_2. For the smaller risk, the surplus available to pay administrative costs associated with taking out insurance is also smaller. Hence the individual is less likely to insure against small risks.

why people *actively* undertake gambles. One avoids transaction costs by not filling in football coupons, and by not placing bets on horses. One incurs them by doing so, and they are, of course, covered by the football pool company or bookmaker shading the odds they offer in their own favour and away from a fair bet. Hence, to take account of transactions costs is to make it even more difficult to explain this type of gambling in terms of the analysis presented in this chapter. Only if one postulates that active gambling yields satisfaction to the individual who undertakes it over and above that which he gets from consuming his winnings (if any) can one explain its occurring. This amounts to saying that some people gamble because they like gambling and is perilously close to being no explanation at all of the phenomenon.

Nevertheless, even though the analysis set out in this chapter does not deal satisfactorily with all the relevant facts, it is still extremely useful. It has many applications: to the behaviour of insurance companies, banks, and other financial institutions as well as firms and individuals. It underlies much of the modern work on inventory theory and on the monetary aspects of macroeconomics. As the reader will appreciate, then, this chapter has provided only the briefest introduction to a most important branch of modern micro theory.

8
Goods and their Attributes

Introduction

Our final examination of consumer behaviour involves an extension and reformulation of the theory of consumer choice rather than another application of it. We can by no means give a complete exposition of this alternative way of coming to grips with the problems we have already considered, partly owing to lack of space and partly because the analysis is still under development. Nevertheless, this new view has provided insights into a number of problem areas in which the more conventional approach is rather unhelpful and even a brief exposition of its salient features enables this to be seen. The approach is mainly due to Kelvin Lancaster.

We still analyse the choice-making situation in terms of three basic components — the objects of choice, the constraint upon choice and the tastes in terms of which the choice is made — but we consider them in a rather different way. We have thought in terms of the consumer deriving utility from the consumption of goods, and the constraint upon his consumption being a financial one given by his income and the prices of goods. The key to the new approach lies in looking more closely at the connection between the possession of goods and the derivation of satisfaction from their consumption.

Goods, Attributes and Choice

The 'goods' which are bought by consumers on the market are virtually never commodities that yield a single well-defined service to their purchaser when he consumes them. Instead, they have a number of attributes and it is reasonable to argue that it is these attributes which yield satisfaction in consumption not the goods themselves. Thus a particular house or flat provides a whole variety of services to its occupier. It has a certain amount of floor space, a definite number of rooms, a particular quality of finish, a specific location relative to transport and recreational facilities, and so on; the list that one could draw up is virtually endless. Housing is a particularly complicated commodity to be sure, but even something as simple as a loaf of bread may be described in terms of attributes: its flavour, texture, colour, to say nothing of its nutritional characteristics which are themselves a complex mixture of attributes.

Thus the new approach to consumer theory views the objects of choice as being not the commodities which are available on the market, but their attributes. The utility function in terms of which choices are made deals not with bundles of goods, but with bundles of these attributes. What about the third ingredient of choice-making behaviour, the constraint upon choice? Instead of it being defined solely in terms of income and prices, it now must be defined in terms of income, prices and the technical characteristics of particular commodities available on the market. The demand for market goods and services is no longer to be regarded as the direct result of choice-making behaviour among bundles of such goods and services, but an indirect result of a more fundamental choice-making process.

A Simple Example – Brand Loyalty

Let us now look briefly at the way in which this new approach helps us to understand particular problems in economics. The reader will by now be used to our simplifying problems so as to use on them the geometry to which the technical armoury of this book is confined, and in this case we must simplify ruthlessly. We shall consider the case of a particular commodity, and shall assume that it has but two attributes. We shall also consider a highly artificial situation in which the consumer's volume of expenditure on that particular good is predetermined. In this way we can easily depict our problem in a two-dimensional diagram.

Let us then consider good X and treat it as having two attributes, L and M. If the reader wishes to give rather more concrete content to the analysis that follows, he may think of X as being baked beans, and L measuring the number of beans and M the amount of tomato sauce, or of X as nut chocolate with the two attributes being an amount of chocolate and a quantity of nuts, or indeed he may find his own example. In figure 8.1 we measure not quantities of a good

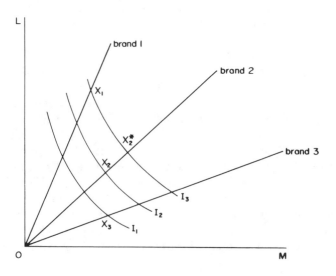

Figure 8.1 L and M are attributes of good X and the indifference curves describe a consumer's tastes *vis-à-vis* those attributes. Three brands of X are available each combining the attributes in different proportions. X_1, X_2 and X_3 represent quantities of these different brands of X that can be bought for a given outlay. If he is constrained to spend just that amount, our consumer will choose to by X_1 of brand 1, since I_3 is a higher indifference curve than I_2 or I_1.

along the axes, but quantities of a particular attribute: any point in figure 8.1 denotes a particular combination of attributes of good X. Now suppose that there were three brands of X available to the consumer, each of which mixed the attributes in different proportions, with the first brand having mostly attribute L and the third having mostly attribute M. Our consumer then can increase his consumption of L and M in fixed proportions by moving out from the origin along any one of the three rays.

Associated with each point on any one of these rays is a price that must be paid to acquire just that combination of L and M. Tins of baked beans, if you like, have a price and, depending on the brand, contain different amounts of beans and sauce. In the artificial example which we are considering, we have endowed our individual with a fixed sum of money to spend on X, and with this sum he can just reach a particular point on each of the three rays. Let these points be X_1, X_2 and X_3 respectively. If our consumer is restricted to buying only one of the brands and is restricted to spending a fixed sum on that brand, then these three points represent the alternatives among which he can choose. They represent a highly discontinuous budget constraint. However, the important characteristic of the budget constraint as it is viewed in this approach is not its discontinuity, but the fact that it is no longer constructed on the basis simply of market data such as income and prices; the technical characteristics of particular goods also enter into it.

Tastes may be treated quite conventionally. We may draw an indifference map of the usual form which shows the consumer's preferences between bundles of attributes. Such a map, displaying a diminishing marginal rate of substitution between the attributes L and M, is drawn in figure 8.1, and the consumer, as always, goes to the point on his budget constraint that yields him the highest level of satisfaction. In this case he has but three points to choose among, and as figure 8.1 is constructed, it is point X_1 that is on the highest indifference curve.

All this seems innocuous enough, and yet this analysis both makes predictions that are not given by the more conventional approach, and enables us to formulate questions about which that approach is silent. Consider first of all the simple question of the individual consumer's response to a fall in the price of a particular good. Conventional analysis predicts that as the price falls, more of the good in question will be bought, and that the bigger the price fall, the bigger will be the consumer's response. Consider, however, the consequences for the individual's behaviour of a fall in the price of just one brand of good X, say brand 2. The lower the price of this brand, the further out along the relevant ray does X_2 lie. However, unless it gets as far as X_2^* — the point at which the indifference curve passing through X_1 cuts ray 2 — there will be no effect whatsoever on our consumer's behaviour. Any price fall that enables him to get beyond X_2^* will cause him to switch his entire consumption of X to this second brand.

Clearly, this is a very different kind of individual response to that predicted by orthodox demand theory. Instead of a smooth and continuous movement from the relatively expensive good towards consumption of one whose price is falling, there is an all or nothing shift whose size is quite unrelated to the extent of the price fall. However, it should be noted at once that though the notion of a smooth downward sloping demand curve is undermined here, it is only undermined at the level of the individual's behaviour. The aggregate demand for a particular brand of a good may still be smoothly downward sloping, but this property would come from the likelihood of different individuals having different tastes and hence switching, at different prices, to a brand whose price is falling.

Now the reader will have noted that in the foregoing discussion we referred to different 'brands' of X. The word did not crop up at all in our discussion of more conventional consumer theory. We derived demand curves for X on the assumption that it could be treated as a homogeneous product. However, product differentiation and the closely associated phenomenon of the use of brand names are widespread and conventional consumer theory has considerable difficulty in dealing with them. To try to apply such analysis to the empirical study of the market, even for so uncomplicated a product as baked beans, immediately leads one to ask questions about whether it is satisfactory to treat all brands as if they were one homogeneous good, or whether each brand should be treated as a separate good. Only *ad hoc* answers are available to this question because the very notion of product differentiation has no place in conventional analysis. It starts after all by taking the product as given, as the basic object of choice. By treating the attributes of products as the basic objects of choice, the new approach enables us to talk about product differentiation as involving goods mixing basic attributes in different proportions. In using it to analyse a consumer's choice between three brands of a particular good, we have shown that there is no reason to expect that smooth substitution relationships will exist between brands of the same good. There is a range of price variation over which the individual will continue to consume a particular brand of X; we have thus given the notion of 'brand loyalty' — the phenomenon of continuing to buy a particular brand even though its price may have risen relative to others — a basis in economic theory, a basis which it does not have in the more conventional approach.

An Elaboration — Combining Brands

One assumption underlying the choice analysed in figure 8.1 was that the consumer was unable to get any mix of attributes other than those made available to him by consuming one or another brand of X. He was not able to mix brands. For some goods this is a reasonable enough assumption, but not for others. If the only difference between brands of baked beans was the ratio of beans to sauce in the tin, then by mixing the contents of different manufacturers' tins in different proportions, a much wider variety of combinations of attributes can be obtained. Indeed, in terms of figure 8.2, a constant outlay could obtain any combination of attributes L and M along a straight line drawn between X_1 and X_2 by combining the first and second brand, between X_2 and X_3 by combining the second and third, and between X_1 and X_3 by combining the first and third. As the figure is constructed, however, the first and third brands would never be combined, since more of the good in question is always available in combinations involving

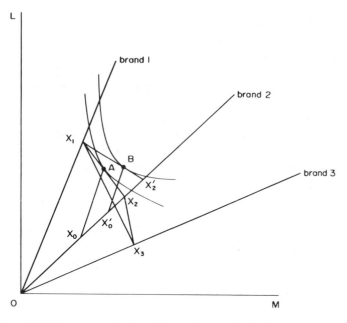

Figure 8.2 If he can mix brands in order to obtain intermediate combinations of attributes, then a constant outlay on X enables our consumer to obtain L and M anywhere along the lines $X_1 X_2$, $X_2 X_3$ and $X_1 X_3$. Given his tastes, he will select combination A. If the price of brand 2 falls this is equivalent to a fall in the price of attribute M, since brand 2 contains relatively more of M than does brand 1. The consumer moves to point B and, for a given outlay, unambiguously increases his outlay on M. Whether this also involves buying more of brand 2 is uncertain. Point A is reached by purchasing X_0 units of brand 2 and $A - X_0$ units of brand 1. Point B is reached by buying X_0' units of brand 2 and $B - X_0'$ units of brand 1. As the indifference curves are drawn, X_0' clearly exceeds X_0 so that more of brand 2 is bought. However, an indifference curve could easily be drawn tangent to $X_1 X_2'$ at a point which would involve X_0' being less than X_0.

brand 2. Given our individual's tastes as depicted in figure 8.2, he will in fact combine brands 1 and 2 and settle at A. Should the price of brand 2 fall, he will make a smooth substitution towards M, so long as this is not a 'Giffen' attribute, but this may involve *either more or less* of brand 2 being purchased as is also shown in the figure.

This analysis is of interest for two reasons. First, it shows that the all or nothing nature of the response to a price change predicted in the previous section of this chapter is dependent upon the individual being unable to combine different brands of the same good in order to reach his own preferred mixture of attributes, or at least unable to do so without incurring costs — which may be merely in terms of time and trouble — that more than offset any advantage that he might gain from so doing. Second, in showing that the demand for a particular brand of a good might fall as its own price falls, even though none of the attributes that make it up are inferior, the analysis warns us that the phenomenon of an upward sloping demand curve might not be quite the practically irrelevant analytic curiosity that orthodox analysis of the 'Giffen good' case might suggest.

Product Differentiation and Advertising

The foregoing considerations lead us immediately into another problem area. It is not unreasonable to suppose that manufacturers of particular goods will find it much easier to vary the proportions in which their output combines various attributes than will individual consumers. Consider figure 8.3. Our consumer with a given outlay to make on X will buy brand 1 so long as he has only three versions of the product to choose from. However, consider that combination of attributes that lies along the ray labelled 4. If some manufacturer can produce a new brand of X that combines L and M in these proportions, and offer it for sale at a price that enables our consumer to reach a point above and to the right of A for his given outlay, he will switch to that brand. Given his particular tastes, he will be better off in so doing. If there are enough consumers with such tastes, and if it is technically feasible, there is a strong incentive for some firm, or firms, to produce brand 4.

The line of reasoning implicit in this very simple example helps us to understand two pervasive phenomena in everyday economic life. First, not every consumer will have the same tastes and hence we can begin to see why it will pay firms, and indeed even the same firm, to produce an array of brands of

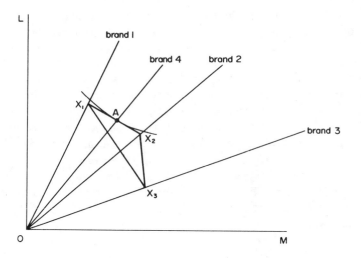

Figure 8.3 If, at going prices, enough consumers prefer L and M combined in the proportion given by A, it might pay a firm to introduce a brand 4 that would appeal to such consumers.

the same good, each one having slightly different attributes. Moreover, there is no reason to suppose that any firm can possibly know *a priori* just how many of its potential customers prefer particular combinations of attributes in a particular product; but without such knowledge it would be all too easy to 'miss the market'. The importance of market research to firms becomes much easier to understand when we look at it in this light.

If product differentiation and market research are phenomena that are illustrated by this new approach to consumer theory, it will come as no surprise to the reader to learn that it is also helpful in the analysis of advertising. Consider what the conventional analysis set out in previous chapters enables us to say about advertising. Consumers have given tastes *vis-à-vis* goods, and, given these tastes, do the best they can for themselves in the light of their incomes and the market prices that rule. The formal analysis makes it difficult indeed to deal with advertising, for everything is presumed to be known to the consumer, but it does not take too much of a stretch of the imagination to realise that consumers in fact do not have perfect information. There is no reason to suppose that a consumer knows the full array of prices ruling in the market at any time, nor is there any reason for him to know just who has what to sell. Clearly, there is room for an industry that specialises in conveying such information, so that there is room for 'informative advertising' in conventional analysis. But even quite casual observation soon convinces one that there is a lot more to contemporary advertising practices than conveying information about who has what to sell at what price. Estate agents' advertisements in local newspapers perform this role, but what about detergent advertisements on television? Prices and names of stockists are seldom, if ever, mentioned.

Such advertising is obviously aimed at persuading consumers to purchase one brand of a good rather than another, and since it hardly makes sense to suggest that consumers do not know their own tastes, the only way to fit such advertising into conventional analysis is to suggest that it is designed to change tastes, to shift the consumers' indifference maps. There is no need to dwell on the social and political implications of this interpretation. However, given conventional consumer theory, there is no other way of interpreting such advertising. The new approach outlined in this chapter does leave room for an alternative interpretation without however ruling out the possibility that advertising's main role is to mould tastes.

If consumers do know their own tastes and advertising does not in fact change those tastes, then it must inform consumers about the objects of choice and about the constraints upon choice. Think of consumers having tastes for the attributes of goods, rather than directly for the goods themselves. Think also of different brands of a particular good combining attributes in different proportions so that the technical characteristics of particular brands are components of the constraint on the consumer's choice. There is no reason for us to suppose that consumers are familiar with the technical characteristics of each particular brand. We may then view advertising as informing consumers about what brands of a particular good are available, where, and at what price, and we can also think of it as informing them about the attributes of particular brands. Thus, advertising that does not stress information about market prices and such, and which, in terms of conventional consumer choice theory, must be interpreted as having to do with an attempt to change tastes, may, in terms of this newer approach, be interpreted as informative. Consider, for example, car advertising that typically stresses such characteristics as fuel economy, passenger carrying capacity, manoeuverability, acceleration, and so on. This is not to say that such advertising *must* be so interpreted, or that it is necessarily correct to so interpret it; only that an alternative hypothesis is available in the context of this new analysis. Which is correct is an empirical question that must await the formulation and performance of empirical tests designed to distinguish between them, but it is a strong point in favour of looking at goods in terms of their attributes that it opens up the possibility of formulating such tests.

Review
all
previous
material

Part III
Production and Costs of Production

9
Production and the Firm

Introduction

Up to now, the analysis presented in this book has concerned itself with consumer choice, and in particular with the allocation of income among expenditures on various goods and services. It hardly needs pointing out that the goods and services which consumers purchase and consume do not simply materialise out of the blue. In large measure they have to be produced. Moreover, we have also seen that important elements in consumer decision making involve, not the purchase of goods and services, but the sale of productive services, not least labour services. Of course, it is these very services that are used in the production of goods which in turn become the objects of the consumer's demand. In short, the analysis of consumer behaviour, vital though it is to an understanding of economic life, cannot tell us the whole story. The study of consumption needs to be supplemented by a study of production and it is to the analysis of production that the next three sections of this book are devoted.

Production

The essential fact about production is so obvious that it hardly needs stating: it involves the use of services of various sorts to generate output. However, productive services do not usually come together spontaneously, their use is typically organised in some way. Clearly, the manner in which production is organised has important social and political, as well as economic aspects, and much of what follows is relevant to more than one form of social and economic organisation. For example, the technical relationships between flows of inputs of productive services and flows of outputs are just as relevant to the student of production processes organised by socialist planners as they are to the student of the private profit-making firm, as indeed is the relationship between such technical relationships and the analysis of costs of production. Production costs are, after all, as relevant to the manager of a collectively owned enterprise as to the manager of a privately owned firm. Indeed, the reader who pursues his studies of microeconomics into the area of the economics of socialism will find that many of the principles which we shall develop below in the context of studying the behaviour of the profit maximising firm also have important applications to questions about how to organise an economy where the means of production are collectively owned.

Nevertheless, the following chapters do take certain social and political conditions for granted inasmuch as they are overwhelmingly concerned with decisions about the production of goods and services as they arise in the context of an economy where such decisions are taken by privately owned, and (in the main) profit oriented firms. We have already noted that production involves the organisation of flows of inputs in order to generate flows of output, and we are going to analyse the decisions that underlie such an organisation as they are taken by privately owned firms. Now of course, in the real world, firms come in many shapes and sizes ranging from the family owned corner business all the way to the giant multi-national, multi-product corporation, and there is no way in which a book as brief as this one could come to grips with all the manifold details of the organisation and operation of such a wide variety of concerns. Thus, the theory of the firm as we shall present it will be abstract and will concentrate on certain properties, one hopes the essential ones, that all such enterprises have in common.

The Firm and the Entrepreneur

The firm, as we shall analyse it, is a social entity that carries out three activities. It buys productive services, organises them so as to produce output, and then sells the output. Its task is to take the decisions upon which the organisation of production depend, and economists have often found it useful to personify this decision making role in the form of being called the *entrepreneur*. There is no need literally to postulate that any one human being in a particular firm takes all the decisions about input purchases, the choice of technology, and the marketing of output, to make the concept of an entrepreneur a useful one. It is sufficient to realise that in any undertaking such decisions must be made in a mutually consistent way in order to see that it might be a useful abstraction to think about those decisions 'as if' they were all taken by one individual.

One thing that the reader should be careful about here is not to confuse the entrepreneur with another personification of a particular social function who sometimes turns up in discussions of the behaviour of market economies, namely the 'capitalist'. The 'capitalist' certainly exists as far as the following analysis is concerned, but only in the background. It is his role to own the capital equipment used by the firm in the production process, and to sell its services to the entrepreneur. His income is derived from his ownership of capital, and is just as distinct from the entrepreneur's income as is his function in the organisation of production. The entrepreneur's 'profit' is what is left to him from the proceeds of sales after the labour force has been paid for its services and the capitalist has been paid for the use of his equipment.

To say that it is the task of the entrepreneur to plan and oversee the execution of the productive activities undertaken by the firm against the background of a market economy raises the following issue. It is often argued that a market economy operates so as to organise in a harmonious way the activities of numerous individual agents without any person or institution having to formulate an overall plan for the economy as a whole. The information and incentives conveyed to individual agents by prices are supposed to be sufficient to ensure that each one of them, pursuing his own self interest, acts in a way that is compatible with the activities of everyone else without supervision of any sort. Such an argument, taken to an extreme position would seem to rule out the existence of firms as social institutions and to give no scope for entrepreneurial activity. It is after all of the very essence of a firm that those who provide productive services to it act under supervision, in accordance with a plan laid down by the entrepreneur, rather than as free agents making voluntary choices about their activities at each and every instant in response to price signals.

The apparent paradox involved here was first noted by Karl Marx who used it to help justify the usefulness of what we would now call socialist planning for an industrial economy. He argued that if planning is useful at the level of the firm, it must be useful at the level of the economy as a whole as well. Much modern work in the field of industrial organisation, particularly that pioneered by Ronald Coase, rests upon an alternative response to this same paradox. The basis of that response is to note that whether any particular set of activities will be coordinated within a firm on a planning basis or between individual agents by the use of market mechanisms, will depend on the relative costs of doing so in one way or the other. According to this view, market transactions *per se* are costly to undertake, so that if an entrepreneur can plan and coordinate aspects of individuals' behaviour more cheaply than they can be organised by market mechanisms, he will be able to compensate them, in the incomes he pays them, for the sacrifice of freedom they make in committing themselves in advance to obeying his orders for the period of time for which they agree to work for him. In short, production activities come to be organised within firms when it is economical to do so.

This line of reasoning has enabled economists to begin to come to grips with a whole range of problems having to do with the factors that determine the extent of vertical and horizontal integration within industries, the way in which mergers between firms come about, not to mention many aspects of the behaviour of bureaucratic organisations both in the private and the public sectors. To deal with this wide range of subject matter would take us far beyond the scope of this book, but as he works through the analysis of the behaviour of the firm that follows, the reader should constantly bear in mind that the analysis in question simply takes it for granted that firms exist. A deeper treatment of the way in which firms operate might go into the question of why they exist, and how they might evolve over time, along the lines so briefly described in the last few paragraphs. As I have already noted, such analysis does exist, and the material that follows in this book should therefore be regarded as constituting an introduction to the analysis of the behaviour of firms and industries, rather than as being anything approaching a comprehensive account of this branch of microeconomics.

Concluding Comment

As has already been remarked, there are certain technical matters inevitably involved in the analysis of production that involve the processes whereby inputs are transformed into outputs, and the properties of the relationships involved here impinge upon all aspects of the behaviour of the firm. Thus in the next chapter, we begin our detailed analysis by considering the *production function* in terms of which these relationships are summarised, and having done that will then proceed to analyse the nature of production costs. Only when we have laid this groundwork will it be possible to proceed to consider the decisions that the entrepreneur will take for the firm *vis-à-vis* its activities in the markets for its outputs and its inputs. These matters form the subject matter of Parts 5 and 6 of this book respectively.

10
Properties of the Production Function

Introduction

Just as market prices and income constrain the behaviour of households, so the technological possibilities of production constrain the decisions taken by the entrepreneur about the behaviour of the firm. The basic framework of the theory of the firm must concern itself to an important degree with the technical relationships involved in the transformation of such inputs as the services of labour and capital equipment into outputs of goods and services. Therefore, we begin our discussion by dealing with these production relationships.

The notion of production is very general. Not only are physical goods produced, but also services, such as transportation, education, insurance and so forth. Any process which involves the transformation of one kind (or kinds) of good or service into another may be thought of as a process of production. However, as with consumption, so with production we can reduce the situation to an extremely basic and simple form and deal in detail with a fairly special case in order to get to grips with the basic issues.

Therefore, in this chapter we will consider the production of good X, and will presume that there are but two inputs to its production. We will refer to these inputs, *factors of production* as they are usually called, as capital (K) and labour (L). It should be noted at the outset that just as the production of X is to be thought of as a *flow* of output, so the inputs into the production process should also be thought of in flow terms: K and L represent machine hours and man hours of productive services, not a stock of capital and a labour force.

The reader should not infer that it is possible to add together the services of all the manifold types of equipment and inventories used in a modern production process to give one unambiguous index number that measures the 'quantity of capital services' employed. Nor may one necessarily aggregate the hours worked by people of many different skills directly involved in production, to say nothing of those indirectly involved in a management or sales promotion role, into some unambiguously measurable quantity called 'the services of the labour force'. Nevertheless, the results of the two input/one output special case are both useful and often capable of being generalised, and are therefore well worth the reader's attention.

Activities and the Isoquant

We start with the most primitive concept in the analysis of production, an 'activity'. Carrying on an activity means combining flows of factor services per unit of time in a particular proportion and getting a particular rate of flow of output from doing so. Thus, in figure 10.1 we depict an activity that involves combining machine services and labour services in the ratio 2/1 by a line labelled 1, another that combines them in equal proportions by a line labelled 2. It is a reasonable initial simplifying assumption that if one doubles the quantities of inputs in any particular activity one will also double output, or, to put it more generally, that equiproportional increases in inputs will lead to equiproportional increases in output. This is the assumption of *constant returns to scale*. An equal distance moved along each activity line in figure 10.1 thus represents an equal increase in both inputs and output.

Now there is no obvious reason why a firm should be confined exclusively to one production activity, or another. It could presumably mix them. Thus, in figure 10.1 it could produce an output of say $3X$ units of X by using all activity 1,

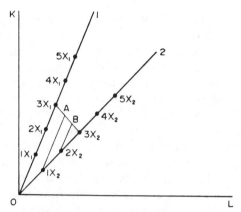

Figure 10.1 Inputs K and L are combined in given proportions along rays 1 and 2 in 'activities' that yield equal increments in the output of X for equal increments to inputs. Activity 1 and activity 2 may be combined at level of output $3X$ (or at any other level of output) to make any combination of capital and labour along the line $3X_1$ $3X_2$ available as a means of producing that level of output.

all activity 2, or by combining these activities in different proportions it could obtain that level of output by combining capital and labour services anywhere along the line joining $3X_1$ and $3X_2$. For example, $3X$ units of X could be achieved by producing $2X$ units by activity 1 and $1X$ by activity 2, thus ending up at point A. The same output could be reached by producing $1X$ unit with activity 1 and $2X$ units with activity 2 thus ending up at point B.

The reader will recognise the similarity between this analysis and that set out in Chapter 8 where we considered the possi- bilities of mixing different brands of a particular good in order to obtain a mixture of attributes between those available from exclusive consumption of one brand or another. He will also realise that there is no reason to confine the analysis to the case of a firm having just two activities available to it. In principle, the analysis can be extended to an indefinitely large number of activities, but, for the sake of clarity alone, in figure 10.2 we depict the case of four available activities, each using capital and labour services in different proportions. Any pair of activities may be used together, and so we have linked up each available pair of activities with straight lines as we did in figure 10.1.

At this point in the argument, even when apparently dealing with purely technological matters, we must introduce an assumption about the firm's motivation and behaviour if we are to proceed further. This assumption is that, whatever motivates those running the firm, they will never use more units of input than are necessary to get a given output. As we have drawn figure 10.2, any output plan that utilises activity 3 requires more inputs for a given output than any plan that does not use it. This activity is said to be *technically inefficient* and will not be used by a firm seeking to minimise the inputs used for any output. Moreover, any combination of 1 and 4 uses more inputs than combinations of 1 and 2 and 3 and 4, or 1, 2 and 4 alone. Thus, the kinked line linking the points $3X_1$, $3X_2$ and $3X_4$ gives the locus of the minimum combinations of factor inputs required for an output of $3X$ given prevailing technology. The line becomes vertical beyond $3X_1$ and horizontal beyond $3X_4$ to indicate that further increases of capital and labour beyond these points add nothing to output.

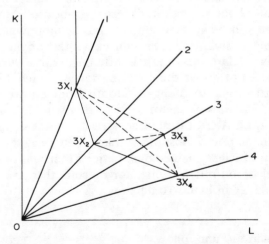

Figure 10.2 With four activities, any pair of them may be combined. Here the solid kinked line passing through $3X_1$, $3X_2$ and $3X_4$ shows the minimum combinations of capital and labour that will produce $3X$ units of output. Above activity line 1, this isoquant becomes vertical and to the right of activity line 4 it becomes horizontal, because further additions to inputs in these directions add nothing to output.

This kinked line is a simple special case of a much used analytic device in the economics of production. The output of X is the same at any point on it, and hence it is known as an 'equal product curve' or an 'iso-product curve' or, most frequently, an *isoquant*. The most important property of an isoquant is already implicit in the simple analysis carried out in figure 10.2. It will never be concave towards the origin, and will in general be convex. In terms of figure 10.2, the isoquant would have been concave to the origin if activity 3 had been used in its construction, for it would have contained the segment $3X_2$ $3X_3$ $3X_4$, but this segment is not part of the isoquant, because for any point on it there is a point on the line $3X_2$ $3X_4$ at which the same amount of output could be produced using fewer inputs.

In figure 10.1, with two technically efficient activities we have a straight line isoquant; in figure 10.2, with three such activities we have an isoquant that is kinked convexly to the origin. But we have already remarked that there is no need to confine ourselves to considering small numbers of activities. The more technically efficient activities there are, each using capital and labour services in different proportions, the more kinks there will be in the isoquant, and the more will it come to resemble a smooth curve, convex to the origin. Just as along a particular consumer's indifference curve we plot all those bundles of goods the consumption of which will yield equal satisfaction, so along a smooth isoquant we plot all those combinations of factor services that will yield an equal level of output. A great deal of analysis is considerably simplified, with no important loss of accuracy, if we treat the various technically efficient factor combinations that will produce a given level of output as lying along a smooth curve such as for example $3X$ in figure 10.3 below.

The Production Function

The previous section of this chapter was concerned with the various ways in which a particular level of output, $3X$ units of X, could be produced. The choice of this output level was, of course, quite arbitrary, and we could have carried out exactly the same analysis for any other level of output. Hence,

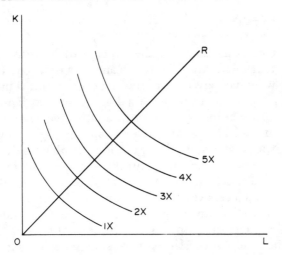

Figure 10.3 A smooth production function. The isoquants show the maximum level of output to be had for each combination of inputs. As we move out along any ray (such as *OR*) drawn from the origin, inputs of capital and labour increase in equal proportions.

there is not just one isoquant implicit in the foregoing analysis, but a whole family thereof, one for each conceivable level of output. A map of such isoquants is shown in figure 10.3, which is a geometric representation of a *production function*. The output of *X* depends on — that is to say, is a *function* of — inputs of capital and labour services into the process. The isoquant map of figure 10.3 tells us, for any combination of factor inputs, what the maximum attainable output of *X* will be. Equivalently, it also tells us, for any given level of output of *X*, what are the minimum combinations of inputs necessary to produce it. Provided that we are willing to think of inputs as being divisible into infinitely small units and of output as being similarly divisible, then we may also think of there being a smooth continuous isoquant passing through every point in figure 10.3. However, as with the indifference map in consumer theory, it suffices for analytic purposes to draw only a selection of these. The rest of this chapter is devoted to looking at the properties of the production function in more detail. Two concepts are helpful in carrying the analysis further — *returns to scale* and *returns to a factor* — and we will deal with them in turn.

Returns to Scale

The reader has already met the concept of 'returns to scale' when dealing with the nature of an 'activity'. The concept refers to what happens to output when every input is increased in equal proportion. In terms of a diagram such as figure 10.3, equiproportional increases in both inputs involve moving out along a straight line, a ray, drawn from the origin. In general, we may speak of production functions displaying decreasing returns to scale, constant returns to scale, and increasing returns to scale. If successive equal increments of all factor inputs yield successively smaller increases in output, we have decreasing (or diminishing) returns to scale, if they yield equal increments in output we have constant returns to scale, and if they yield successively increasing increments in output we have increasing returns to scale.

Strictly speaking, statements about returns to scale characterise what happens over a particular range along a given ray through the origin, and do not necessarily describe the whole production function. If all we require of our isoquants is that they be smooth and convex to the origin, then it is easy indeed to construct a production function which yields constant returns along some rays and diminishing (or increasing) returns along others, or which yields successively increasing, constant and diminishing returns along the same ray. Nevertheless, there are special types of functional relationships for which what is true of one section of one ray through the origin is true of all sections of all rays. One class of such functions is called *homogeneous functions*. Because they are, mathematically speaking, relatively simple in form, they are much used in empirical work on production and hence are worthy of brief description here.

The first characteristic defining a homogeneous function is that *all* the isoquants that cut *any one* ray through the origin do so with the same slope. This characteristic is known as *homotheticity*. Homothetic isoquants which are equidistant from one another along any one ray are also equidistant along any other. To move from one isoquant to another represents a definite cardinally measurable change in the level of output. The second characteristic of a homogeneous production

function is that is displays the same returns to scale characteristics along any ray regardless of the input combination
represented by that ray. Figure 10.4, in fact, depicts a special
case of such a relationship: the constant returns to scale
special case. Such a production function is often described as
displaying *homogeneity of degree one*.

Now the production function derived from activity analysis
obviously displays constant returns to scale and the question
must arise as to how any production function could display
any other characteristic? The key simplifying assumption that
yields this property is that it is possible to carry on any
activity, with equal efficiency, at any level of output. This
need not always be so. In agriculture, for example, it is not
the case that, simply by halving all inputs, including the size
of the field, one also halves output, nor that output can be
doubled merely by doubling all inputs. There are technical
indivisibilities here that make it impossible to utilise certain

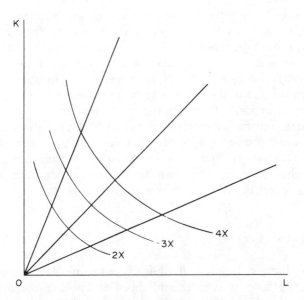

Figure 10.4 A 'homogeneous of degree one' production function. As
we move out along any ray through the origin, equal increments in
input yield equal increments in output. All isoquants have the same
slope as they pass through any particular ray.

types of technology at small output levels and that make it preferable to switch from one technical process to another as the scale of output changes. The type of harvesting equipment used on large North American type farms cannot be used effectively on the small farms that at one time dominated British agriculture, and are still widespread on the Continent of Europe. Or, to give another example, in the battery production of eggs, if one wishes to double the number of hens housed, it is far from clear that it is technically most efficient to double the air space of the buildings in which they are housed. There is no reason to suppose that the amount of inputs needed to heat the henhouses in question will be doubled for, even if one did just double the airspace of the building by, for example, doubling its floor area one would not double the area of its outside surfaces, nor would one double its propensity to heat loss. Nor, of course, would one double the building materials required to erect the building by doubling its air space.

We could multiply examples like this *ad nauseam*, but enough ought now to have been said to convince the reader that a production function that everywhere displays constant returns to scale is a special case, albeit, perhaps, a useful and relevant special case. *A priori*, there is nothing in general that can be said about the returns to scale characteristics of production functions. One can have decreasing, constant or increasing returns to scale, or indeed a combination of all three in any production function. It depends upon the nature of the technology that is available to a particular industry. As we shall now see, it is possible to be more definite about the characteristics displayed by returns to a factor.

Returns to a Factor

The production function is basically a technical relationship; economics takes it as given and classifies the characteristics it may display. However, this does not mean that it displays no dominant characteristics of particular importance to economics. When it comes to *returns to a factor* we may say something very definite about its nature, namely that, in the region that is relevant for analysing the behaviour of firms, the production function displays *decreasing* or *diminishing returns to a factor*. The concept of returns to a factor refers to what happens to output as successively equal increments of one input are combined with a fixed quantity of other inputs. In terms of figure 10.5, we analyse returns to labour by seeing what happens to output as we move along a line drawn perpendicular to the capital axis. To postulate diminishing returns to either factor involves postulating successively decreasing increments in output for equal increments in the factor in question.

To say that diminishing returns to a factor always exist in the region that is relevant for analysing the behaviour of the firm is to say two things: first, that it is usual for production

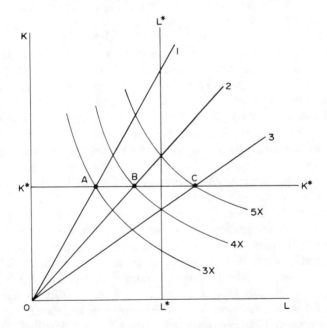

Figure 10.5 This homogeneous of degree one production function displays constant returns to scale but diminishing returns to a factor. Thus, as we move along K^*K^*, the movement from A to B to C involves successively greater increases in labour input for equal increments in output. Note that this movement takes us from ray 1 to 2 to 3, so that the isoquants become progressively less steep as we move to the right.

functions to display in some region diminishing returns
to a factor regardless of their returns to scale characteristics; second, that firms behave in such a way as to ensure
that that tendency exists in the region of the production
function upon which they choose to operate. Since we have
not yet said anything about what motivates this behaviour of
firms, we cannot take up this second point at this stage, but
it is easy to show that the tendency to diminishing returns is
present in almost any production function.

In figure 10.5 the production function which we have
drawn displays constant returns to scale along any ray drawn
out from the origin, and the isoquants that describe it are
convex to the origin. These two properties are enough to
ensure diminishing returns to both capital (as we move along
$L*L*$) and to labour (as we move along $K*K*$) because along
either of these lines isoquants showing successively equal
increases in output are growing further and further apart.
That this must be the case is easily seen. Let us consider the
case of increasing labour inputs. The isoquant that cuts $K*K*$
at C is more shallowly sloped than that which cuts it at B,
which in turn is more shallowly sloped than A. The further to
the right we move along $K*K*$ the more rapidly is each isoquant moving away from the one to the left of it, and the
wider the horizontal gap between successive curves. Only if
the isoquants were straight lines touching both axes would
there be no tendency for diminishing returns to a factor when
returns to scale are constant.

Even the simple isoquant map based on the existence of
two activities presented in figure 10.1, and drawn here as
figure 10.6, would display diminishing returns, and in a
dramatic way. With a given quantity of capital of $K*$ we
would have constant returns to labour up to output $3X$. Here
there is enough labour to make activity 1 fully viable. We
would then have constant positive returns to labour (but at a
lower rate) between level of output $3X$ and level of output
$5X$. At the latter point, activity 2 would be the only one in
use and further increments of labour could not be productively employed without adding to the capital stock. In short,
returns to labour, holding capital constant, would suddenly
diminish to zero at output level $5X$.

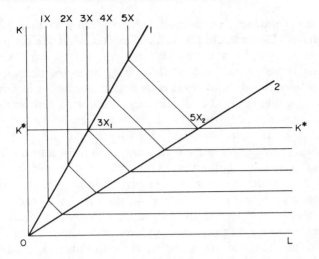

Figure 10.6 Diminishing returns to labour with but two constant returns to scale activities. Equal increments in labour yield equal increments in output along $K*K*$ until point $3X_1$. Thereafter increments to output continue but at a smaller size until point $5X_2$. Thereafter, further increments to labour inputs add nothing to output.

If returns to a factor always end up diminishing when returns to scale are constant, it should be obvious that they also diminish when returns to scale decrease. If, in terms of figure 10.5, successive increments of capital, or labour, holding the other factor constant, lead to successively smaller increases in output when equal movements along any ray through the origin yield equal increments in output, they must also do so when equidistant movements out from the origin yield successively smaller increments in output. Diminishing returns to scale accentuates the tendency of a production function to display diminishing returns to a factor. If a production function displays increasing returns to scale this can offset the tendency to diminishing returns to a factor, and indeed it is mathematically possible to write down formulae for production functions in which returns to scale increase so rapidly that returns to a factor never begin to diminish. However, what is mathematically possible is not always empirically plausible, and such cases are logical curiosities rather than practically relevant examples.

In the real world, it is clear that the tendency to diminishing returns to a factor is ubiquitous. No matter what the technical process of production is like, and no matter what might happen to its productivity if all inputs into it are increased in proportion, if only one input is increased, sooner or later that input is going to find it harder and harder to find units of other inputs to cooperate with; it may even begin to get in the way of production simply by its physical presence. The contribution of extra units of this factor to production is then inevitably going to diminish. One cannot indefinitely cram more and more machines into a given building with a given labour force; one cannot indefinitely add men to a production line; one cannot put more and more hens into a given hen-house; one cannot put more and more fertiliser on a given plot of land and not expect to see the extra units of the input that is being varied make a diminishing contribution in terms of additions to output.

Concluding Comments

It might be helpful to summarise the points developed in this chapter. We have argued that the production function is a technical relationship between the rate of flow of factor services put into a production process and the rate of flow of output emerging from it. When inputs are increased in equal proportion we describe the consequences for output in terms of the concept of returns to scale, and we have seen that a production function may be characterised by decreasing, constant or increasing returns to scale. Indeed, it may exhibit a combination of these characteristics as output increases over different ranges. When only one factor is varied, holding constant the quantities of all the others, we speak of the consequences in terms of returns to that factor. Though certain production functions *may*, logically speaking, display a tendency to increasing returns to a factor, the overwhelming general tendency here is for returns to a factor to diminish, and as we shall see below, competitive firms always operate in the region of the production function where they do diminish. The importance of all this, as far as the behaviour of firms is concerned, is that the production function provides a vital link between their behaviour in goods markets with that in markets for factors of production. We shall begin to investigate this link in the next chapter.

11
Cost Functions

Introduction

The production function is central to the economics of the firm because it is the relationship that enables us to translate market prices of individual factors of production into costs of production for output, and to derive from market prices of output the costs which firms are willing to incur in order to obtain factors of production. This chapter uses the production function to clarify the way in which production costs vary with the level of output.

As the reader might guess, it is always logically possible to construct peculiar special case production functions that in turn yield peculiar relationships between output levels and costs. In what follows, we stick to dealing with homogeneous (or at least homothetic) production functions (described on page 130) in order to keep the analysis manageable, and so some results are not quite general. Nevertheless, they are sufficiently widely applicable that they serve quite adequately as a basis for the analysis of firm behaviour that is dealt with subsequently.

We said earlier that a firm would seek to produce any given output utilising no more inputs than were necessary. Such behaviour is a consequence of a more basic proposition about the behaviour of firms, namely that whatever level of output they choose to produce, they will do so at the minimum possible cost. This in turn is an implication of the basic assumption of the so-called neo-classical theory of the firm, that the entrepreneur's motive is to maximise his profit. We will discuss this assumption at some length below but, for the moment, the reader need only accept the weaker cost minimisation hypothesis as a basis for the following analysis.

Isocost Curves

Let us assume that the firm whose behaviour we are to study produces only good X, and uses the services of labour and capital in its production. Let us further assume that, in relation to the markets for these inputs, the firm stands in very much the same way as did the consumer of Part I in relation to the markets for X and Y. That is to say, the prices the firm must pay for labour services and for capital services do not vary with the amounts bought. The measurement of input prices, though straightforward, is worth explicit attention. As we have seen, inputs are measured in flow terms – in man-hours or man-weeks per week or per month as far as labour is concerned; as to capital, the appropriate input measure is also a flow, e.g. hours or weeks per week or month. Thus, the relevant price for labour is the wage per man-hour or per man-week, and the relevant price of capital is emphatically *not* the price of a new machine. Rather it is the weekly or hourly rental price of a machine. Though machinery is sometimes leased, it is more typically owned by the firm that uses it, but the reader might find it helpful to think of the firm renting the machine from itself. The rental price of the machine is given by what the firm forgoes, per hour, or per week, by owning the machine: that is clearly the interest that the firm could earn per hour or per week on the funds tied up in the machine, (the normal net rate of return on capital in the economy times the value of the machine) plus any depreciation (or minus any appreciation) in its value. It is the *opportunity cost* of owning the machine.

In figure 11.1 we consider a situation in which the prices of labour and capital services are given to the firm. We construct a relationship analogous to the budget line of consumer theory.

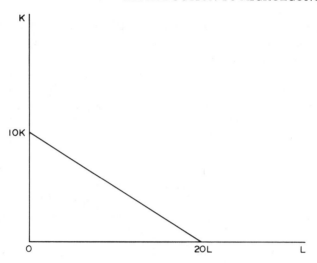

Figure 11.1 An isocost curve, showing the quantities of capital and labour services that can be bought per unit of time for an outlay of £1,000 per unit of time when their prices are £100 and £50 per unit respectively.

Let the prices of capital and labour be £100 and £50 respectively. Then for an outlay of £1,000 per week we see that the firm can acquire 10 units of capital, 20 units of labour, or any combination of inputs along the line joining 10K and 20L. This is called an *isocost* or *equal outlay* curve, and for given factor prices we may construct a family of such curves each one representing a given, higher, outlay as we move upward and to the right. Now minimising the cost of production of X means two equivalent things. One may say that the firm, for a given outlay on factors, maximises production of X or, for a given level of output, minimises the cost of obtaining the factors necessary to produce that level of output. In geometric terms, cost minimisation takes place where an isoquant representing a particular level of output is just tangent to an isocost curve. By exact analogy with arguments developed in Chapter 2, we may say that costs are minimised where the marginal rate of substitution between inputs in production, the slope of the isoquant, is equal to the ratio of factor prices, the slope of the isocost curve. Any other combination of factors along the isoquant in question, other than that at

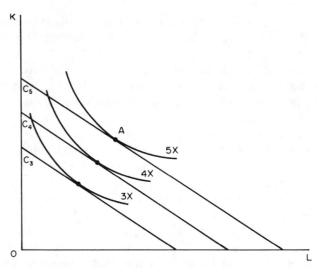

Figure 11.2 A family of isocost curves superimposed upon the production function. At point A we have the cheapest way of producing output $5X$ since any other point on that isoquant must be above isocost curve C_5. Equivalently, an output of $5X$ is the maximum output that can be had for an outlay of C_5 on factors of production. Any point other than A on isocost line C_5 is on a lower isoquant than $5X$. Similarly, C_3 and C_4 are the minimum costs of producing $3X$ and $4X$ units of output.

which this condition holds, will result in more expense for no extra output, and any other point on the same isocost curve will mean the same expense for less output. So much should be obvious from inspection of figure 11.2.

Long-Run Total Cost, Average Cost and Marginal Cost

We are now in a position to derive a curve relating the total cost of producing X to its level of output; a *total cost curve*. We first of all consider a situation in which the firm is free to vary all inputs at will, a state of affairs usually described as 'the long run'. The assumption of cost minimisation ensures that, in these circumstances, the outlay on factors incurred in producing a given output level will be that underlying the isocost curve that is tangent to the relevent isoquant. Thus, the returns to scale properties of the production function are critical in determining the nature of the relationship between costs and output.

Figure 11.3(a) shows the long-run total cost curve (LTC) when returns to scale are constant. It is derived from figure 11.2 where the production function was drawn to display this property. Equiproportional increases in outlay on factors lead to equiproportional increases in their quantity devoted to producing X, and hence in equiproportional increases in output. The long-run total cost curve is, therefore, an upward sloping straight line. The reader should satisfy himself that a production function that everywhere displays decreasing returns to scale produces a long-run total cost curve that slopes upwards at a rate that increases with output, figure 11.3(b), and one that displays increasing returns to scale produces a long-run total cost curve that slopes upwards at a rate that decreases with output, figure 11.3(c).

Two other cost/output relationships are implicit in figure 11.3. There is a relationship between *average cost* and output and between *marginal cost* and output. Average cost is simply the total cost of producing a given volume of output divided by the volume of output. In terms of figure 11.3, it is measured by the height of the total cost curve at any point divided by

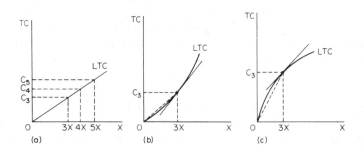

Figure 11.3 Long-run total cost curves (LTC) showing (a) constant returns to scale (this curve is explicitly derived from figure 11.2 by relating the value of each isocost curve to that of the isoquant tangential to it), (b) decreasing returns to scale, (c) increasing returns to scale. At a particular level of output, average cost is given by dividing total cost by output (e.g. $3X / C_3$). Long-run marginal cost at any level of output is given by the slope of the total cost curve at that level of output.

its distance from the vertical axis or, in other words, by the slope of a straight line drawn from the origin to that point on the total cost curve. As the reader will readily discern, when returns to scale are constant, average cost does not vary with output; when they diminish, average cost increases with output; when they increase, average cost systematically falls with output. He should also note that this set of propositions depends upon our having assumed that the production function is homogeneous.

Now consider the relationship between marginal cost and output. Marginal cost per unit of output is the ratio of the additional cost incurred by making a small (in the limit, infinitesimal) addition to output, to that addition to total output. It is thus measured by the slope of the total cost curve — in just the same way as the marginal propensity to consume a good is given by the slope of an Engel curve (Chapter 2), or the marginal utility of wealth is given by the slope of the total utility of wealth function (Chapter 7). It should be obvious from figure 11.3(a) that when returns to scale are constant, marginal cost is equal to average cost and does not vary with output. Figure 11.3(b) implies that decreasing returns to scale involves marginal cost increasing with output and exceeding average cost, while in figure 11.3(c) we find marginal cost falling with output and being below average cost.

Long-Run Costs with Varying Returns to Scale

Now we remarked in the previous chapter that there was no need to confine our attention to production functions that everywhere display the same returns to scale characteristics; that it was quite conceivable that the technical conditions of producing a particular good were such as to result in increasing returns to scale at low output levels and decreasing returns at higher output levels. Such a production function is, in fact, most useful in the analysis of the behaviour of the competitive firm, as we shall see in the next chapter, and the long-run cost curves implicit in it are worth consideration at this point.

In figure 11.4, we draw the long-run total cost curve implied

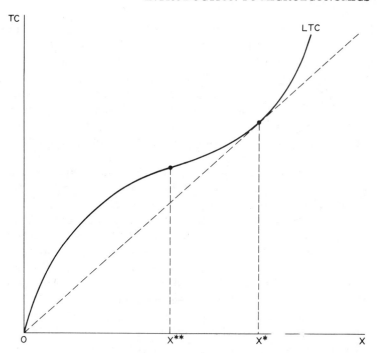

Figure 11.4 A long-run total cost curve showing first increasing and then decreasing returns to scale. Average cost is given by the slope of a straight line drawn from the origin to the curve. The slope of such a line, and hence average cost, is at a minimum at output X^* where the relevant line is tangent to the total cost curve. This straight line through the origin has the same slope as the total cost curve and hence, at output X^*, average cost and marginal cost are equal to each other. The slope of the total cost curve, and hence marginal cost, is at a minimum at output X^{**}, which is lower than X^*.

by such a production function, still assuming that factor prices are fixed to the firm. Total costs first increase with output at a decreasing rate and then at an increasing rate. Long-run average cost, measured as it is by the slope of a straight line drawn from the origin to the total cost curve, at first falls with output, and then rises; it reaches a minimum at level of output X^* where such a line is just tangent to the total cost curve. As we have already said, long-run marginal cost at any level of output is given by the slope of the total cost curve. At first this too falls with output, and at levels of output lower than

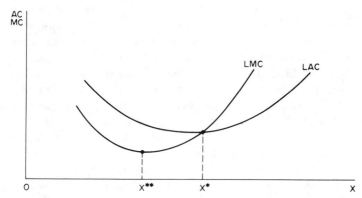

Figure 11.5 Long-run average and marginal cost curves implicit in figure 11.4. Marginal cost cuts average cost from below at the minimum point of the average cost curve.

X^* is below average cost — as the reader should easily be able to verify by inspecting figure 11.4. However, marginal cost begins to rise at X^{**} before output X^* is reached and becomes equal to average cost at X^*; at this level of output the slope of a straight line from the origin to the total cost curve is just equal to the slope of the total cost curve. Beyond X^* marginal cost continues to rise, and the reader should satisfy himself that marginal cost is above average cost at higher output levels than X^*. The relationships between long-run marginal cost, long-run average cost, and output implicit in figure 11.4 are displayed in figure 11.5. The average cost curve (LAC) takes a form that is often called U-shaped, and is cut at its minimum point by a rising marginal cost curve (LMC). The reader will become very familiar with curves of this general shape in the chapters that follow.

The Concept of Short Run

Now the curves with which we have been dealing so far are, as we have remarked above, 'long-run' curves. They tell us how costs vary with output on the assumption that the firm may move freely and without difficulty to any point on its production function, that it may use any combination of

inputs with equal ease, and that it always chooses the minimum cost combination. Movements such as this take time; the
use of some inputs can be varied more rapidly than that of
others. It is easier to hire more hourly paid labour than it is
to order and install new machinery. It is easier to cut back on
outlays on hourly paid labour than it is for the firm to rid
itself of machinery once acquired. In ignoring such problems
we were implicitly assuming that the firm had sufficient time
to overcome them: hence the phrase 'long-run' to describe the
relationships so far discussed.

In constrast, we define the 'short run' as that period of time
over which the services of at least one factor input flowing to
the firm are fixed as a result of past decisions. For the two-
factor case it is usual to think of this fixed factor as being
capital. Inasmuch as capital consists of machinery, it is physically fixed in place, owned or leased by the firm and it is by
no means straightforward to vary the amount of it. The labour
force, on the other hand, is more likely to be on short-term
contract, weekly or monthly, easily reduced by short-time
working and dismissals and just as easily expanded by overtime
and new hiring. Thus, in the following analysis, we assume
that in the short run only labour can be varied and capital is
fixed.

This is nevertheless a naïve assumption made, in the main,
to keep the analysis simple. There is no particular reason why
in any actual firm every type of capital should be only slowly
variable and every type of labour rapidly variable. It is true
that some types of labour are on short-term contract and
easily hired and fired, but by no means all types. Equally,
plant and equipment may be difficult to expand and contract
quickly, but inventories of raw materials are just as much a
part of capital and in some cases they may easily be adjusted.
For any firm, there is a time horizon over which all inputs
may be varied, but there are many, not just one, shorter
horizons over which some inputs are fixed. Moreover, it is not
necessarily the case that any type of labour may be varied
more rapidly than any type of capital.

When in the following analysis we define the short run as
the period over which labour but not capital inputs can be

varied, we are not attempting directly to decribe any kind of empirical reality. We are constructing a simplified special case in order to make certain analytic notions clear. Any attempt to apply the short-run/long-run distinction to a real world problem that simply takes it for granted that there is a factor called labour whose services can be varied more rapidly than those of capital and does not instead look carefully at the whole array of inputs involved in the particular situation to see which is the most easily varied is likely to be misleading.

Short-Run Cost Functions

With the above caveat in mind, let us proceed to the analysis of short-run costs and their relationship to long-run costs. Just as the returns to scale characteristics of the production function underlie the shape of the long-run cost curves, so the nature of short-run cost curves depends upon the returns to the variable factor (labour in this simplified example) character- istics that it displays. We will explicitly analyse only the relatively complex case of a production function that displays increasing, followed by decreasing, returns to scale, but the reader will find it helpful to carry out the same analysis for at least one simpler case — say that of constant returns to scale.

We fix K at some historically given level K^* in figure 11.6 and note that, given the prices of labour and capital, long-run cost minimisation would involve the firm producing at A. If it wishes to vary its output over short periods it must move along the line K^*K^* rather than along the ray through the origin. We may construct a short-run total cost curve from figure 11.6 by relating to one another the values of the iso- quants and isocost lines that intersect K^*K^*. In this case, as we have drawn figure 11.7, like the long-run curve, the short- run total cost curve displays first increasing and then decreasing returns, but these are returns *to the factor* and not returns *to scale*.

Now A represents a point that is both on the short-run total cost curve (STC) and on the long-run curve (LTC) as drawn

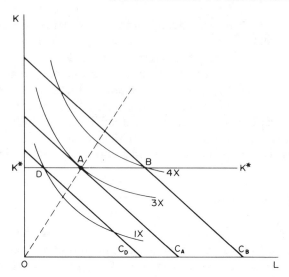

Figure 11.6 Given factor prices, the firm would produce level of output
$3X$ at point A, using K^* units of capital services, even if it was free to
vary the capital stock. With capital fixed at K^* any other level of output
(e.g. $4X$ produced at B or $1X$ produced at D) will be produced at greater
cost than it would be were the firm free to vary its capital input. C_D and
C_B are the minimum short-run costs of producing $1X$ and $4X$. Note that
the isoquants are here drawn to display first increasing and then
decreasing returns to scale.

in figure 11.7. The level of output here is the only one for
which short-run and long-run total costs of production are
equal. The short-run total cost of producing any other level
of output is higher than the long-run cost, for at any other point
on K^*K^* the isocost lines *intersect* the isoquant and are not
tangent to it. If, at level of output $3X$, the long-run curve and
the short-run curve coincide, and at all other levels of output
short-run costs are higher, there is obviously a tangency
between the two curves at level of output $3X$.

The derivation of the short-run average cost curve and the
short-run marginal cost curve from the short-run total cost
curve is, analytically speaking, exactly the same exercise as
the derivation of the relevant long-run curves and there is no
point in repeating it explicitly. Because the long-run and short-
run total cost curves touch tangentially at output $3X$ we may

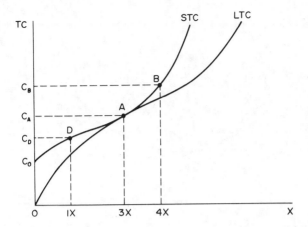

Figure 11.7 A short-run total cost curve for a particular level of the capital stock will be tangent to the long-run curve at A — corresponding to point A in figure 11.6. C_0 here represents outlay on the services of K^* units of capital. It is a cost that must be met in the short run, even if output is zero.

make inferences about the relationship between short-run and long-run average costs at that output, and between the two marginal cost curves. The average and marginal cost curves are drawn in figure 11.8. First, the slopes of the two total cost curves are equal at A, in figure 11.7, so short- and long-run marginal cost are equal at output $3X$. Immediately to the left of A the short-run total cost curve is less steeply sloped than the long-run curve, and to the right of A it is more steeply sloped. Hence, the short-run marginal cost curve (SMC) cuts the long-run curve (LMC) from below and to the left at level of output $3X$.

Short- and long-run average costs coincide at this level of output, $3X$, too, but here we have tangency between the two rather than an *intersection*. At any other level of output, total and hence average costs are higher in the short run than in the long run. Note that this does *not* mean that short-run average cost (SAC) is at a minimum at level of output $3X$. The tangency of the two total cost curves means only that short-run average costs will fall *less rapidly* or rise *more rapidly* than long-run average costs as output expands, or contracts, not

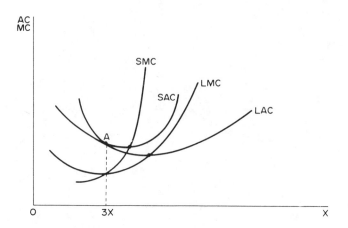

Figure 11.8 The relationship between long- and short-run average and marginal costs. The two average cost curves are tangent to each other at A — corresponding to point A in figure 11.7, while the two marginal cost curves intersect at the same level of output ($3X$).

that they will necessarily rise in absolute terms. As figures 11.7 and 11.8 are drawn, both short-run and long-run average costs are, in fact, falling at level of output $3X$.

Short- and Long-Run Average Cost — The 'Envelope'

Now we carried out the foregoing analysis on the assumption that there was a given level of capital that could not be varied. The amount we chose was quite arbitrary. There is in fact a different array of short-run curves for every level of the capital stock and, as the reader should see from figure 11.9, the higher the level of the capital stock, the higher is the level of output at which the lines representing this stock ($K*K*$ and $K**K**$) intersect the ray through the origin along which the long-run cost curves are derived. Hence, the higher the level of output at which the two total cost curves coincide. For every level of the capital stock there is a short-run average cost curve tangent to the long-run curve, and a short-run marginal cost curve intersecting the long-run curve. Figure 11.10 depicts a few of these curves, and its very appearance explains

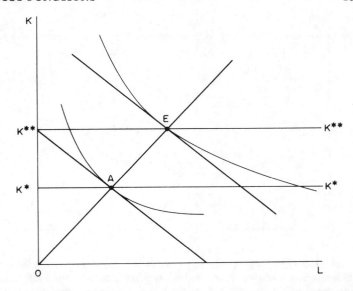

Figure 11.9 The higher the given level of the capital stock, the higher the level of labour input, and of output associated with the firm having the long-run cost minimising ratio of inputs. Point A here corresponds to point A in figure 11.6. Point E is a similar point; it would yield a tangency between long-run and a particularly short-run total and average cost curves, the latter derived for a higher fixed level of capital services (K^{**}).

why the long-run average cost curve is often referred to as being the 'envelope' of the short-run curves. As should be clear from the analysis presented earlier, the 'U' shape of the long-run average cost curve in figure 11.10 depends upon the assumption that we are dealing with a production function characterised by increasing returns to scale at low levels of output and decreasing returns to scale at higher levels. Such a production function was presented in figure 11.6 above.

Fixed and Variable Costs

Now we have included outlays on capital services in the short-run costs with which we have been dealing. However, because capital input is fixed, outlay on it is fixed. It is often helpful

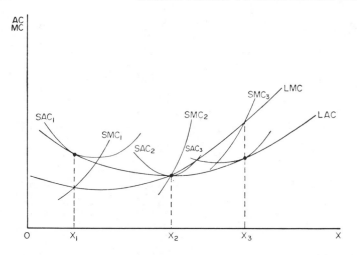

Figure 11.10 The long-run average cost curve is an 'envelope' of short-run average cost curves, each of the latter being derived for a different, fixed, level of capital services. There is a short-run marginal cost curve associated with each short-run average cost curve. It cuts the latter at its minimum point. It intersects the long-run marginal cost curve at the same level of output at which the short-run average cost curve is tangent to the long-run average cost curve. X_1, X_2 and X_3 are the output levels at which this happens for the three sets of short-run curves shown here. The curves labelled SAC_2 and SMC_2 are associated with a level of the capital stock which permits long-run average costs to be minimised. Hence SAC_2 equals LAC at the lowest point in the latter curve and SMC_2 intersects LMC where each curve cuts its associated average cost curve.

to distinguish between the fixed and variable components of short-run costs. In the long run, of course, all costs are variable because, by definition, the level of all inputs can be varied as the firm desires. To obtain total variable costs from total short-run costs one simply subtracts the fixed outlay on capital. The short-run total cost curve depicted in figure 11.7 and reproduced in figure 11.11 cuts the vertical axis at C_0, for in the short run, at zero output, the firm must still pay this amount for capital services even if they are not utilised. To get the total variable cost curve (TVC), one simply shifts the short-run total cost curve (STC) down until it cuts through the origin, as shown in figure 11.11. Since marginal cost measures the slope of the total cost curve, the distinction

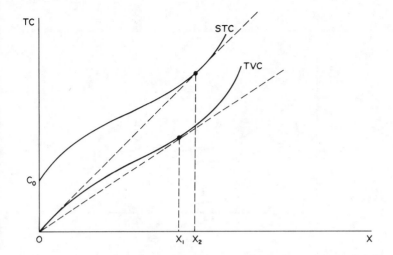

Figure 11.11 Total variable cost is equal to short-run total cost minus fixed costs (C_0). Average variable cost (the slope of a line drawn from the origin to TVC) is at a minimum at a lower level of output, X_1, than is short-run average cost (the slope of a line drawn to STC). The latter is minimised at X_2.

between variable and total cost does not affect the short-run marginal cost curve. After all, if fixed costs are fixed, then they do not vary with increments to output.

However, the distinction between fixed and variable costs is relevent to the discussion of average costs. If we average fixed costs over an increasing level of output, their contribution to overall average cost diminishes, as is shown in figure 11.12. Average variable cost may be obtained from average overall cost by subtracting average fixed cost (AFC). Alternatively, the slope of a line drawn from the origin to the total variable cost curve in figure 11.11 measures average variable cost. These two methods of obtaining the average variable cost curve are, of course, equivalent and the minimum point of the average variable cost curve lies to the left of that of the overall short-run average cost curve. The marginal cost curve, of course, cuts both average cost curves at their minimum points. All this is shown in figure 11.12. The reader who doubts any of the foregoing propositions will find it helpful to derive them for himself.

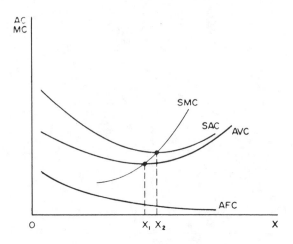

Figure 11.12 Average variable cost (AVC) is equal to short-run average cost (SAC) minus average fixed cost (AFC). The latter is simply a constant divided by an increasing level of output and hence declines systematically with output. Thus AVC and SAC move closer together as output increases. The short-run marginal cost curve cuts both of these two curves at their minimum points at X_1 and X_2.

Concluding Comment

Now the analysis of cost curves is quite tricky and if it was being carried out only for its own sake, it would be tedious as well. However, cost/output relationships such as those we have discussed here are a basic ingredient to the price and output decisions of the firm. We have now dealt with them in sufficient detail to begin discussing, in the next part of this book, the entrepreneur's decision making about the quantity of output to be produced and the price at which it is to be sold.

Part IV
The Firm in the Output Market

12
Perfect Competition

Introduction

As we remarked at the end of the last chapter, the analysis of cost functions is important because the nature of these relationships impinges upon the price and output decisions of the firm; the precise manner in which they impinge depends upon the institutional setting in which the firm finds itself and upon the motivation of those who take the relevant decisions. In this and following chapters we will concern ourselves with a variety of institutional settings, perfect competition, monopoly, discriminating monopoly, and a variety of forms of imperfect competition, but mainly with one assumed motive — profit maximisation.

The Profit Maximisation Hypothesis

The maximisation of profits is not the only conceivable motive for the operator of a firm, whom we designated earlier as the 'entrepreneur'. However, if he is a utility maximising individual who gains utility solely from the consumption of goods and services sold on the market, then maximising profit is consistent with achieving that end. To the extent that an individual draws satisfaction from less tangible factors, such as power, the esteem of his friends and neighbours and so forth, it is possible to construct arguments that suggest that the size of the firm (perhaps measured by the value of sales) or the rate of growth of the firm would be a more appropriate variable for him to maximise. Moreover, when one recognises that the world in which any actual firm operates is far from being a certain one, so that it is seldom clear which particular decision among the alternatives available will indeed result in maximum profits, motives based upon acquiring security, cutting down the effort put into decision making, and such also begin to look appealing.

A large part of the literature of that field of economics known as industrial organisation is devoted to careful analysis of the questions just raised about motivation. There simply is not space enough here to go into this, even superficially. Because we assumed that consumption alone yielded utility when dealing with the consumer, and because we are going to adopt, albeit usually implicitly, the assumption that uncertainty about the future does not exist when dealing with the firm, consistency suggests that we adopt profit maximisation as well. It is not an uncontroversial assumption about motivation, but it does yield relatively simple and useful analysis. Its implications are worth pursuing for that reason alone. Moreover, in the last analysis, any firm, whatever the motivation of its owners and managers, must earn profits if it is to survive. There must always be an element of profit seeking in the behaviour of any firm and it is not perhaps unreasonable to approximate this with the simplifying assumption of profit maximisation. Remember, though, that the following pages do not represent a comprehensive survey of the theory of the firm, dealing as they do mainly with the theory of the profit maximising firm operating in conditions of certainty.

The Perfectly Competitive Firm's Output Demand Curve

We will now analyse the so-called perfectly competitive firm, sometimes called a *price-taking* firm. As the latter name implies, the firm is one that takes the price of its output and of its inputs as given and makes decisions only about the volume of its output and the quantities of inputs it will employ.

It is usual to think of the price-taking firm as being a suffi-ciently small part of the industry of which it is a member that its own activities could not possibly have a noticeable effect on the price of the industry's output. A single farm producing a particular crop is the archetypal example here, which is one of the reasons why agricultural economists find the perfect competition model so attractive and useful. For whatever reason, however, the demand curve for its output that such a firm faces takes the form of a horizontal line at a given price such as that depicted in figure 12.1. The curve shows an infinite price elasticity of demand, since the smallest fall in its selling price will lead to an infinite increase in the quantity that the firm can apparently sell. From this demand curve it is trivially easy to construct a relationship between revenue and output — a total revenue curve. One simply sums the revenue obtained for each unit of output to obtain the straight-line relationship labelled TR in figure 12.2. Note that, as for the total cost curve of the previous chapter, there are *average*

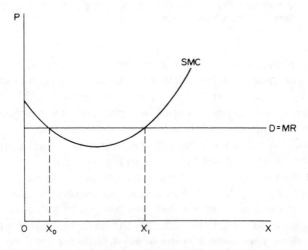

Figure 12.1 For a perfectly competitive firm the demand curve is infinitely elastic. Marginal revenue therefore equals price. Profits are maximised in the short run where marginal cost cuts the marginal revenue curve from below (at output X_1). At output X_0 marginal cost cuts the marginal revenue curve from above and losses are maxi-mised. Figure 12.2 presents the same analysis in terms of total revenue and total cost functions.

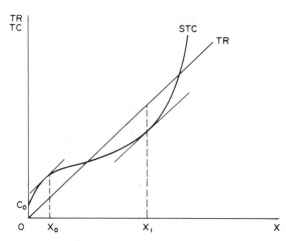

Figure 12.2 Short-run profits are maximised where short-run total cost is at a maximum distance below total revenue. This is at level of output X_1 where the slopes of the two curves are equal (i.e. where marginal cost equals marginal revenue) where the slope of the total cost curve is increasing. At X_0 the slopes of the two curves are equal, but here costs exceed revenue and the slope of the total cost curve is falling. Hence short-run losses are maximised here.

and *marginal* revenue curves related to this total revenue curve. So long as a firm sells each unit of its output at the same price, the terms 'price per unit of output' and 'average revenue' are synonymous and the demand curve is in fact the average revenue curve. When the total revenue curve takes the form of a straight line through the origin as it does in figure 12.2, and as it inevitably must given the assumption of a horizontal demand curve, then marginal revenue will be equal to price (average revenue). Note that average and marginal revenue are *not* synonymous terms; they just happen to be equal when the demand curve that the firm faces is horizontal. When price does not vary with the volume of sales, then marginal revenue (the amount added to total revenue per unit of output when a small addition is made to output — and hence to sales) is simply price per unit of output. If the price the firm received did vary with output, this would not be the case, as we shall see in the next chapter.

The Firm's Short-Run Supply Curve

What, then, about profit maximisation? First, let us consider the *short-run* situation. There are two equivalent ways of finding the level of output at which profits are maximised in the short-run. They are depicted in figures 12.1 and 12.2. Consider first figure 12.2 where a short-run total cost curve that displays, at first increasing and then decreasing, returns to labour is set alongside the total revenue curve. Profits are equal to total revenue minus total costs which, in terms of figure 12.2, is the vertical distance between the two curves. This distance is obviously at a maximum at output level X_1, where the total cost curve is below the total revenue curve and they are parallel to each other. At any lower level of output, revenue is rising faster than cost, and at any higher level it is rising more slowly. Note that, by a similar argument, maximum losses would be made at output X_0.

Now we have seen that the slope of some 'total' curve yields a 'marginal' curve. If it is a condition of profit maximisation that the slope of the total revenue curve be equal to that of the total cost curve, then this also means that marginal cost should be equal to marginal revenue. This could take place at either X_0 or X_1 in figure 12.1, but output X_0 is one that maximises losses. It is also a condition of profit maximisation then that the marginal cost curve cuts the marginal revenue curve from below. This, of course, is at a level of output at which there are diminishing returns to labour. We have here an example of the condition asserted in Chapter 10, that the firm will always operate in the region of the production function characterised by diminishing returns to a factor.

Now for a price-taking firm, marginal revenue and price are equal to one another. Thus, in the short run, a profit maximising price-taking firm will fix output at that level whose marginal cost of production (on the upward sloping segment of the marginal cost curve) is equal to market price, with one qualification that we must now discuss.

It is always open to the firm to produce nothing at all, and there are circumstances where this is the most profitable (in the sense of being the least costly) thing it can do. In the short run, the firm must always pay its fixed costs, regardless of its level of output. It only incurs variable costs if it produces output, and it is easy to construct a case in which both the total cost curve and the total variable cost curve lie above the total revenue curve at every level of output. In such a case price is below both overall average cost and average variable cost at any positive level of output. Figure 12.3 depicts just such a situation. If this firm *must* produce something then it will certainly maximise profits (that is minimise losses; the terms are synonymous) at output X_1 where marginal cost and marginal revenue are equal. However, by producing X, it would make greater losses than it would incur if it produced nothing at all. If it produced nothing, it would lose only its fixed costs, whereas by producing X_1 it is making a loss in its variable costs also. Unless a firm can reduce its losses by producing, it will not produce, and it can only do this if the price it receives for its output exceeds the minimum value of average variable cost.

At any price above this level, which just covers average variable cost, profit maximising output is found by inspecting

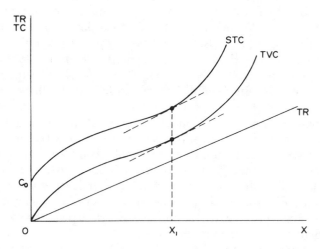

Figure 12.3 If total revenue is everywhere below total variable cost, then losses are greater at output X_1 (where they are nevertheless minimised for any positive level of output), than they would be if the firm produced nothing and incurred a loss of C_0 — its short-run fixed costs.

the marginal cost curve, but below this level the firm will produce no output at all. Notice what has just been said: above the minimum point of the average variable cost curve the marginal cost curve relates the firm's profit maximising output to price. Since the firm is a profit maximiser, this will be its actual output. Hence, for the individual competitive firm in the short run, *the marginal cost curve is its supply curve.*

Price Determination in the Short Run

We are now in a position to investigate how the price, taken as given by the individual firm, is in fact determined, at least in the short run. The market demand curve for X may be obtained by summing up the individual demand curves derived in Part I (using the constant real income rather than constant money income curves if we wish to deal with a fully employed economy). Just as the individual's demand curve tells us how much he will buy at a given price, so the market demand curve tells us how much all the individuals in the market for X will together buy at a given price. By analogous reasoning, we may derive the short-run market supply curve for X on the assumption that input prices are constant for all producing firms, regardless of their output. The short-run marginal cost curve above the minimum point of the average variable cost curve tells us how much X any individual firm will supply at a given price. Adding up the amounts of X over all firms tells us how much the whole industry will supply. Figure 12.4(b) portrays the relevant market supply and demand curves. Their intersection at P^*, X^* determines the overall output of X and its price. This is the price which is given to the individual firm whose situation is depicted in figure 12.4(a). At this price, the consumption plans of consumers and the output plans of firms are just compatible. We have an *equilibrium* situation.

Now the situation for the particular firm shown in figure 12.4(a) has it producing X_1 at the going market price. Since the average cost of producing that level of output is AC_1, the firm is clearly making a total profit of $(P^* - AC_1)X_1$. A

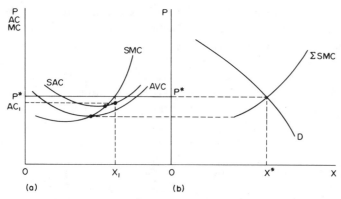

Figure 12.4 The short-run industry supply curve, when factor prices are given, is the horizontal sum of each firm's marginal cost curve above the minimum point of each firm's average variable cost curve (ΣSMC). The interaction of supply and demand at the industry level determines industry output at X^* and price at P^*. At this price the individual firm produces X_1 units of output and makes a total profit of $(P^* - AC_1)X_1$. Note that, to keep the diagram manageable, the scale on the horizontal axis of panel (b) is greatly reduced from that which is used on the same axis of panel (a), so that a given horizontal distance from the origin of (b) represents a greater volume of X.

number of questions arise. First, suppose we looked at the behaviour of this firm over a rather longer time period. Would it still be the case that this is the level of output it would choose? Once it is free to vary its capital inputs, might there not be some other level of output that was more profitable at that price? Second, the supply curve used to determine the market price was obtained by adding up the marginal cost curves of all firms in the industry. It is only valid to aggregate individual short-run marginal cost curves in this way if we assume that input prices do not vary even when all firms in the industry vary their output levels. We have also been assuming that there is a given number of firms in the industry. Now, over a time period where the individual firm cannot vary its capital stock, it is quite reasonable to make this latter assumption. But what determined how many firms were in the industry in the first place? When we consider a horizon long enough to make all factors of production variable, we must also consider the possibility of firms entering and leaving the industry. In short, we must consider the determination of price and output in the long run.

The Firm and the Industry in the Long Run

The foregoing analysis showed, with input prices constant, that the short-run supply curve of the perfectly competitive firm is that section of its marginal cost curve that lies above its average cost curve. If, still holding factor prices constant, the reader will simply substitute the long-run total cost, average cost, and marginal cost curves for their short-run counterparts in the arguments embodied in figures 12.1, 12.2 and 12.4, he should readily satisfy himself that the firm's long-run supply curve is given by that section of its long-run marginal cost curve that lies above the minimum point of the long-run average cost curve. However, it does not follow from this that the industry's long-run supply curve is simply some horizontal summation of the individual firms' supply curves. The reason for this is that, in the long run, each firm is free to vary the quantities of all the inputs that it uses, and if existing firms can do that, then they can, if they choose, leave the industry, while new firms can enter it. In the long run, therefore, the number of firms in the industry is variable.

In order to carry our analysis further, suppose that there are no special resources or limited skills necessary to produce X so that the production function underlying the cost curves of the particular firm we have been considering is available to any firm. Suppose also that each firm is able to buy its inputs at the same price as any other. It then follows that the short-run and long-run cost curves for any firm will be identical to those for any other.

Now consider figure 12.5. Here we show the short- and long-run cost and supply curves for a typical firm in the industry. It is assumed in drawing this figure that the firm is in a situation in which price is equated to both long-run and short-run marginal cost, so that, given the price ruling in the market, the firm has the right sized plant. If this is true of

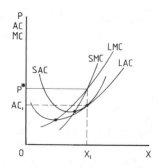

Figure 12.5 Suppose that price is given by P^*. At this price the typical firm will, in the long run, wish to sell X_1 of X. At this scale of output there are associated short-run average and marginal cost curves, the latter cutting the long-run marginal cost curve from below at output level X_1. As this figure is drawn, the firm makes positive profits at an output of X_1. From the point of view of the industry, this cannot be a long-run equilibrium situation.

each firm, there will be no internal tendency for it to change its output at all: each one will be making profits of $(P^* - AC_1)X_1$ — the maximum available. However, from the point of view of the industry as a whole, the situation depicted in figure 12.5 is not a tenable one. If the technology underlying the production function is readily available to all comers, and if anyone may enter the industry, existing firms will not be allowed to remain undisturbed in the situation shown in figure 12.5.

The profit which each firm is depicted as making is the difference between revenue and outlay on both the wage bill and on the rental of all its capital equipment. It is a pure surplus, because any 'normal rate of return' is already included in the rental price of capital, as we pointed out in the previous chapter. This profit is a rate of flow of extra income that is available simply as a result of being in the industry. New firms will obviously be attracted by the existence of this profit and will set up in the production of X. Only when such profit is completely competed away will there be no further entry. The means by which such profit is competed away are easily analysed. As each new firm enters the industry its output must be added to the output of the firms already in the industry. Because the market demand curve for X slopes downwards, the market price of X will fall as industry output

is increased in this way. Firms will continue to enter the
industry until market price has fallen to such an extent that
no profits are being made by any firm. At this point, with
neither entry nor exit, each firm may be said to be of equilibrium size and the industry to contain an equilibrium number
of firms. As the reader should be able to satisfy himself, when
the industry is of equilibrium size, the output of each firm
in it will be lower than in what we now know to be the non-
equilibrium situation depicted in figure 12.5.

For there to be neither entry nor exit, the industry's
output must be at such a level that the price facing each firm
in the industry just enables it to cover its costs while maximising profits. Maximum profits means that marginal cost must
equal price and zero profits means that average cost must
equal price. Marginal and average cost are only equal to one
another at the minimum point of the average cost curve. Thus,
if firms are free to come and go in the industry, the price of
output will always return to this same level in the long run.
The long-run supply curve for the industry will be a horizontal
line at the minimum value of long-run average cost for any
firm in the industry, as we show in figure 12.6, and each firm
will produce an output of X^{**}.

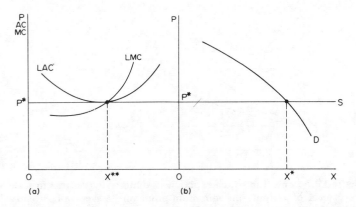

Figure 12.6 The existence of positive profits will entice new firms into
the production of X. If factor prices are constant and all firms are
equally efficient, price will always tend, in the long run, to be equal to
the minimum attainable level of long-run average cost. Hence the long-
run industry supply curve will be horizontal at this price. Each firm will
produce X^{**} at price P^*.

Now so far we have confined our analysis to what the reader might think of as a rather special case: namely, an industry of equally efficient firms each one having a U-shaped long-run average cost curve, and each one facing the same, invariant, set of prices for its inputs. Now we shall look at the special assumptions involved here in more detail. Only the assumption of the U-shaped cost curve plays more than a simplifying role in the analysis of perfect competition, and so we shall take up this matter first.

Alternative Assumptions about Returns to Scale

The returns to scale characteristics of the firm's production function that underlie the U-shaped long-run average cost curve assumed above play an important role in the theory of perfect competition, and this is best seen by examining what would happen if these characteristics were different.

Consider, first of all, the long-run average and marginal cost curves of a firm that faces diminishing returns to scale at any

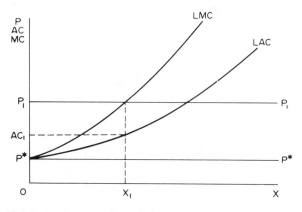

Figure 12.7 For a firm which experiences diminishing returns to scale at every level of output, the minimum point on its average cost curve is arbitrarily close to the vertical axis. In perfect competition with all firms equally efficient, then each such firm would end up making zero profits at an output approaching zero. The assumptions of consistently decreasing returns to scale together with that of equally efficient firms are not useful in the context of perfect competition.

level of output. They will be as depicted in figure 12.7. Clearly, at any price above P^*, say P_1, this firm will be making positive profits. If every firm, actual and potential, faces the same cost conditions, the existence of positive profits will lead to an expansion of the industry. This expansion should go on until each firm is producing at the lowest point on its long-run average cost curve, but that would be at a level of output approaching zero. The prediction that an industry will end up in the long-run situation of having a number of firms approaching the infinite, each producing an output verging on zero, does not make much empirical sense, and we may rule this case out on these grounds alone. If the perfectly competitive firm is to have a finite equilibrium size in the long run, then the minimum point on its average cost curve must not coincide with the vertical axis.

When the firm's production function is everywhere characterised by constant returns to scale, its long-run average and marginal cost curves coincide and are horizontal lines. This case produces indeterminate rather than nonsensical results at the level of the analysis of the individual firm. In figure 12.8, the long-run equilibrium price at the industry level is given at P^*, and the demand curve faced by the individual firm will be horizontal at that price, coinciding at every point

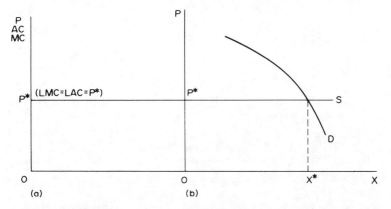

Figure 12.8 If all firms are equally efficient and experience constant returns to scale, industry output is determinate at X^*. However, the firm's output is indeterminate since the marginal cost, average cost and marginal revenue curves coincide when zero profits are being made.

with the firm's marginal and average cost curves. Thus, the number of firms in the industry and their sizes are left indeterminate in this case. One firm or many could equally efficiently produce the whole industry's output. Constant returns to scale at the level of the firm cannot be reconciled with a useful analysis of the behaviour of the individual perfectly competitive firm, not at least in terms of the simple analysis upon which we base this chapter.

Finally, consider the case of the invididual firm benefiting from continuously increasing returns to scale. The appropriate cost curves are depicted in figure 12.9. This case, though empirically plausible, is incompatible with the existence of perfect competition. When there are continuously increasing returns to scale up to the level of output that will satisfy the entire market demand for the industry's output, one firm can produce the whole industry's output at a lower average cost than can two or more firms, and that firm could therefore always undercut and drive out any smaller firms that tried to compete with it. We have here what is known as *natural monopoly* and the perfectly competitive model may not be applied in this case. The theory of monopoly, dealt with in the next chapter, is the appropriate device to use in its analysis.

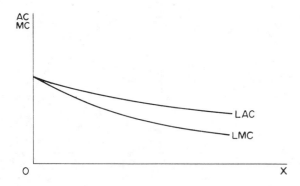

Figure 12.9 When returns to scale are always increasing, long-run average cost falls continuously and marginal cost is below it. There is no meaningful price and output equilibrium to this case in the context of perfect competition. Increasing returns to scale naturally lead to monopoly.

The U-Shaped Average Cost Curve and Managerial Inputs

The reader will by now appreciate the importance of postulating a U-shaped long-run average cost curve in the context of the theory of perfect competition and, unless there is some good reason for believing that it is likely to be empirically a particularly relevant phenomenon, its importance for this model might be regarded as undermining the status of perfect competition as a useful piece of analysis. The following argument is often advanced as a plausible justification for using this type of cost function. The production process is not solely an engineering matter; there are also administrative problems involved in getting goods produced. Someone has to organise the factors of production to ensure that they do end up cooperating in the technically most efficient manner, and someone must decide upon output levels and so forth. There is, in effect, a third input into our production process, namely the managerial skill of the organiser of the firm, the entrepreneur. Thus, when a firm expands output by equiproportional increases in labour and capital services, this does not represent equiproportional increases in *all* inputs. Managerial skill is being held constant. If, at very low levels of output, this skill is under-utilised, the firm will be able to do an increasingly effective job of organising capital and labour as output expands — to get, that is, decreasing average costs of production — up to a certain level. But, as output expands further, this same amount of organisational skill is likely to become increasingly overtaxed: hence at higher output levels a tendency to rising average costs.

The existence of a third, fixed and indivisible, factor of production called the organisation skill of the entrepreneur may thus be called in to justify the postulate of a U-shaped long-run average cost curve for the firm, but when this is done, something needs to be said about how that entrepreneur gets paid for his services. The answer here, as we noted in Chapter 9, is that he gets paid out of the firm's profits, that competition does not bid these down to zero, but that it bids them down to some minimal acceptable level known as *normal profits*. One can reconcile the existence of normal profits with the mechanics of the analysis set out in the previous chapter in two equally acceptable ways. First, one can note that the entrepreneur, were he not working in one industry, would be in some other. Hence, to engage in organising a firm in the production of X, he is giving up the profit that he could have earned by organising a firm in some other industry. The normal profits he could have earned elsewhere are then a cost of production of X in addition to outlays on capital and labour. It then becomes reasonable to think of these as being included in the factors lying behind the firm's long-run cost curves. Alternatively, one may simply suppose that these normal profits, when spread over a sufficiently large equilibrium volume of output, make such a small difference between the minimum point on the firm's average cost curve and the price of output as to be negligible. The reader may take his pick here since it makes no difference to the mechanics of the analysis whether normal profits are thought of as being included in the firm's costs or are simply ignored.

Just because the arguments presented here are often invoked to justify the existence of a U-shaped long-run average cost curve does not mean that they present no difficulties. Two points in particular should be noted. Their basis is that entrepreneurial capacity represents an indivisible factor of production, but the 'entrepreneur' may just as well be a management team as an individual person. Once that is realised, the case for treating entrepreneurial capacity as indivisible begins to lose much of its initial appeal. Furthermore, the management decisions that need to be undertaken by those in charge of a firm operating in the kind of perfectly competitive industry we are envisaging here, are trivial to the point of being negligible. Our analysis abstracts from all the uncertainty about markets, about technical change, about the behaviour of competitors, and so on, that make entrepreneurial activity so taxing in the real world. Thus, arguments to the effect that the indivisibility of entrepreneurial inputs lies at the root of the U-shaped long-run average cost curves that we attribute to perfectly competitive firms are better regarded as attempts to extend the logical completeness of an already rather abstract, but not for that reason irrelevant, model than as attempts to bring that model closer to reality.

Inter-Firm Differences in Efficiency

Let us now turn to relaxing certain other assumptions made in the previous chapter. As we shall see, these are by no means as critical for the perfectly competitive model as is that of a U-shaped long-run average cost curve. When we made the assumption that all firms in the industry are equally efficient, the long-run industry supply curve turned out to be infinitely elastic at a price given by the minimum point of the typical firm's long-run average cost curve. One way of looking at this case is to note that, by adding firms to the industry, one is adding to the production process units of the third input, the skill of the entrepreneur, and that constant returns to scale are emerging at the level of the industry rather than at the level of the firm. Be that as it may, there is no reason to suppose that firms will in fact be equally efficient. If they are not, then if every firm already in a particular industry is observed to be making positive — or above normal — profits, new firms will still be attracted into that industry. If the factors that make existing firms more efficient are specific to the particular industry in which they find themselves, rather than arising from general advantages that could be exploited in any industry, and if they are not available to newcomers, then the new entrants will be less efficient in the sense that the minimum long-run average cost of production that they can achieve will be higher than that incurred by those already there, even though they pay the same price for other inputs. The entry of new firms will bid down the price of output, and this will continue to fall until the least efficient firm in the industry is producing at the minimum point of its long-run average cost curve. This least efficient firm is often called the marginal firm, for obvious reasons. All other firms in the industry, having lower average costs, will be making positive (or above normal) profits.

The long-run equilibrium described here is depicted in figure 12.10, and this diagram should be self-explanatory. The important implication of the analysis set out in the figure is that in this case the industry's long-run supply curve slopes upwards even when the number of firms varies. This is because

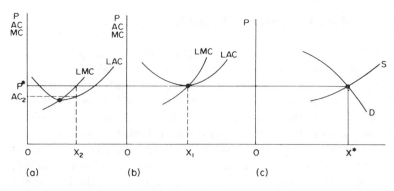

Figure 12.10 When all firms are not equally efficient, even when factor prices are constant, the industry's long-run supply curve with the number of firms variable (S) slopes upwards. Only the marginal firm, panel (b), makes no profits at its equilibrium output of X_1. Any intra-marginal (i.e. more efficient) firm such as that depicted in panel (a) will make positive profits at its profit maximising level of output (X_2). Note that the intra-marginal firm does not produce at a scale of output that minimises long-run average cost, but at a larger scale with an average cost of AC_2.

as output expands, less and less efficient firms, with higher and higher average costs of production, enter the industry. At each level of output, equilibrium price is given by the minimum average cost of the marginal firm, and the higher the level of output, the less efficient is that marginal firm.

It should be noted that if some firms are more efficient than others because the entrepreneurs running them are in general more skilful, and if their greater skill could be utilised effectively in any industry, then the extra return that it yields in the X industry should properly be regarded as a cost, because it could also be earned elsewhere. In this case, as the reader should be able to satisfy himself, the industry long-run supply curve would be a horizontal straight line, and there would be no uniquely identified marginal firm.

Variations in Factor Prices in the Short Run

So far we have dealt with the effects on supply conditions of the technical conditions of production within the industry and within firms. We have, throughout the analysis, held input prices constant. Let us now relax this particular assumption, and deal with the consequence of what are frequently called economies and diseconomies of scale external to the firm, which impinge upon firms' behaviour through the variations that they produce in factor prices. They are so called to distinguish them from the economies and diseconomies internal to the firm that, being the consequence of increasing and decreasing returns to scale in the production function, are under the control of the firm itself, i.e. are internal to its decision-making process. We will explicitly analyse external effects only in the case of an industry made up of equally efficient firms, but the reader might find it helpful to reproduce for himself the analysis modified to fit the case of an industry where the firms vary in efficiency.

Consider first of all the effects of factor prices rising as the whole industry expands. If any particular firm is sufficiently small that no variations it makes in its scale of operations can influence factor prices, but if the industry as a whole is large enough relative to factor markets to bid up input prices when it expands, and bid them down when it contracts, then such factor price variations are outside the control of the firm, and hence are indeed external to its decision making. Because such variations result from changes in the industry's size, they may be referred to as internal to the industry.

Let us analyse an industry's short-run response to an increase in the demand for its product at any given price. In figure 12.11 the industry demand curve shifts; each firm moves up its short-run marginal cost curve, and the industry as a whole moves up its short-run supply curve, which is of course just the sum of these short-run marginal cost curves. Now suppose that the effect of the increased demand for labour implicit in this move is to increase the price of labour. Then the short-run average and marginal cost curves of each firm are obviously shifted vertically upwards as is the industry's short-run supply curve. The movement to a new short-run equilibrium in this case involves in part a movement along and in part a shift upwards of marginal cost curves and the new equilibrium is to be found at a point such as $P_2{}^*X_2{}^*$ in figure 12.11. Now we can perform the experiment of shifting the demand curve

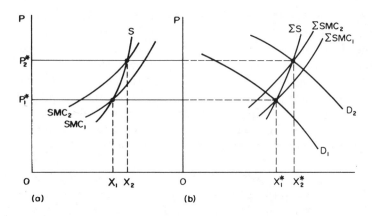

Figure 12.11 The short-run supply curve when prices of factors increase with an increase in their employment: industry demand increases from D_1 to D_2, each firm attempts to move out along SMC_1 and hence industry supply tends to shift along ΣSMC_1. However, the price of the variable factor rises as output expands shifting every firm's short-run marginal cost curve upwards. Equilibrium is re-established at X_2* and P_2*, as opposed to the initial equilibrium of X_1*, P_1*. Here the price of the variable factor is higher, so that each firm is on SMC_2 and the industry is on ΣSMC_2. The supply response of the firm from X_1 to X_2 is a mixture of a movement along a marginal cost curve and shift of such a curve; which may be summarised into a movement along a curve such as S, which is the firm's short-run supply curve of X when the whole industry is expanding its output of X and the price of the variable factor of production increases with its utilisation. The industry's short-run supply curve is the sum over all firms of curves such as S, ΣS. It is more steeply sloped than the supply curve derived holding factor prices constant.

about many times and the consequence will always be this combination of movements along curves and shifts of curves, the resulting equilibrium price and output combinations for the industry lying along a line such as ΣS, which may then be interpreted as the industry's short-run supply curve *when factor prices rise with output*. Such a curve will clearly be more steeply sloped than the summed marginal cost curves at any given level of factor prices. The reader may easily satisfy himself that, were the price of labour to fall as output increased, the resulting short-run supply curve would have a shallower slope.

Factor Price Variations in the Long Run

Long-run supply relationships must be modified in a way similar to the short-run response when factor prices are allowed to vary. Output increases, the prices of both capital and labour services tend to increase and so the minimum level of average cost attainable by any firm in the industry shifts upwards. Thus, the supply curve derived from permitting the number of firms to vary acquires an upward slope. All this is shown, at the industry level, in figure 12.12.

What happens at the level of the particular firm when, in the long run, factor prices increase as the industry expands is not altogether clearcut. It is certain that each firm's cost curves shift upwards and also that, when the industry is in

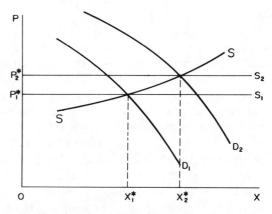

Figure 12.12 When all firms are equally efficient, but inputs prices vary positively with the industry's demand for them, a shift from D_1 to D_2 in the demand for X leads in the long run to an increase in the number of firms in the industry, and an increase in factor prices that shifts up the minimum point on each firm's average cost curve. Hence the long-run supply curve permitting the number of firms to vary, but holding factor prices constant, shifts up from S_1 to S_2. The industry's supply response is thus a mixture of a shift along such a curve and a shift up of such a curve and may be summarised in a movement from P_1*X_1* to P_2*X_2* along a curve such as S. This is the industry's long-run supply curve, when we permit the number of firms in the industry to vary and the prices of factors of production to rise systematically with output.

long-run equilibrium with an expanded number of firms, each firm will once more be producing at the minimum point of its long-run average cost curve. This much is clear, but what cannot in general be predicted is what will happen to the individual firm's scale of output. This is because one would not in general expect the prices of capital and labour to increase equiproportionately as the industry expands. Thus, the firm will change the proportions in which it employs labour and capital towards the relatively cheaper factor. (In terms of figure 10.4 it will shift from one ray through the origin to another along which the cheaper input is used in relatively greater quantities.) When factor proportions are thus changed it is not necessarily the case that the minimum point on the long-run average cost curve will occur at the same level of output at the two different sets of factor prices. It may, or may not. Everything here depends upon the specific nature of the production function.

Factor prices may fall rather than rise as output increases. This would happen if there existed some economies of scale in other industries producing inputs, or if the quality of inputs increased with their scale of use. If all firms are equally efficient, the long-run supply curve would then slope downwards. This is a point of some interest because it enables us to be precise about the extent to which average costs that fall as the level of output increases are compatible with competition. We have already seen earlier that falling average costs produced by increasing technical returns to scale — economies internal to the firm — lead to monopoly. So it is only when average costs fall as a result of declining input prices — as a result of economies external to the firm — that competition and decreasing costs are compatible.

Such external economies as these most often arise when we have a regionally localised industry requiring specialised skills on the part of its labour force. Thus, in the case of Britain, the localisation of the cotton industry in Lancashire, lace-making around Nottingham, and the pottery industry around Stoke, for example, led to a tradition among the local labour force that perhaps reduced the costs of training labour — hence effectively lowering the price of the services of skilled labour to individual firms. Moreover, the importance of this phenomenon tends to vary with the size of the industry, so that, for example, the advantages to a textile firm of locating in Lancashire now, as compared to say seventy years ago, have probably considerably diminished, as the scale of the industry in that area has diminished.

Perfect Competition and the Supply Curve

Now in this chapter we have been continually discussing the supply curve. We have seen that, as for the demand curve, there is no unique way of deriving a supply curve. Just as we could have demand curves for individuals and market demand curves, so we have here had firm and industry supply curves. Moreover, just as one gets different demand curves depending upon what it is that is conceptually held constant, so we have had different supply curves for the short run, for the long run, for constant factor prices and for variable factor prices.

Again, as with the demand curve, there is no uniquely correct way to define a supply curve; the appropriate choice must always depend upon the situation under analysis and hence upon one's assessment of which factors it is appropriate to hold constant in a particular instance. Nevertheless, *the ability to generate a relationship between quantity supplied and price, to complement that between quantity demanded and price, so that the tools of supply and demand may be utilised, is an important one. Of all the forms of industrial organisation that we will consider in this book, perfect competition is the only one that enables us to generate this relationship.* Quite apart, then, from all the other results obtained in this chapter, this is surely more than enough reason for taking seriously the theory of the profit maximising perfectly competitive firm and industry.

13
Monopoly, Discriminating Monopoly and Monopolistic Competition

Introduction

The perfectly competitive firm with which we dealt in the last chapter faced a horizontal demand curve and was able to sell all it pleased at the going market price. The monopolistic firms we shall analyse in this chapter face downward sloping demand curves. As we shall see, there is no unique set of influences which ensures that the demand curve faced by every monopolist is the market demand curve for his product, but for the moment it will suffice if the reader thinks of him as being the sole seller of a good in an industry where, for one reason or another, the entry of competitors is quite impossible. In such a situation the market demand curve for the good does indeed become the demand curve that faces the monopolist.

The Demand Curve and Total Revenue

The monopolist's demand curve is downward sloping, and his total revenue function is not therefore an upward sloping straight line along which revenue is proportional to sales. A demand curve is, by definition, an average revenue curve, and if all we know about that curve is that it slopes downward, a wide variety of shapes is available for the total revenue function.

It must only have the property that straight lines drawn to it from the origin slope less steeply at higher and higher levels of output; the slope of such lines measures average revenue, which is, of course, demand price. Figure 13.1 displays a number of such curves and, curiously shaped though some of them are, all are compatible with a downward sloping demand curve. The curve in figure 13.1(c) is the one upon which we shall concentrate since it is derived from a straight-line demand curve, and the use of such a demand curve will make the exposition simpler. Simplicity is the only reason for preferring a straight-line demand curve, however; there is no theoretical or empirical reason for preferring it.

Now the reader will recall that as price falls and quantity demanded increases, total expenditure by consumers increases when the price elasticity of demand is in excess of unity: expenditure remains the same at unit demand elasticity and falls when elasticity is less than unity. Note that total expenditure by consumers is just the monopolistic firm's total revenue by another name and consider the linear demand curve of figure 13.2, which has a constant slope dX/dP. Elasticity is defined as $(dX/dP)/(X/P)$. At point A it is clear

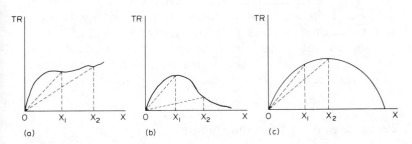

Figure 13.1 Three possible shapes for a total revenue curve associated with a downward sloping demand (average revenue) curve. The slope of a straight line from the origin to any one of these curves falls systematically as output increases. The movement from X_1 to X_2 gives an example of this. Panel (c) shows the total revenue curve associated with a straight-line demand curve. Around level of output X_2, total revenue is constant as output varies. Thus, price must be changing in equal but opposite proportion to quantity and the elasticity of the demand curve must be unity at this point. At lower levels of output than X_2 demand must be elastic, and at higher levels inelastic.

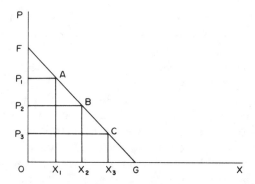

Figure 13.2 A straight-line demand curve. Its slope is constant at OG/OF. Halfway between F and G, at point B, the ratio OX_2 to OP_2 is equal to the slope of the curve, so its elasticity is equal to unity at this point. (OFG, P_2FB and X_2BG are similar triangles; FB equals BG and is half of FG. Thus X_2B which equals OP_2 is half of OF, and similarly OX_2 is half of OG.)

that X/P is smaller than dX/dP. Hence elasticity is greater than one and total revenue is increasing with quantity. By similar argument, at C, it is clear that X/P is greater than dX/dP. At this point, elasticity is smaller than unity and total revenue is decreasing. At B which lies halfway along the curve, dX/dP and X/P are equal. Elasticity is unity and total revenue is not changing with quantity. The straight-line demand curve encompasses all elasticities from infinity at its intersection with the vertical axis to zero at the horizontal, and the shape of the total revenue curve in figure 13.1(c) reflects this.

Profit Maximising Price and Output

There is no reason to suppose that a monopolist's cost functions differ in any qualitative way from those of a competitive firm and, with the exception that entry of new firms is ruled out, our previous analysis of the long-run/short-run dichotomy still holds.

There is no need for us to repeat all this then, and we may immediately analyse monopoly pricing in the long run. The analysis of short-run behaviour simply involves the substitution

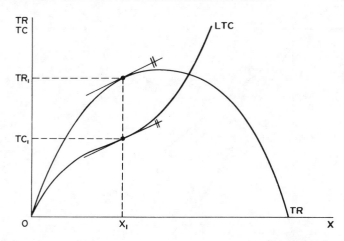

Figure 13.3 Long-run profit maximisation for a monopolist facing a straight-line demand curve, and endowed with a long-run cost function characterised by increasing followed by decreasing returns to scale. Maximum profits occur where the slopes of the two curves are equal (i.e. where marginal cost equals marginal revenue). Profit is equal to $TR_1 - TC_1$. So long as total costs increase with output, profit maximisation requires that output be fixed on the rising section of the total revenue curve, i.e. where the elasticity of demand for the product is greater than 1 in absolute value.

of short- for long-run cost curves in what follows. Figure 13.3 superimposes a long-run total cost curve upon the total revenue curve. Profits will be maximised where the vertical distance between the two curves is at its greatest (with revenue in excess of costs) and this occurs at output X_1, where the two functions have equal slopes. This statement about equality of slopes is another way of saying that profits are maximised where marginal cost equals marginal revenue. Figure 13.4 depicts the same profit maximising solution in terms of explicitly drawn marginal cost and marginal revenue functions.

For a monopolist, marginal revenue and price are not equal because the total revenue function is not a straight line through the origin. Thus, the slope of the total revenue function is not the same as the slope of a line drawn to it from the origin. Indeed, if we call price by its other name, average revenue, it becomes obvious that a downward sloping demand curve implies continually falling average revenue. It must also be

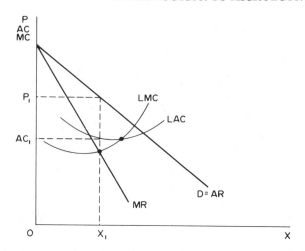

Figure 13.4 The profit maximising monopolist will fix output where marginal cost equals marginal revenue at X_1 and charge the maximum price that he can get for that quantity of output, P_1. This diagram repeats, in more familiar terms, the analysis set out in figure 13.3. Profits are given by $(P_1 - AC_1)X_1$ which is equal to $TR_1 - TC_1$ in figure 13.3.

the case that the relationship between average and marginal revenue must be exactly the same as that between average and marginal cost. Thus it clearly follows that the marginal revenue curve will everywhere lie below a downward sloping demand curve. This, be it noted, is *not* the same as saying that marginal revenue is always falling, as the reader may determine for himself by reproducing the relevant panels from figure 13.1 and deriving the average and marginal revenue curves implicit in them. The exercise should convince him both of our wisdom in sticking to the special case of the straight line demand curve for purposes of exposition, and the dangers inherent in over-generalising from analysis based upon it. In this case the marginal revenue curve is always downward sloping. There is in fact a precise relationship between the elasticity of the demand curve and marginal revenue.* Where the elasticity is accorded its negative sign, it is given by:

---

* The geometric proof of this is extremely tedious. However, a little calculus enables it to be very simply shown:

$$\text{Marginal revenue} = \text{price} \left(1 + \frac{1}{\text{elasticity}} \right) \qquad (13.1)$$

We will find this relationship useful in the analysis that follows.

Now, what can we say about the properties of the long-run price and output decision of the monopolist set out in figures 13.3 and 13.4? First, it shows him making positive profits equal to $TR_1 - TC_1$ as measured in figure 13.3, or $(P_1 - AC_1) X_1$ as measured in figure 13.4. That positive profits are earned is not a necessary consequence of monopolistic behaviour. It results from the assumptions about costs and revenues which we have built into the diagrams and nothing else. Thus, in figure 13.5(a) we have a situation in which the cost and revenue functions are such that the maximum available profit is zero, and in figure 13.5(b) a situation in which losses would be made at any level of output, so that in fact no production would take place in the long run.

The second characteristic of figure 13.4 worth noting is, however, a general property of monopoly behaviour (unless certain types of price discrimination to be dealt with below take place): the price charged is greater than marginal cost. Now, in perfect competition, in the long run, price is equal to the long-run marginal cost of the least efficient firm in the

---

$TR = PX$

$MR \equiv \dfrac{d(TR)}{dX} = P\dfrac{dX}{dX} + X\dfrac{dP}{dX}$

$= P + X\dfrac{dP}{dX}$

Multiply through by $1 \equiv \dfrac{P}{P}$

$MR = P\left(1 + \dfrac{X}{P}\dfrac{dP}{dX} \right)$

$= P\left(1 + \dfrac{1}{E} \right)$

where $E \equiv \dfrac{dX}{dP}\dfrac{P}{X}$

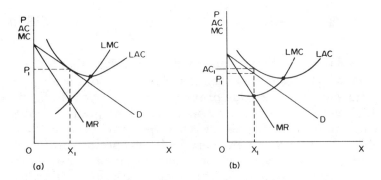

Figure 13.5 A monopolist whose profit maximising level of output X_1 yields (a) zero profit, and (b) a loss of $(AC_1 - P_1)X_1$. In panel (a), if LAC is just tangent to D, then MR equals LMC at this level of output, for at this level of output the total revenue curve would just be tangent to the total cost curve from below.

industry. If it is the case that the monopolist's marginal cost curve is the same as that which would yield the long-run supply curve of a competitive industry, then the monopolist will charge more and produce less than a competitive industry.

Finally, the monopolist produces where marginal cost equals marginal revenue. Therefore, so long as marginal cost is positive, he will produce at a price and output level at which total revenue increases as output increases — a point where the elasticity of demand for output is greater than unity. It is a common misconception that monopolists are particularly likely to exist where demand for products is inelastic. Any monopolist finding himself in such a situation can increase his profits by curtailing output and raising price until he is on an elastic segment of his demand curve. Inelastic demand and profit maximising monopoly (at least non-discriminating monopoly) are incompatible. The formula given above (13.1) confirms this point. If elasticity lies between 0 and −1, it yields a negative value for marginal revenue. Now this is the second time that we have referred to price discrimination and we shall now discuss this behaviour in the following section of this chapter.

Price Discrimination

Price discrimination involves nothing more than selling different units of the same good at different prices. It is a widespread phenomenon and we will consider it in two forms: first, charging different prices to different consumers and second, charging the same consumers different prices for different units of the good. Obviously these are not mutually exclusive practices — more complicated cases do indeed exist and may be analysed with the tools we shall now develop.

Suppose that, for some reason, the market for X facing the monopolist with whom we have so far been dealing were to expand by having a new group of consumers added to it. We would analyse the results of this by adding the demand of our new consumers on to that of those already in the market, deriving the new marginal revenue curve and thereby solving for price and output. We do this in figure 13.6. The only point

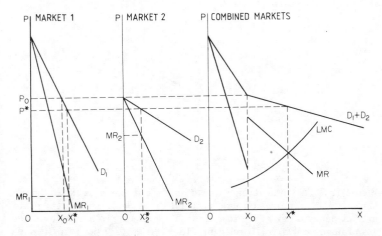

Figure 13.6 A monopolist sells in two different markets, but being unable to separate them sells at the same price P^* in both of them, X_1^* in market 1 and X_2^* in market 2. Thus marginal revenue is different in the two markets and profits could be increased by charging different prices in the two markets and equalising marginal revenues. A unit of output withdrawn from market 1 and transferred to market 2 would add more to revenue in the second market than it subtracted from revenue in the first since at P^*, MR_1 is below MR_2.

here that is new to the reader is the discontinuity in the marginal revenue curve for the aggregate market. This arises because, at P_0, the price at which the new group of consumers comes into the market, there is a kink in the summed demand curve. If the reader will translate this back to a property of the total revenue curve he will see that there will be a kink there too, as shown in figure 13.7, and that there is therefore a discontinuity in that curve's slope, in marginal revenue.

The profit maximising solution depicted in figure 13.6, where marginal cost equals marginal revenue in the aggregate market, is an output of X^* sold at a price of P^*. Both groups of consumers are paying the same price for X; note that this implies that the marginal revenue accruing from selling to each group is different except in the special case where each group's elasticity of demand for X at that price is the same. Now marginal revenue is the addition to be made to total revenue from a small increment in the quantity sold (or the loss accruing from reducing quantity sold). As we have constructed

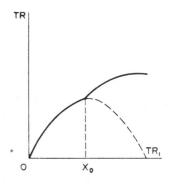

Figure 13.7 The total revenue curve implicit in summing the individual market demand curves of panels (a) and (b) of figure 13.6 to get a total market demand curve. Up to output X_0, goods are sold only in market 1 and hence only TR_1 is relevant. However, at X_0, price is sufficiently low that purchasers in market 2 begin to buy the good. Hence total revenue is now that earned in both markets and there is a kink in the total revenue curve at this level of output that corresponds to the kink in the total demand curve. The slope of the total demand curve (marginal revenue) thus increases discontinuously at output X_0. Note that this total revenue curve is derived on the assumption that the good X is sold at the same price in both markets. It is not relevant to the analysis that follows when different prices are charged in the two markets.

figure 13.6, holding output, and hence costs, constant, one could increase revenue by withdrawing units of X yielding a low marginal revenue from market 1 and selling them in market 2 where marginal revenue is higher. Gains would arise from doing this up to the point where marginal revenue was equated in the two markets. Such equating of marginal revenues, though, would involve charging different prices to the two groups of consumers, in short, there would be price discrimination between them.

Demand Elasticity and Price Discrimination

A monopolist does not necessarily have the power to charge different prices to different people. It depends what good he is selling and how easy it is to identify and keep separate members of the two (or more) groups. If the good is such that one consumer can sell it to another after purchase at trivial cost in time and trouble, then discrimination is not possible, for any attempt to charge a higher price to one group would result in them having members of the lower price group make their purchases for them. Thus a cinema might offer a price discount to old age pensioners, but not a bookshop; a football ground might offer a discount to school children, but not a sweet shop. The reader may readily construct further examples of his own. If we assume that our two groups can be identified, and that the good is such that they can be kept from retrading it between them, it will pay the monopolist to charge them different prices. Moreover, we may predict who will pay the higher price.

The reader will find it helpful to recall at this point that, just as the slope of the total revenue curve is equal to marginal revenue and just as the slope of the long-run total cost curve is equal to long-run marginal cost, so the area under the marginal revenue curve measures total revenue and the area under the long-run marginal cost curve measures long-run total cost. These relationships were set out in Part I (Chapter 4) in the context of total and marginal utility, but they hold equally for any total marginal interrelationship, and are particularly useful in the analysis of price discrimination. So also is the relationship between marginal revenue, price, and the elasticity of demand:

$$\text{Marginal revenue} = \text{price} \left(1 + \frac{1}{\text{elasticity}} \right)$$

If to maximise his profits a discriminating monopolist is to equate marginal revenue between two markets, then the higher the absolute value of the elasticity of demand in either one of them, the lower will be the price. In terms of figure 13.8, which reproduces figure 13.6 and extends the analysis, the gain in profits from price discrimination is given by the area $CDX_2{}^*X_2$ minus the area $ABX_1X_1{}^*$. This is the gain in revenue from lowering price in market 2, minus the loss from raising it in market 1. Equivalently, it is given by the area GEF which is the difference between the area under the curve that is marginal to the summed demand curves of markets 1 and 2, and that under the summed marginal revenue curves of these markets. These two curves are *not* the same. The first is $HGFEJ$ and the second is $HGEJ$. The first marginal revenue curve tells us how marginal revenue changes with quantity *when that quantity is sold to yield an equal price* in each market. The second deals with a situation when *that quantity is sold so as to yield the same marginal revenue*. The summed demand curve is irrelevant in the second case: it is the sum of the marginal revenue curves in the individual markets that is important.

This distinction is crucial when analysing the special case where the firm's marginal cost curve just passes through the discontinuity on the curve that is marginal to the summed demand curves. Here the inability to discriminate might lead to a price being set at which one group of consumers buys nothing. The ability to discriminate allows the latter group to be charged a lower price, and actually results in output increasing from the no discrimination situation. The reader will find it instructive explicitly to carry out the analysis and satisfy himself that this is indeed the case.

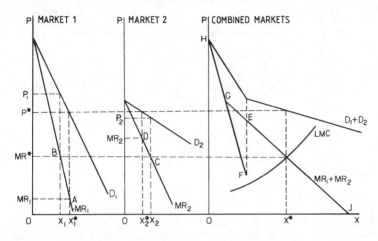

Figure 13.8 Price discrimination between two markets. Prices are set in the two markets so as to equalise marginal revenue, so that P_1 is above P_2. The higher the elasticity of demand in a particular market, the lower the price charged. The increase in profits relative to charging the same price (P^*) in both markets is given equivalently by the areas $(CDX_2^*X_2 - ABX_1X_1^*)$ or GEF. Sales in the first market, panel (a), contract from X_1^* to X_1 and those in the second market expand from X_2^* to X_2. There is no change over all output X^* from the no price discrimination case and hence no change in costs of production. That is why revenue changes may be used to measure profit changes in this case.

Perfect Price Discrimination

To charge different prices to different groups of consumers is only one form that price discrimination can take. As we saw when we dealt with the theory of consumer's surplus, it is of the very essence that a consumer faced with a single price for a commodity gains from being able to purchase it; it is only the marginal unit purchased that is worth no more to the consumer than he is asked to pay for it. Consider figure 13.9 where a typical consumer's demand curve has been drawn, and let us make the Marshallian assumptions that permit us to treat the area under that curve as an approximate measure of the maximum amount that an individual would be willing to pay to obtain any particular quantity of the good. If the price is P_1, our consumer buys X_1 units of X spending in

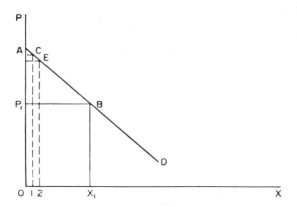

Figure 13.9 An individual's demand curve for X derived on Marshallian assumptions (*cf.* Chapter 4). A perfectly discriminating monopolist could acquire revenue of $OABX_1$ if it sold X_1 units of X to this consumer.

total P_1X_1, but he would be willing to spend up to ABX_1O to obtain this quantity.

If the firm selling X was able to charge him a different price for each unit that he bought, it could charge him the area under the curve between A and C for the first unit, that between C and E for the second and so on. It would obtain a total revenue of $OABX_1$ from the sale of X_1 units, and would thereby increase its profits by ABP_1. Such 'perfect price discrimination', as it is called, would obviously be adopted by the profit maximising firm if it was able to do so. Figure 13.10 shows what the situation would be from the point of view of the total market for X, rather than from that of the individual consumer (but still dealing with a demand curve based on Marshallian assumptions).

If the monopoly depicted there were able to price discriminate to perfection, its total revenue would be given by the area under the market demand curve for X, its total costs by the area under the long-run marginal cost curve; profits, the difference between the two, would obviously be maximised where the price of the last unit sold was just equal to long-run marginal cost. In this case, the market demand curve in effect becomes the firm's marginal revenue curve, rather than its average revenue curve. Now such perfect price discrimination

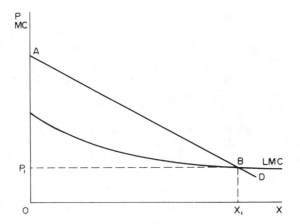

Figure 13.10 A profit maximising perfectly discriminating monopolist would charge P_1 for the last unit of X that he sold and get a total revenue of ABX_1O. Equivalently, if he could operate a multipart tariff scheme he would charge P_1, i.e. long-run marginal cost per unit of X and have available the area AP_1B as the maximum amount he could collect by way of a fixed charge for the privilege of buying X at price P_1.

as this is a limiting case of a very general phenomenon. Any consumer who faces a multi-part tariff for the use of electricity or gas, or who pays a cover charge at a restaurant, is on the receiving end of a discriminatory pricing scheme.

Perfect price discrimination appropriates to the seller of a good all the consumer's surplus that each consumer would get from buying it at a constant price. A two-part tariff for gas or electricity, whereby a consumer may buy as much as he likes at a given price, after he pays a rent for the right to receive any supply at all, takes some consumer's surplus in the form of this rental payment. If a profit maximising seller knew the exact form of the consumer's demand curve, he would fix his rental equal to the area ABP_1 in figure 13.9 and obtain exactly the effect of perfect price discrimination. Similarly for the restaurant that imposes a cover charge. Lack of perfect knowledge about the exact form of each customer's demand curve and the fact that it is expensive to acquire such knowledge even imperfectly — to say nothing of the administrative costs of running a different pricing scheme for every customer — leads such firms to set a uniform fixed charge which leaves some consumers with a surplus, some with none and persuades others to refrain from consuming the good at all where the charge is in excess of their surplus.

Price discrimination of the type just analysed can occur wherever it is possible for the seller to identify an individual consumer and face him with a two-part choice: whether to consume the good at all, and how much of it to consume, given that some is to be consumed. The possibility of imposing such a choice depends very much on the technical nature of the good being supplied. Electricity and gas consumption require the installation of supply facilities in individual houses and factories, the consumption of a restaurant meal requires that a particular table be occupied. Hence rental, or cover, charges may be imposed. The reader is invited to think up some further examples of his own where discrimination is possible. Doing so will not only help him to master the foregoing analysis but will convince him of the ubiquity of the practice.

How much output will a discriminating monopolist of the type just described sell, and at what kind of price structure? If he wishes to maximise profits, the first step is to set his price on the margin in such a way as to maximise the possible gain to himself from charging a higher price for intra-marginal units. The possible gain in question is of course equal to the profits that would be made by a perfect price discriminator and these are maximised, as we have seen, by setting price on the margin equal to marginal cost. In terms of figure 13.10, output would still be equal to X_1 and price on the margin would be set at P_1, even if perfect discrimination were not feasible. How much of the consumer's surplus existing in the area ABP_1 the monopolist would appropriate to himself, and with what kind of price structure, would depend upon how much he knew about the shape of the demand curve and how ingenious he was at devising a suitable pricing scheme. The important implication here is that the monopolist who is able to price discriminate by using multi-part tariffs will produce exactly the same output as a perfectly competitive industry, if his long-run marginal cost curve is indeed the same curve that would be such an industry's long-run supply curve. It is only monopolists who do not have the power to discriminate who will restrict output below its competitive level. Where price discrimination of the type just analysed is possible it is the amount of profits obtained, and not the level of output, that differentiates the consequences of monopoly from those of competition.

Monopolistic Competition

It is a widely held view that perfect competition and monopoly represent two extreme ends of what might be termed a spectrum of different forms of market organisation. This view has spawned a whole literature on alternative models of the behaviour of the firm, under conditions that lie between these two alleged extremes, and one of the best known of these models deals with a situation known as *monopolistic competition*.

The pure monopolist with whom we dealt earlier in this chapter ended up with the possibility of making positive profits in long-run equilibrium. We did not consider the question of why competitive firms did not spring up to take these profits away from him. There are abundant reasons why a monopolist may be able to remain a monopolist at least for a significant time. There may be legal barriers to other firms producing the same good as a monopolist; he may have patent protection for his product; he may have access to some trade secret that gives him a significant cost advantage in producing his product; he may be in an industry where the technology is characterised by increasing returns to scale; and so on. At the opposite extreme, if other firms can reproduce his product to perfection at no cost disadvantage, the industry becomes perfectly competitive. What about intermediate cases in which a similar, but not identical, product can be produced by other firms at no cost advantage? It is precisely with such a case that the theory of monopolistic competition seeks to deal.

However, the theory was built up at a time before economists had available to them that approach to the theory of demand, some of whose rudimentary characteristics are set out in Chapter 8. It was not clear at that time that goods could be looked upon as constituting bundles of attributes, an approach to their definition that opens up the possibility of giving some sort of precision to ideas like 'similar but not the same goods'. Thus, there has always been an element of imprecision to this particular theory of firm behaviour that has made it very difficult to make it relevant to particular empirical circumstances, however apparently relevant its basic characteristics might seem to be when they are viewed in a more general perspective.

Be that as it may, the basic outlines of this approach are easily enough set out. Figure 13.11 shows a monopolist in long-run equilibrium making profits equal to $(P - AC_1)X_1$. Now suppose that it was possible for other firms to set up and produce a different brand of the same product under the same cost conditions as this monopolist. The effect of this would be both to make the demand curve for our monopolist's product more elastic at any particular price (the introduction of close substitutes is bound to do this) and to shift the curve in to the left as he lost customers to these other firms. Now if there are no barriers to entry of new firms, this

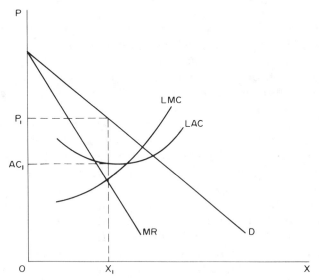

Figure 13.11 A monopolist in long-run equilibrium earning profits of $(P_1 - AC_1)X_1$. This diagram is similar in all respects to figure 13.4.

process would continue until there were no profits being made to attract new entrants. Thus, our original monopolist and all his competitors would find themselves in an equilibrium such as portrayed in figure 13.12. Here the firm is making no profits, it is in equilibrium at a level of output at which long-run average cost and price are equal. Because competitors are producing 'similar' but not identical products, the demand curve facing each firm slopes downwards so that with price being equal to average cost where profits are maximised, each firm is necessarily producing on the downward sloping segment of its long-run average cost curve. Thus, it is sometimes argued, a firm involved in monopolistic competition is *inherently* less efficient than its perfectly competitive counterpart since it ends up producing output at more than minimum average cost.

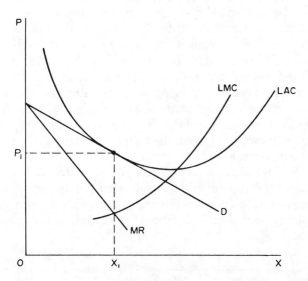

Figure 13.12 A typical monopolistically competitive firm in long-run equilibrium. The existence of positive profits attracts new firms which produce a similar but not identical product to X. The expansion of such firms results in the demand curve for X shifting until it is just tangent to the firm's long-run average cost curve at $P_1 X_1$. This figure is similar in every essential respect to the zero profit special case of a monopolistic firm portrayed in figure 13.5(a).

Now the foregoing analysis is certainly superficially appealing, but we must ask whether it really adds anything to the monopoly model with which we dealt earlier. Monopoly differs from perfect competition in its analysis of the behaviour of the firm in one respect only: the monopolist's demand curve slopes downward. So also does that of the monopolistically competitive firm, and in long-run equilibrium it is just a special case of monopoly where zero profits are being made. If this analysis does add anything to our understanding of firms' behaviour, it must be because it tells us something about the interactions between firms in an industry, for it tells us nothing new about the individual firm.

But there is a problem at this level too. The monopolistically competitive industry is made up of firms producing 'similar', though not identical, products that are therefore 'close', but not perfect, substitutes for each other. The question upon which the analysis founders is 'how close is close?' Are different brands of tea 'similar' products? And if they are, is coffee a sufficiently 'close' substitute that we should talk about a 'beverage' industry? And if we do, are cocoa producing firms part of it? The model does not tell us how to draw the boundary around an industry and hence leaves it up to the individual economist carrying out his analysis to decide whether to treat a particular group of firms as individual monopolies or as members of a monopolistically competitive industry. Since no one has ever suggested that there are no substitutes for an individual monopolist's output, and that changes in the price of those substitutes will not shift the demand curve he faces, it would appear that the notion of the monopolistically competitive industry adds nothing to our ability to understand firms' behaviour that is not already inherent in the theory of pure monopoly.

Concluding Comment

Now to say that the theory of monopolistic competition does not seem to add much to our ability to understand the behaviour of firms is not to say that perfect competition and monopoly between them provide a complete theory of their behaviour. They do not touch on several problems arising from firms' interactions. Taking the demand curve that faces it as given exogenously, the problem for each firm is to pick the point on that curve which will maximise profits; for the perfect competitor this involves choosing output alone, and for the monopolist it involves choosing a combination of price and output.

Lying behind the demand curve, whether of a monopolist or a perfect competitor, are the prices of other goods. An implicit assumption behind the theories we have so far discussed is that the decisions taken by the firm under analysis have very diffuse effects on the demand curves facing other firms. If this assumption is granted, there is no need to consider the possibility of other firms reacting to the actions taken by the firm under analysis in such a way as to cause the demand conditions under which it is operating to change, and the theories of perfect competition and monopoly are adequate tools of analysis. However, if this assumption does not hold and firms' demand curves do in fact become significantly interdependent in any circumstances, then these theories begin to break down. Oligopoly theory, certain aspects of which we will discuss in sections of the next chapter, represents an attempt to come to grips with such matters.

14
Further Topics in the
Theory of the Firm

Introduction

The theories of monopoly and perfect competition with which we have dealt in the last two chapters are the basic building blocks of the theory of the firm, but, as we have already hinted in a number of places, there is a rich literature in the field of Industrial Organisation which encompasses a wide variety of other models of firm and industry behaviour. In this chapter we deal with a selection of these alternative models in order to give the reader at least the flavour of this extensive literature. We make no pretence at comprehensiveness. It would take a textbook by itself to survey the material currently available to those who wish to study industrial organisation. However, it is hoped that the following pages will provide a useful introduction for those who will later carry their studies of this area further.

Oligopoly and the Kinked Demand Curve

The theories of perfect competition and monopoly have in common the assumption that the decisions taken by any particular firm have such diffuse effects on the environment in which other firms operate that the individual firm can safely neglect this reaction to its behaviour in making its own decisions. However, it is easy to think of circumstances in which this is not a sensible assumption. In particular, where a small number of large firms dominate a particular industry producing identical or closely substitutable products, one would expect the likely response of other firms to be a major factor influencing any price/output decision. Such a state of affairs is central to the form of industrial organisation known as *oligopoly* — competition among a few firms. Conventional profit maximising theory has not got very far in analysing oligopoly; there are serious problems involved with the 'kinked demand curve' model of oligopolistic behaviour which is one of the best known.

The basic properties of the model are set out in figure 14.1, and are derived in the following way. We deal with a firm, one

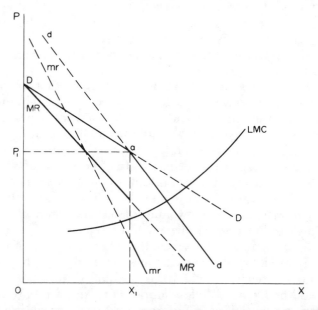

Figure 14.1 The kinked demand curve model of oligopoly. With price fixed at P_1 the firm believes that if it raises price, other firms will not follow suit. Hence the response of quantity demanded of X to such a move will be relatively large. However, the firm believes that others will follow a price cut so that the response of quantity demanded to such a move will be relatively small. Thus the firm thinks itself confronted by a demand curve kinked at point a, and hence as facing the discontinuous marginal revenue curve $MR - mr$. Note that cost fluctuations that do not shift LMC outside of the discontinuity in the marginal revenue curve will not result in the firm changing either price or output.

of a small group of firms producing closely related products, which produces output X_1 and sells it at price P_1. Consider the demand curve for this product. If the prices charged by competing firms are held constant, then we have a conventional demand curve such as DD. This curve has been drawn with a relatively shallow slope to reflect the fact that some of the other goods whose prices are being held constant are close substitutes for X. It is by no means obvious that the producers of these close substitues will set their prices independently of the price of X. We can draw another demand curve for X that reflects the response of quantity demanded to price, on the assumption that other firms would also alter their prices in the same direction as the price of X when it was varied. Such a curve would obviously be more steeply sloped than DD and in figure 14.1 it is drawn as dd. There is a marginal revenue curve for each of these demand curves, and they are labelled as MR and mr respectively.

Now suppose that the firm takes the view that its competitors will react asymmetrically to a price change, that they will follow a price cut but will not follow a price increase. Then the demand curve that faces the firm will appear to be given by Dad, a kinked relationship. There is an element of *a priori* plausibility about this demand curve because, if one firm out of a small group of firms raises its price, all the others who at the old price were happy with the volume of sales they were enjoying, would see that volume of sales increase without their doing anything. Hence they might be expected to be reluctant to follow a price increase. On the other hand, one firm lowering its price would take customers from them if they did not respond. Hence, to avoid this possibility, these other firms would be likely to follow a price cut. And not only is there *a priori* plausibility here; there is also a certain amount of evidence from questionnaires circulated to firms that they do indeed tend to expect their competitors to react this way — not following a price increase, but following a price cut.

If the demand curve which a particular firm thinks it faces does take the form of Dad, then it will also think of the marginal revenue curve which it faces being a discontinuous relationship. The reader who is uncertain as to why there should be this discontinuity in the marginal revenue curve should construct for himself the total revenue curve implicit in a kinked demand curve such as *Dad*. He will find that, at the level of output corresponding to the kink, there is a kink in the total revenue curve. Its slope will discontinuously become less at that level of output and this is equivalent to saying that marginal revenue will discontinuously become lower.

As we have drawn figure 14.1, the firm's long-run marginal cost curve passes through the discontinuity in the marginal revenue curve and so the firm is in equilibrium at price P_1 and X_1. Note that, in this situation, fluctuations in costs that do not take the marginal cost curve out of the range of the discontinutiy in the marginal revenue curve will not result in price changes.

The analysis looks appealing then, and yields the prediction that for an oligopolist, the price of output will be relatively rigid in the face of cost changes. What then is the problem with it? The analysis begs an important question we might want it to answer. The theory of perfect competition tells us how price and quantity of output are determined, as do the theories of monopoly and discriminating monopoly. This model does not. We have to know in advance what price and quantity are before we can locate the kink in the demand curve. The model does not explain how that particular price and quantity, rather than any other, happened to get established. Nor is there any way of knowing where equilibrium will be re-established if the marginal cost curve moves out of the discontinuity in the marginal revenue curve. In other words, figure 14.1 gives us a portrait of a particular situation in which a firm might find itself, but contains no information as to how the situation in question arose in the first place. It is a theory that explains why price, once set, may be rigid, but it does not explain how price gets set.

Collusion between Firms

One way in which the output price of an industry in which there are but a small number of firms may be set is by way of collusion among the firms. They may form a cartel, and

agree not to compete with one another; rather they set a
price for output that maximises the profits accruing to the
industry as a whole and then share those profits out according to some formula or other. In such a case, the industry as
a whole comes to act like a single monopolistic firm. Figure
14.2 depicts the essentials of the behaviour of such an
industry.

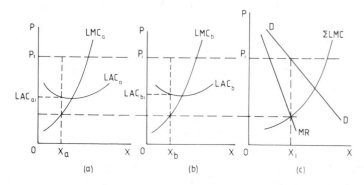

Figure 14.2 A two-firm cartel. Firm *a*, panel (a), and Firm *b*, panel (b),
collude to fix price and output at the industry level to maximise their
joint profits, panel (c). Each firm takes P_1 as given, and hence has an
incentive to cheat on the cartel arrangement by expanding its output
up to the point at which its long-run marginal cost equals P_1.

Suppose, purely for the sake of keeping the diagram of
manageable size, that there are but two firms in the industry
producing X, and that the market demand curve for X is given
by the curve DD in figure 14.2(c). If industry profits are to
be maximised, then industry marginal revenue must be equated
to industry marginal cost, just as in the case of the conventional single firm monopolised industry. The curve labelled
MR is the relevant marginal revenue curve, while the industry
long-run marginal cost curve is obtained by horizontally
summing the long run marginal cost curves of the individual
firms depicted in figure 14.2(a) and (b). Hence, industry
profit maximising output is determined at X_1, while price is
given by P_1. Each firm then agrees to produce that quantity
of output at which its marginal cost is equal to that of the
industry at the aggregate profit maximising level of output,
so that firm *a* produces X_a and firm *b* produces X_b.

Suppose that the industry's rule for profit sharing was simply that each firm kept the revenue raised from its own sales. Though there is no logical necessity that such a rule be adopted, it does have the merit of requiring no machinery to administer it and hence would be a likely one for a cartel to adopt. In that case the profits accruing to firm a would be given by $(P_1 - LAC_{a1})X_a$ and to firm b by $(P_1 - LAC_{b1})X_b$.

Notice that the essential property of the agreement between the firms which we are discussing here is that each one of them takes as given to it the industry's output price which is determined by a joint profit maximising decision taken in collusion. Each individual firm, from its own narrow vantage point, becomes a price taker, and hence P_1 becomes its marginal revenue. Inspection of figure 14.2 will confirm that P_1 is obviously and necessarily greater than the marginal cost of production to either firm at the levels of output which each of them must maintain if industry-wide profits are to be maximised. Hence, each firm has an incentive to increase its output a little in order to increase its profits at the expense of the other; in other words each firm has an incentive to cheat.

Cheating and Retaliation

There is nothing in general that economics can say about such a state of affairs. If the industry under analysis is one in which it is very easy for each firm to monitor the output and the pricing policies of the other (or others), then of course any attempt at cheating would be met by prompt retaliation, and each firm would know this in advance. If the retaliation was likely to involve price cutting by its competitors, then each firm would come to think of itself as facing a kink in its demand curve at its current price and output level, and the analysis of the previous section of this chapter would become relevant to its behaviour. Note though that the previous analysis is now modified and expanded because the last few paragraphs have given us a way of explaining how price and output are determined in the first place. Even so, many other kinds of retaliation aimed at keeping cartel members in line, other than simple price cutting, are possible in the real world, depending upon the nature of the particular industry. A price cutting airline might well find itself having difficulty in obtaining landing rights at key airports, or, under private medical care systems, the doctor who charges less than the medical association's 'recommended' fees sometimes loses his hospital privileges. These are but two examples of the way in which cartel pricing arrangements may be enforced without resort to retaliatory price cutting.

Of course, to consider retaliatory action at all presupposes that the cheater gets caught, and not every industry is one where each firm finds it easy to police its competitors. Surreptitious discounts to particular customers, preferential after sales service involving for example 'secret warranties', priority delivery dates to particular favoured customers, are but a few of the more obvious ways in which firms who wish to cheat on cartel agreements may act in order to keep hidden what they are doing. All economic theory can say in general about these matters is that an agreement among firms to collude so as to maximise industry profits *automatically* creates an incentive for each participant to cheat if he can. Whether he will do so, by what methods, and to what extent; whether his cheating will be detected, and if so by what means it will be punished; all these matters depend upon the nature of the specific case under analysis.

The analysis that we have set out so far in this chapter is all in one way or another related to problems that arise when any particular firm in an industry takes into account the specific reactions of other firms to its own behaviour when making its decisions. There is a rich body of analysis dealing with these issues, with which the reader who carries his studies of microeconomics on into the field of industrial organisation will soon enough become familiar. Considerations of space, not to mention questions of mathematical difficulty, do not permit us to deal in any general way with such analysis in this book. However, there is one model which is particularly useful, which uses no more complex analysis than we have already developed, and to which we now turn. It deals with the phenomenon known as *price leadership*.

Price Leadership

Its very name expresses the essential properties of the price leadership model. It deals with an industry in which there is one *dominant firm* from which all others take the lead as far as pricing policy is concerned. The dominant firm takes the reactions of the other firms into account when making its decision about price and output, but they take his price as given in settling on their own behaviour. The phenomenon involved here is therefore called *price leadership*.

Consider figure 14.3. In panel (a) we have the market demand curve for X, and a long-run market supply curve derived from the behaviour of a group of perfectly competi-

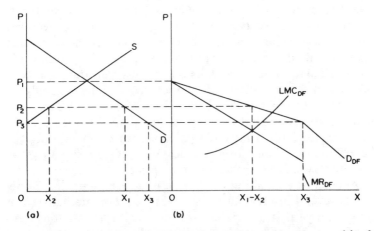

Figure 14.3 Price leadership. The industry demand curve, combined with the supply curve of a number of perfectly competitive firms is depicted in panel (a). The demand curve of the dominant firm D_{DF} is derived by substracting the competitive supply curve from the industry demand curve. Faced with this demand curve in the long run the dominant firm equates marginal cost (LMC) to marginal revenue (MR_{DF}). Price is determined at P_2, competitive firms supply X_2, total demand is given by X_1 and the dominant firm sells $X_1 - X_2$. Note that, unless it can produce a positive output at price less than P_1, the equilibrium price in its absence, the dominant firm will not exist. Thus a firm can only achieve dominance if it has a significant cost advantage. If its profit maximising price was P_3 or below, the dominant firm would be the only firm in the industry.

tive firms. For simplicity we assume that given factor prices
lie behind this curve and that it derives its upward slope from
declining efficiency of new firms as supply expands. Now
suppose that a new relatively large (and hence 'dominant')
firm was considering entering the market for X. How would
he view the demand conditions facing him? Clearly at price
P_1, the already existing competitive firms would supply the
entire market and he would be able to sell nothing. However,
were he to set his price at P_2, below P_1, less efficient competitive firms would drop out of the market. Those remaining
would supply X_2, leaving $X_1 - X_2$ to be sold by the large
firm. In other words, the quantity demanded from the dominant firm at any particular price, is found by taking the
market demand at that price and subtracting from it the
quantity that would be supplied by the competitive firms.
Obviously, at price P_3 the resulting demand curve becomes
the market demand curve. There is a kink in the dominant
firm's demand curve at this point and hence a discontinuity in
its marginal revenue curve. This is *not*, however, the same type
of kinked demand curve as we met in the previous analysis,
as ought to be obvious. As we have drawn figure 14.3 the price/
quantity solution that emerges is one at which price is fixed
at P_2 by the large firm. The total amount demanded is X_1, of
which the dominant firm supplies $X_1 - X_2$ leaving X_2 to be
supplied by small firms at the going price.

As well as explaining how price is determined, this model
yields several interesting insights. First, a dominant firm can
only emerge if it is capable of producing a 'substantial' proportion of the industry's output at a lower price than would
emerge under competition among relatively small firms. The
example of the supermarket in comparison to small groceries
as a purveyor of retailing services comes to mind here. Second,
it is not just existing competitors that affect the elasticity of
a demand curve facing a firm, but potential competitors as
well. Thus, a downward sloping demand curve facing a firm is
by no means necessarily synonymous with the market demand
curve for the good in question — *even if that firm is the sole
producer of the good in question.*

To make this point quite clear consider figure 14.4 which is

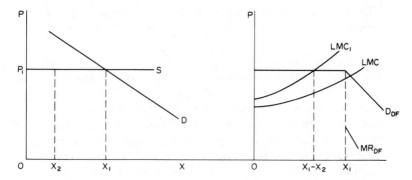

Figure 14.4 Price leadership when the long-run competitive industry supply curve is horizontal. If the dominant firm's marginal cost curve is given by LMC it produces the whole industry's output, but sells it at the competitive price P_1. If it is given by LMC_1 it sells a proportion of the industry's output, $X_1 - X_2$, at the competitive price with competitive firms selling X_2. In neither case does the dominant firm have any monopoly power, even when it is the only firm in the industry.

a variation on the theme developed in figure 14.3. It differs from figure 14.3 in two ways only. First it is assumed that all small firms are equally efficient and second it is assumed that in drawing its marginal cost curve as LMC the large firm's cost advantage is such as to permit it to take the whole market for X. Nevertheless, this firm, even as the sole producer of X, has no power to raise its price above P_1. That is to say, a sole seller of a good who is in that position simply by virtue of a cost advantage is far less a 'monopolist' than one whose advantage stems from some legal barrier to competition. The latter can treat the market demand curve as the one that faces him, but not the former.

Another variation on figure 14.4 is also worth considering. Suppose the large firm's marginal cost curve lay at LMC_1. It would produce a large part of the industry's output, but would in fact be a perfect competitor as far as its pricing behaviour was concerned. The number of firms actually in an industry is not then, *in and of itself*, any indicator of the competitiveness of that industry.

The Revenue Maximising Hypothesis under Perfect Competition

The material dealt with so far in this book on the theory of the firm has been based on the assumption that the individual firm seeks to maximise its profits, but it has been hinted on more than one occasion that there are alternative hypotheses about the firm's motivation. Some people, for example, follow the lead of William Baumol, and argue that it is more reasonable to think of firms attempting to maximise their sales revenue. We could argue indefinitely about whether or not this hypothesis is or is not 'realistic', but an *a priori* debate about assumptions is seldom profitable. More to the point is to see whether this alternative hypothesis enables us to say anything about the way in which firms might behave that is different from what is implied by profit maximisation. That is the issue which we shall now, briefly, take up.

To begin with, note that it is quite unreasonable to postulate that the firm seeks to maximise its revenue and leave it at that. A perfectly competitive firm, which faces a given price for its output can always increase its revenue simply by increasing output, at least up to the level of taking over the whole industry. However, we have already seen that when the perfectly competitive industry is in equilibrium with each firm maximising profits, the actual level of profits that will be made by a particular firm, unless it happens to have some special advantage not available to its competitors, will be zero. Thus, to expand output beyond this profit maximising level for the sake of increasing revenue would involve the perfectly competitive firm in making losses.

The above argument has two important implications. First, because no privately owned firm can stay in business if it continually makes losses, the revenue maximisation hypothesis does not, when taken by itself, make sense. It must be qualified by saying that firms seek to maximise sales revenue up to a level of output that ensures some minimum acceptable level of profits, which cannot be negative. The second implication follows immediately from this first one. The perfectly competitive profit maximising firm is, as a result of market forces, put in a position of producing its output at a level which in the long run yields zero profits. Hence, it is already up against a minimum acceptable profit constraint, and its behaviour is going to be no different from a firm that seeks to maximise its sales revenue subject to that same constraint in perfectly competitive conditions.

This conclusion is of considerable interest. The conventional theory of the firm has often been criticised for the 'unrealistic' nature of its underlying assumptions, and the profit maximisation hypothesis in particular has been singled out for criticism along these lines. There are many who would regard the revenue maximisation postulate as more acceptable, and yet we have now seen that, in the important case of perfect competition, without which we could not derive the supply curve which is so widely used in applications of simple microeconomics, the 'realistic' revenue maximisation hypothesis leads us to exactly the same conclusions about behaviour as does that of profit maximisation. Revenue maximising firms behave 'as if' they were interested only in maximising profits, and may safely be analysed on the basis of this latter 'unrealistic' assumption. This illustrates a general principle first explicitly proposed by Milton Friedman and often invoked by economists in defence of their highly abstract models; namely that debate about whether or not a model's assumptions are 'unrealistic' or descriptively 'inaccurate' is usually futile; the degree of conformity to reality of the conclusions it yields provides a more constructive basis for criticising a model.

The Revenue Maximising Hypothesis under Monopoly

Now as it happens the revenue maximisation hypothesis does not always yield the same results as does profit maximisation. Consider the case of monopoly. We have already seen that a profit maximising monopolist whose marginal production costs are positive will choose a point on the demand curve facing him where the absolute value of the elasticity of demand is greater than one. This means that such a firm could increase its revenue by lowering price and increasing output. So long as we were dealing with a typical case, in which maximum attainable profits were positive, the firm could do so without violating the requirement that it make some minimum level of profits. Thus, under conditions of monopoly, the revenue maximising firm would produce a greater output than the profit maximising firm. Just how much greater depends upon the cost conditions facing the firm.

Recall that sales revenue will be maximised at a level of output at which the elasticity of demand is equal to −1, and consider figure 14.5 which depicts two possible cases. In panel (a) we depict a firm whose long-run average production costs are rather 'low' so that they are still below price at the level of output at which the elasticity of demand is equal to minus 1. This firm will settle at this level of output and will make

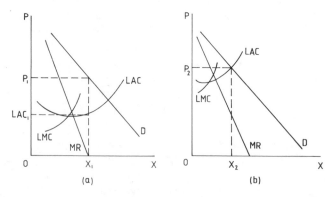

Figure 14.5 Two possible solutions for the revenue maximising monopolist. (a) Long run average costs are 'low' so the firm produces X_1 and sells it at P_1; at this point the elasticity of demand is −1 and profits are positive at $(P_1 - LAC_1)X_1$. (b) Long run average costs are 'high' so the firm produces X_2 for sale at a price of P_2. At this output profits are zero, and because demand is still in the price elastic range, revenue is not at its unconstrained maximum. In either case, output is higher than the profit maximising (LMC=MR)level.

The imposition of a lump-sum tax shifts the long-run average cost curve upwards by the amount of the tax divided by output, but does not shift the marginal cost curve. So long as the tax is less than $(P_1 - LAC_1)X_1$, its imposition will not affect the price and output of the firm (a); if the tax is greater than this amount firm (a) will come to act like firm (b) and set its price equal to long-run average cost including the tax. The imposition of such a tax on firm (b), rgardless of its amount, will shift the LAC upwards and will cause output to fall and price to rise.

positive profits. In panel (b) we depict a firm with rather 'high' average costs which become equal to price while output is still in the elastic range of the demand curve. If minimum acceptable profits are zero, this firm will settle at a level of output at which price equals average cost, and profits are zero.

It is also worth noting that, in either case described above, the reaction of the firm to a lump sum tax levied on its profits may be different from that of a profit maximiser, who will not react to the imposition of such a tax. After all, the price and output that maximise profits will also maximise profits net of some constant deduction unless the tax is greater than maximum profits, in which case the firm will simply go out of business. In the case of the revenue maximising firm depicted in panel (a) of figure 14.5, the imposition of such a tax, depending upon its size, will either leave its price and output unchanged if net of tax profits are still positive, or cause it to lower its output to a point of higher profit if the amount of the tax is greater than the profit it was making at revenue maximising price and output. In the case of the firm depicted in panel (b), the imposition of any such tax will cause it to lower output and to raise price. As with the profit maximising firm of course, it is possible to set the tax in question sufficiently high that the revenue maximiser will be driven entirely out of business by its imposition.

Now the point of the last few paragraphs has been to show that the equivalence of the sales revenue maximisation hypothesis and the profit maximisation postulate that exists under assumptions of perfect competition does not exist under conditions of monopoly. The reader should note that this lack of equivalence was established, not by arguing about the relative degrees of 'realism' that might be attributed to the alternative *assumptions*, but rather by showing that there are circumstances under which they lead to *different conclusions* about the way in which we would expect to see firms behave. Whether the circumstances in question are sufficiently widely observed in the real world as to make the revenue maximisation hypothesis an important alternative to profit maximisation is perhaps a moot point. Lump sum taxes are something of a rarity and real world 'profit' taxes are typically levied on the rental rate earned by capital equipment owned by the firm as well as on any pure monopoly profit that it might be earning, and hence are not quite equivalent to the profits tax we postulated.

Nevertheless, if the foregoing analysis convinces the reader that there is an alternative theory of what it is that motivates firms to the simple pursuit of profit, that the theory in question does not always yield the same predictions about behaviour, and that the profit maximisation hypothesis should not therefore be taken for granted as a foundation for the theory of the firm, its presentation will have served its purpose.

Concluding Comments

Now in this chapter we have briefly discussed four well-known models of firms' behaviour in the product market that try to deal with problems which conventional monopoly and perfect competition theory leave untreated. There are a host of phenomena with which we have not dealt and a host of models that we have not discussed. The reader is entitled to be reminded of the problems *not* discussed here, if only to put the analysis that has been dealt with in perspective.

No mention has been made of the many models of oligopolistic behaviour that explicitly treat two or more firms reacting to each other's decisions so as to produce a time path for output and prices that may or may not be stable. We have not analysed so-called 'non-price competition' through product differentiation and advertising, although the reader is reminded that these issues were touched on earlier in Chapter 8, which he might care to review at this point. Neither have the problems of firms whose main customer is not the consuming public but rather the government or some other large firm been mentioned.

Obviously, many important questions have been left to one side. Nevertheless the reader who has mastered the analysis which has been presented should now be in a position to approach and critically appraise at least the basic literature on these issues as and when he comes across it.

Part V
Factor Markets

15
The Demand for Factors of Production: Perfect Competition

Introduction

We have dealt above with the way in which profit maximising firms would choose the price and quantity of their output. Implicit in this choice are decisions about factor utilisation and payments to factors of production. We now turn to an explicit analysis of those decisions. It is important to note that we are not here analysing new or different decisions taken by the firm. We are looking at exactly the same decisions with which we dealt earlier, but from a different point of view: from the point of view of the market for the inputs used by the firm rather than from that of the markets for its outputs.

The Physical Productivity of a Factor

It is convenient to begin where we began before, with the two input production function (figure 15.1), but this time with the aim of deriving the demand curve for a factor of production rather than with the aim of deriving cost functions and from them a supply curve for output. The relationship between price and quantity is not uniquely defined merely by the term 'demand curve'. We must specify what other things there are that we are holding constant before we can be precise in this respect. We will concern ourselves initially with deriving the demand curve for labour of a perfectly competitive firm *in the short run*; that is to say when the

217

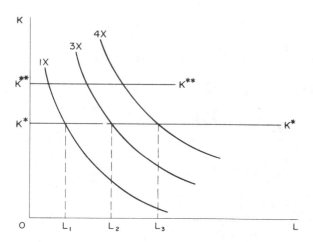

Figure 15.1 A production function displaying first increasing then decreasing returns to scale and two short-run paths along which output can be expanded holding capital fixed — K^*K^* and $K^{**}K^{**}$.

amount of capital services in the production process is given and when the price of output is given. Thus, we are concerned with what happens to the price that the firm is willing to pay for labour as it moves along a path such as K^*K^* in figure 15.1. The first step in the analysis involves investigating what happens to the 'physical productivity' of labour as its quantity is varied.

In figure 15.2 we plot what is known as the *total physical product curve*. This relates the level of output, read off from the isoquants of figure 15.1, to units of labour input read off the horizontal axis. The precise shape of this relationship will, of course, depend upon the technical nature of the production function. However, as we have already seen (in Chapter 10), when we go on adding more and more units of one particular input to the production process, holding all others constant, we eventually run into diminishing returns to that factor, whatever the returns to scale characteristic of the production function. Thus, eventually, the rate of increase of total physical product begins to decrease. The total physical product curve plotted in figure 15.2(a) does in fact display increasing returns to labour at low levels of labour input and

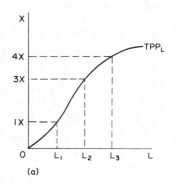
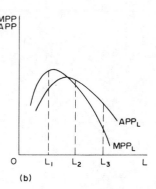

Figure 15.2 (a) The total physical product curve of labour (TPP$_L$) implicit in the production function displayed in figure 15.1. (b) The average and marginal physical product of labour curves (APP$_L$ and MPP$_L$) implicit in panel (a).

the reader may think of it as having been derived from a production function where increasing returns to scale exist at low levels of output. However, nothing hinges upon this because, as we shall see the firm always ends up operating in the region of diminishing returns to a factor.

As the reader will by now have anticipated, where there is a total physical product curve there are also average physical product and marginal physical product curves for labour. These are derived from the total product curve in the usual way and are drawn in figure 15.2(b).

Revenue Productivity and the Short-Run Demand for a Factor

Now the firm is not concerned with the physical productivity of any factor of production for its own sake. Its objective is to make profits and it is the revenue that a factor produces, rather than the physical output, that is ultimately of interest. We need to transform physical productivity measures into what are termed 'revenue productivity' measures as the next step in our analysis. This is done in figure 15.3, where we simply multiply units of X by the price of X — a constant

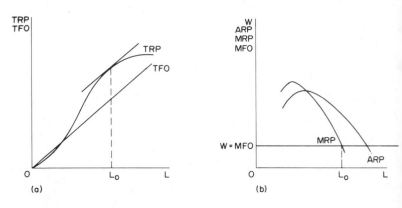

Figure 15.3 (a) Profits are maximised where the vertical distance between the total revenue product of labour (TRP) and total outlay on that factor (TFO) is maximised, that is at the level of employment L_0 where their slopes are equal. (b) An alternative portrayal of the profit maximising level of employment. Here the marginal revenue product of labour (MRP) is equal to marginal outlay on labour (MFO). Since the wage rate is given at W, MFO is constant and equal to W.

since we are here dealing with a perfectly competitive firm to which output price is given. Our firm is a profit maximiser, and given that the level of capital inputs, and hence cash outlay on capital inputs, is constant, profits will be maximised if total revenue minus total outlay on labour is maximised. If we assume a constant price for labour, total outlay on that output is proportional to the quantity of its employed, and we may draw a straight line *total factor outlay* (or cost) *curve* in figure 15.3.

Profits are then maximised where the *slope* of the total factor cost curve is equal to the *slope* of the total revenue product curve, that is, where marginal revenue product is equal to marginal factor cost. In this case, constancy of the price of X means that we may also refer to the marginal revenue product of labour as the *value of the marginal product* of labour.

Now the reader will no doubt have been struck by the similarity between this analysis and that by which the short-run supply curve of the individual firm was derived in Chapter 12. What we have been doing here is to look at exactly the same set of conditions which we discussed there from a different point of view. We said in Chapter 12 that profits would be maximised where marginal cost was set equal to marginal revenue. Short-run marginal cost of production is given by the extra outlay on labour per unit of output necessary to produce a small addition to output; it is thus equal to the marginal outlay on labour per unit of labour divided by the marginal physical product of labour; or, to put the same point in other words, short-run marginal cost is the additional cost of employing an extra unit of labour divided by the amount that that unit will add to output. Writing MFO for marginal factor outlay, MPP for marginal physical product, MR for marginal revenue and MC for marginal cost of output, the condition that marginal cost be equal to marginal revenue may be written as:

$$MC \equiv \frac{MFO}{MPP} = MR$$

But we have just shown that, when looking at the factor market, profit maximisation requires that marginal factor outlay be equal to the marginal revenue product of the factor, that is

$$MFO = MR.MPP$$

Obviously this condition is already implicit in the requirement that marginal cost equals marginal revenue in the product market.

If the perfectly competitive firm will always set its employment of the variable factor at a point where its marginal revenue product equals the price of that factor, then this curve becomes the firm's short-run demand curve for the factor. This is a mirror image of the proposition that the firm's short-run supply curve of output is its short-run marginal cost curve. Note also that, for the equality of marginal factor outlay and marginal revenue product to be consistent with profit maximisation, the latter curve must cut the former from above. Total outlay and total revenue must be closer together at all other levels of output, to put the matter in terms of figure 15.2. Thus, the firm will always be operating at a level of output where there exist diminishing returns to the factor in question.

Now the industry's short-run demand curve for labour will not just be the sum of the firm's demand curves. When analysing the individual firm it makes sense to hold the price of output constant, but when we consider the whole industry expanding its labour input, and hence its output of X, we must remember that this will affect the price of X. This price will fall as output expands so long as the demand curve for X does not shift. Hence, the *industry's* demand curve for labour in the short run will be more steeply sloped than the sum of the *firm's* marginal revenue product curves. The latter slopes downwards only because the marginal productivity of labour diminishes. The industry's demand curve slopes more steeply because, in addition, the price of X falls as the industry's output increases. Figure 15.4 shows this.

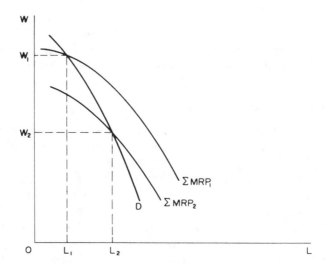

Figure 15.4 A short-run industry demand curve for labour. It is more steeply sloped than the sum over all firms in the industry of their marginal revenue product curves at a constant output price because, as employment and hence output increases, the price of output falls. Thus, when the wage rate falls from W_1 to W_2, the summed marginal revenue product curve shifts down from ΣMRP_1 to ΣMRP_2 and employment increases from L_1 to L_2. The industry's demand curve for labour is given by D.

Factor Demand in the Long Run

Now there is a different set of physical productivity curves for labour for every quantity of capital that could be employed. A higher level of the capital stock, say K^{**} in figure 15.1 would involve at any given level of labour input a higher total, average and marginal physical productivity for labour. This is important when we come to consider the nature of the demand curve for a particular factor of production in the long run when all factor inputs may be varied. Consider first the firm's long-run demand curve for labour. It is easy to show that in the long run the firm's demand for a factor will be more elastic than it is in the short run, provided that output price is held constant.

As we have seen, a fall in the price of labour involves more labour being employed by the firm, even if capital cannot be varied: costs of production unambiguously fall and at a given price output expands. However, an increase in the employment of labour is usually assumed to raise the physical productivity of capital.* If this is the case, with the price of output given, there is an increase in the marginal revenue product of capital. With a given supply price for capital services, employment of capital will increase in the long run, and the short-run marginal revenue product curve of labour will shift to the right. The long-run demand curve for labour, then, is the result of movements along and shifts of the short-run curve, and hence is more shallowly sloped. This is illustrated in figure 15.5.

The analysis of the industry's long-run demand for labour is less clear-cut than that of the firm because we must drop the assumption that output price is given when operating at this level. Two considerations now affect the marginal revenue product of capital services when the quantity of labour employed varies, and in opposite directions. Increased labour input increases capital's *physical productivity,* but expanding industry output lowers the price of output and hence drives its *productivity in revenue terms* downwards. The net effect

---

* We rule out an analytic curiosity, the 'inferior factor of production', with this assumption.

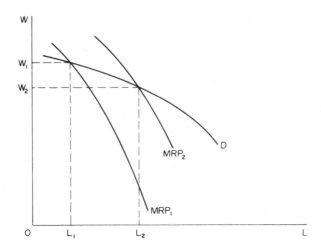

Figure 15.5 The firm's long-run demand for labour, holding the price of output constant. An increase in employment of labour following a fall in its price from W_1 to W_2 increases the productivity of capital and hence leads to an increase in its employment in the long run, thus shifting the *MRP* of labour to the right. The firm's long-run demand curve, D, is a compound of a shift along and a shift of the *MRP* curve and hence is more shallowly sloped, generating a change in the demand for labour from L_1 to L_2.

of these two tendencies may go either way. We may end up with more capital employed and hence have a long-run industry demand curve for labour that, though more steeply sloped than the simple summation of firm's demand curves, is nevertheless more shallowly sloped than the short-run industry demand curve. On the other hand, it is possible for the demand for capital actually to fall, and for the long-run demand curve for labour to be less elastic than the short-run curve. Figure 15.6 illustrates both cases.

The Elasticity of Substitution — a Measure of Factor Substitutability

Now the results of the foregoing analysis are intuitively plausible. What happens to the demand for capital when the price of labour falls is the result of two competing tendencies.

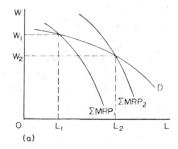 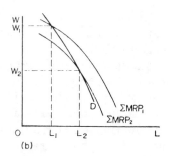

Figure 15.6 D is the industry's long-run demand curve for labour. (a) D will slope more shallowly than ΣMRP if, when the wage rate falls from W_1 to W_2, the consequent expansion of employment and output and the fall in output price on balance increase the revenue productivity of a given stock of capital. More capital inputs will be used, ΣMRP of labour will shift to the right and employment will increase from L_1 to L_2. (b) D will slope more steeply than ΣMRP if a fall in the wage rate from W_1 to W_2 produces responses that lead to a fall in the revenue productivity of a given stock of capital. In this case, a cut in capital input shifts ΣMRP of labour to the left, though employment still increases from L_1 to L_2.

First, there is a tendency for labour to be substituted for capital and hence for the demand for capital to decrease, but second, there is a tendency for output to increase and the demand for capital to increase. If the first tendency dominates, the amount of capital used will fall in the long run, the physical productivity of labour at any scale of input will diminish, and the industry's long-run demand for labour will be less elastic than the short-run curve along which the level of capital utilisation is held constant. Such a situation will be associated with a degree of substitutability between factors that is high relative to the elasticity of demand for output. Cases where the long-run demand curve for labour is more elastic than the short-run curve will occur where substitutability between factors is relatively low and the elasticity of demand for output is relatively high.

In the foregoing argument, we have referred more than once to the degree of 'substitutability' between factors of production, and it is worthwhile being a little more precise than we have been so far about what we mean by the term. Substitutability has to do with the extent to which the ratio in which capital and labour will be used changes in the long run when the ratio of their prices change. A higher degree of substitutability involves a greater change in this so-called 'capital/labour ratio' for a given change in the price ratio of inputs. In terms of isoquants, the flatter they are, the less convex towards the origin, the greater is the degree of substitutability between factors, as figure 15.7 illustrates. Economists sometimes find it useful to have a quantitative measure of the degree of substitutability between factors. That most commonly used is the *elasticity of substitution*; it may be defined as the ratio of a proportional change in the capital labour ratio to the proportional change in the price ratio of capital and labour that brings it about. However, in the long run the cost minimising firm will always use capital and labour in proportions such that their marginal revenue productivities equal their prices. This implies that the ratio of their marginal physical productivities is equal to the ratio

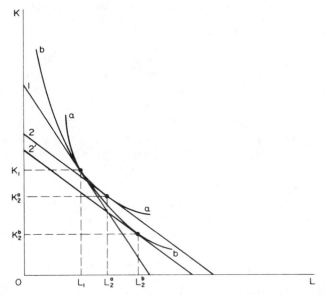

Figure 15.7 Curves a and b are isoquants from different production functions. For a given change in the ratio of factor prices from isocost line 1 to 2 and 2', the capital labour ratio shifts from K_1/L_1 to K_2^a/L_2^a along curve a and to K_2^b/L_2^b along curve b. Along the latter curve there is greater substitutability between capital and labour.

of their prices.* Thus, if we confine ourselves to cost minimising equilibria, it is possible to replace a proportional change
in the ratio of factor prices with a proportional change in the
ratio of the marginal physical productivity of factors in the
above definition of the elasticity of substitution. Hence, it
may be, and usually is, defined solely in terms of the technical
properties of the production function.

Determinants of the Industry's Elasticity of Factor Demand

The concept of substitutability is important because the
extent to which factors are substitutes for one another has
a great deal to do with determining the degree to which the
long-run industry demand for a particular input is sensitive
to its own price. It should be immediately obvious that, other
things being equal, the greater the degree of substitutability
between factors of production, the more elastic will be the
demand for a particular factor. However, as we have seen, the
long-run responses of the demand for a particular factor — let
us take the case of labour — to a change in its price does not
consist solely of a substitution of labour for capital at a given
level of output. A fall in wages leads to a fall in marginal
production costs and hence to a fall in output price and an
increase in the volume of output. Clearly, the larger the
increase in output as a result of a given fall in the wage rate,
the greater will be the resulting change in the demand for
labour for a given degree of substitutability between labour
and capital. There are two steps between a change in the
wage rate and a change in output. The first step is a fall in

---

* Where R is the rental price of capital and all other symbols have their
conventional meaning,

if MRP_K $= R$
and MRP_L $= W$

then $\dfrac{MRP_K}{MRP_L} = \dfrac{R}{W}$

Divide top and bottom of the left-hand side by MR:

$\dfrac{MPP_K}{MPP_L} = \dfrac{R}{W}$

output price, and the larger is that part of production costs made up of payments to labour, the larger will be the fall in output price as a result of a given fall in the wage rate. The second step is the response of the demand for output to a change in its price, and the more elastic the demand for output the greater will this response be.

Thus, for a given price of other inputs, the greater the degree of substitutability between labour and these other inputs, the greater is the proportion of production costs made up of wages, and the more elastic the demand for the final output, the more elastic will be the demand for labour. However, there is no reason to treat the price of other inputs as necessarily remaining constant. If a fall in the price of labour causes the demand for other inputs to increase in the long run, then the less effect this increase in demand has on the prices of other inputs, the smaller will be the extent to which the effect of a fall in wages on output price will be offset by price increases of other inputs. If the fall in wages leads to a fall in demand for the other factor, then the smaller the effect this has on their prices the less tendency is there for substitution towards labour as a result of the initial fall in wages to be offset. In short, to the three influences on the elasticity of demand for labour already derived, we must add a fourth, namely the elasticity of supply of other factors. The higher this is, holding other influences constant, the higher will be the elasticity of demand for labour.

Factor Payments and the Value of Output

Lying behind the various demand curves for labour whose properties we have been considering in this chapter is the marginal productivity of labour. We could, of course, just as easily have concerned ourselves with the demand for capital, for from a formal point of view the two pieces of analysis are absolutely identical. This observation leads us into a problem area that at one time much concerned economists and even now is worth some brief discussion. Consider again the firm in the long run. Suppose that in terms of figure 15.8 the firm is in long-run equilibrium employing L_1 units of labour

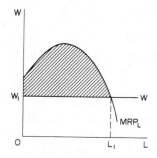
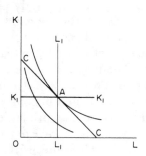

Figure 15.8 (left) The marginal revenue product of labour. The wage bill is given by $W_1 L_1$ leaving the shaded area available for payments to capital. If factor payments exhaust the value of output this area should equal $R_1 K_1$ in figure 15.10.

Figure 15.9 (right) The firm in long-run equilibrium at point A, with employment of labour at L_1 and of capital at K_1. The ratio of factor prices is given by the slope of the isocost line CC and equals the ratio of the marginal productivities of the inputs given by the slope of the isoquant at point A.

services at a wage rate of W_1. Implicit in the assumption that the firm is in long-run equilibrium is the proposition that a certain flow of capital services is also being utilised, the marginal revenue product of which is also equal to the price of capital services. In terms of a production function diagram, the firm is at a position such as A in figure 15.9 where the marginal rate of substitution between factors is equal to the ratio of their prices, as the reader will recall from Chapter 11 (pp. 139–40 above).

Associated with the employment of capital services at rate K_1 is a marginal revenue product curve for labour that passes through the long-run demand curve at $L_1 W_1$ and is derived by moving along the line $K_1 - K_1$ on figure 15.9. Now, the area under this marginal revenue product curve between the vertical axis and L_1 measures the total revenue accruing to the firm at its equilibrium output level. Since payments to labour amount to $W_1 \times L_1$, it is clear that an amount equal to the shaded area in figure 15.8 is left over to make payments to capital. (The return to the factor that is fixed in the short run is often called a *quasi-rent* for reasons that we shall go into below.) An exactly parallel argument may be developed in terms of the demand for capital services. Variations in the marginal revenue product of capital as one moves along a line such as $L_1 - L_1$ in figure 15.9 may be plotted in a diagram exactly similar to figure 15.8. Figure 15.10 is such a diagram; here the area $R_1 \times K_1$ represents payments to capital and the shaded area then becomes what is left over to meet the wage bill. Now we may put an interesting question: are the alternative measures of wage payments and capital payments depicted in figures 15.8 and 15.10 consistent with one another? Do factor payments exhaust the value of output?

This is a question which bothered economists for many years. It seemed to boil down to a technical question about what kind of production function had the properties which would, in general, ensure that the sum of the marginal revenue product of each factor of production multiplied by the quantity of that factor being utilised, when added up over factors, would just turn out equal to the value of output. To put it in symbols for the two-input case, under what circumstance will it be the case for a competitive firm engaged in producing X that

$$P(\mathrm{MPP}_K . K + \mathrm{MPP}_L . L) = P.X$$

or, to divide through by output price,

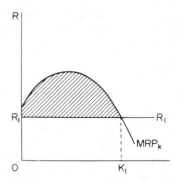

Figure 15.10 The marginal revenue product of capital. Where R is the rental price of capital, outlay on capital is $R_1 K_1$ leaving the shaded area available to meet the wage bill. If factor payments exhaust revenue this area should be equal to $W_1 L_1$ in figure 15.8.

$$\text{MPP}_K . \ K + \text{MPP}_L . \ L = X$$

If we ask what are the mathematical properties of a production function that will guarantee that the above equality always holds, the answer given by the so-called Euler theorem turns out to be a production function homogeneous of degree one. Among its other properties such a function everywhere displays constant returns to scale — as we mentioned in Chapter 10. If we were forced to require that the production function be of this restrictive mathematical form before payments to factors add up to the value of output, we might regard a theory of the demand for factors of production based on perfectly competitive profit maximising behaviour with a certain amount of scepticism.

However, notice that the question 'do factor payments exhaust the value of output?' is the same question as 'do total costs equal total revenue?' When the question is put this way it becomes apparent that it does not concern only the production function but also the way in which firms behave. Suppose that the area under the marginal revenue product curve of labour is less than total expenditure on factors of production at that scale of output. The firm of which this was true would leave the industry since it would be making long-run losses. Firms would continue to leave the industry until such long-run losses had been eliminated. Similarly, if the area under the marginal revenue product curve of labour were to exceed total factor payments as measured by their prices times the quantity of them employed, then this would imply the existence of positive profits, price would be above long-run average cost, and firms would enter the industry until these profits were eliminated.

So long as each firm has the same production function, then profit maximising behaviour ensures that each firm will achieve just that level of output at which factor payments do indeed exhaust revenue. That is to say, each firm will produce at zero profits at the minimum point of its long-run average cost curve, but that is precisely a point at which cost per unit of output is neither rising nor falling, a point at which returns to scale may be said to be constant.

In an industry in which different firms are of different

levels of efficiency this will be true only of the marginal firm, of course. All others will be earning positive profits and factor payments will not exhaust their revenues. There is no need to elaborate further on all this. We have already been through the analysis in some detail in Chapter 12. The important point to notice here is that whether or not factor payments exhaust the revenue of a perfectly competitive firm is a question that must be answered with reference to market behaviour and not just to the technical nature of the production function.

Concluding Comment

In this chapter we have discussed the theory of the demand for factors of production solely from the point of view of perfect competition. Just as dropping the assumption of perfect competition led us to modify our analysis of price/ output behaviour, so our analysis of the demand for factors of production changes somewhat when we depart from perfectly competitive assumptions. We will take up some of the major problems involved here in the next chapter.

16
Factor Demand: Monopoly, Monopsony and Bilateral Monopoly

Introduction

For the monopolist, just as for the perfectly competitive firm, the demand for factors arises as a corollary of profit maximising price and output decisions, and not as the solution to some separate and distinct set of problems. Moreover, the basic nature of his decision is the same as that of the competitive firm. He will continue to expand his employment of any factor of production just as long as he increases his profits by so doing. That is to say, as long as the expansion adds more to revenue than it does to costs. In short, the condition that marginal revenue product be equal to marginal factor cost underlies the monopolist's demand for factors just as it does that of the competitive firm, and is but another way of stating the product market condition that marginal cost should equal marginal revenue.

The Monopolist's Factor Demand Curve

However, this is not to say that the monopolist's behaviour does not differ at all from that of a competitive firm. As long as he is a price taker in the market for factor inputs, as long as their supply price does not vary with the quantity he purchases, then the market price of the input is equal to marginal factor cost, and this side of the market is the same

233

as it was in our analysis of the competitive firm. To the competitive firm though, the price of output and marginal revenue are identical. Thus the short-run demand curve for the factor which related its marginal revenue product to the quantity of it utilised was obtained by multiplying the factor's marginal physical product by a constant output price. Marginal revenue product was equivalent to the value of the factor's marginal product. To the monopolist, price declines with output, and marginal revenue is thus less than price. The value of the marginal product of a factor of production employed by a monopolist is obviously marginal product multiplied by price, but marginal revenue product is obtained by multiplying marginal physical product by marginal revenue. The two magnitudes are different for a monopolist, marginal revenue product being always the lower of the two.

Figure 16.1 shows the two relationships, the difference between them reflecting in the factor market the gap between the price of output and the marginal revenue accruing from the sale of one extra unit of output. If the demand curve for output faced by the monopolist was the same as that which would be faced by a competitive industry, if his production function was the same as would characterise that industry, if the wage rate W_1 that he faced was the same as would face a competitive industry, then such a competitive industry's short-run demand curve for labour would be given by the value of the marginal product curve in figure 16.1 and its employment of labour would be equal to L_2 instead of L_1, the quantity employed by the monopolist. This tendency of the monopolist to curtail the use of factor inputs relative to what might be demanded by a competitive industry is simply a reflection in the factor market of his tendency to restrict output relative to a level that would be realised by a competitive industry.

There is little to be said about the monopolist in the long run. The demand for a particular factor may be more or less elastic in the long run than in the short run, depending upon the outcome of two competing tendencies. A fall in the price of one factor leads to more of it being used and hence raises the marginal physical product of the other factor. It also

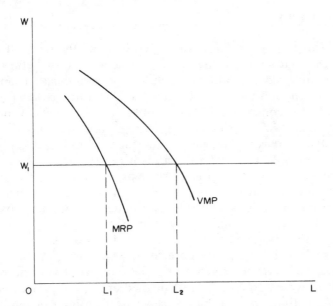

Figure 16.1 For a monopolist, marginal revenue is below output price. Hence the marginal revenue product or MRP (marginal physical product times marginal revenue) of a factor is below the value of its marginal product or VMP (marginal physical product times output price).

leads to increased output and lower marginal revenue. The net effect of these competing tendencies can lead either to an increase or a decrease in the quantity of the other factor employed. Thus a monopolist's long-run demand curve for a factor of production may either be more or less elastic than the short-run relationship.

Finally, it should be noted that the question of factor payments exhausting revenue does not arise in the context of monopoly. If it just happens that the monopolist's profit maximising price for output equals long-run average cost of production, then factor payments will equal revenue. If he makes positive profits then they obviously will not. As with perfect competition, what happens in this regard is a matter of the firm's behaviour and not simply of the nature of the production function.

Monopsony

The analysis carried out so far has been of the demand side of the market for a factor of production; and whether the firm under consideration is a competitor (as in the last chapter) or a monopolist (as in this one), as far as the market for his product is concerned, the assumption has been made through-out that he is a perfectly competitive purchaser of his factor inputs. That is to say, each firm we have considered has been assumed able to buy as much as it pleases of any factor of production at a given price, a price presumably determined in some broader market for the factor in question of which the firm under analysis makes up a small part. In other words the firm faces a horizontal supply curve of the factor.

There is no need to restrict our analysis of factor markets to such a situation any more than, when discussing product markets, it was necessary to restrict ourselves to dealing with a firm which could sell all it pleased at a given price. Just as we can think of a particular seller of a product being faced with a downward sloping demand curve for his output, so we can think of a particular purchaser of a factor of production being faced with an upward sloping supply curve for that input, so that the price he pays for the input varies with the quantity purchased. Such a purchaser is called a *monopsonist.*

Faced with an upward sloping factor supply curve, the firm must distinguish between the price (i.e. the average cost) of the factor on the one hand, and the marginal cost of obtaining it on the other. The total factor outlay curve associated with the horizontal supply curve that underlay the analysis of the last chapter would clearly be a straight line through the origin. Figure 16.2 shows an upward sloping factor supply curve (a straight line for simplicity) — which may be termed an 'average factor outlay' (or 'average factor cost') curve — as well as the associated total factor outlay curve. Total factor cost here increases at an increasing rate with the quantity of the input purchased, and the slope of the total factor cost curve is everywhere steeper than the slope of a straight line drawn to it from the origin. That is to say, marginal factor cost everywhere lies above the market price of the factor. Though figures 16.2 and 16.3 show the relationship

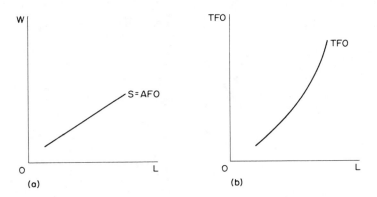

Figure 16.2 (a) An upward sloping supply curve of labour yields (b) a total factor outlay curve that slopes upwards at an increasing rate. Hence, marginal factor outlay lies above the factor supply curve.

in question for the special case of an upward sloping, but linear, factor supply curve, the reader must bear in mind that its properties, though analytically very convenient, are those of a case that is every bit as special as the straight line demand curve which we used in Chapter 12 when we considered the behaviour of a monopoly seller of a good.

The profit maximising firm will purchase that flow of inputs for which marginal revenue product equals marginal factor outlay and will choose the price which it pays for that quantity as the minimum which it needs to pay in order to obtain it; that is to say, the price it pays will be given by the factor supply curve. All this is shown in figure 16.3 with L_1 units of labour being employed at a wage rate of W_1. Just as it is inappropriate to refer to the monopolist's marginal cost curve as a supply curve since it does not relate quantity supplied to price, so it is inappropriate to refer to the monopsonist's marginal revenue product curve as a demand curve for a factor. A further parallel with monopoly in the product market is worth noting here: as compared to perfect competition, monopsony leads to a restriction of input use just as monopoly leads to a restriction of output. Figure 16.4 shows the combined effects of these tendencies for a firm that is both monopolist in its product market and monopsonist in its factor market. Perfect competition in both markets

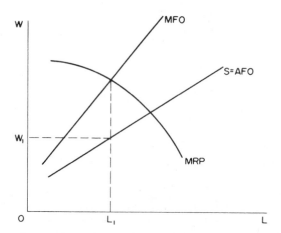

Figure 16.3 A monopsonist equates marginal factor outlay to marginal revenue product in order to determine the profit maximising level of employment for a factor, L_1 in this case, paying it the wage rate given for that quantity by the supply curve, W_1 in this case.

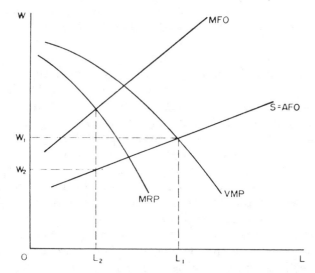

Figure 16.4 A monopsonist in a factor market who is also a monopolist in his product market employs less labour at a lower wage than would a competitive industry. The latter would equate the value of labour's marginal product to the wage rate and would employ L_1 at a wage rate of W_1, while the former equates marginal factor outlay to marginal revenue product, thus employing L_2 of labour at W_2.

would result in the market price of the factor being set at W_1 and L_1 of it being employed. The combination of monopoly and monopsony results in a lower price of the factor (W_2) and a smaller quantity of it being utilised (L_2).

Discriminating Monopsony

As the reader may well have suspected, the parallels between product market monopoly and factor market monopsony run further than we have so far taken them. Thus, we can have discriminating monopsony in the factor market. Consider a situation in which a monopsonist has two sources of supply for a particular factor input, sources of supply that he is able to keep separate in the sense that it is impossible for the owners of the services he buys from one source to begin to provide them instead by way of the other source. Then, as we show in figure 16.5, it will pay our monopsonist to equate the marginal costs of obtaining the factor from each source of supply and this will result in his paying different prices to factors obtained from the two sources.

The argument here is exactly parallel to that already set out when we discussed the price and output behaviour of a discriminating monopolist. Suppose our monopsonist initially was unable to discriminate between his two sources of supply. He would then pay the same price to each unit of the factor regardless of where he bought it. But the marginal cost to him of obtaining an extra unit of input from market 1 is, in these circumstances, higher than it is in market 2. If the monopsonist acquires the power to pay different prices in the two markets, it will pay him to reduce his purchases in the first market and increase his purchases in the second, thus cutting down on his total outlay on this particular factor without reducing the quantity of it available to him for employment. As the reader will see from figure 16.5, this results in the *factor* price being *lower* in the market where the elasticity of *supply* is lower. Again, the parallel with discriminating monopoly ought to be obvious, for there the price of *output* was *higher* in the market with the *lower* elasticity of *demand*.

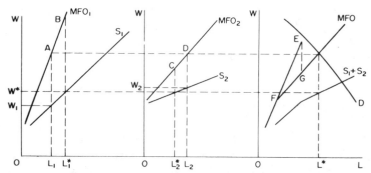

Figure 16.5 A firm which buys its labour in two markets will employ
L^* units of it at a wage of W^* if it cannot discriminate between markets.
If it can discriminate, it will equate marginal factor outlay in the two
markets. The wage rate will fall to W_1 in the first market with employment falling from L_1^* to L_1; in the second market, wages will rise to
W_2 and employment will expand from L_2^* to L_2. The overall level of
employment will remain the same, the increase in expenditure on labour
in the second market is given by $CDL_2L_2^*$, and the cut in expenditure
in the first market is $ABL_1^*L_1$. The gain in profits from being able to
discriminate is given by the difference between these two areas, or
equivalently by the area EFG which is the difference between the area
under the marginal factor outlay curve that corresponds to the summed
factor supply curves of the two markets – which is relevant in the no
discrimination case – and the area under the summed marginal factor
cost curves of the two markets, which is relevant when discrimination
takes place.

It is often asserted that discriminatory wage fixing in the
labour market between men and women may be explained by
the fact that women, having fewer alternatives for employment than men, face any potential employer with a less
elastic supply curve for their services. However, the reader
is warned that many other factors contributing to lower
productivity on the part of female workers must also be
taken into account in any particular instance before one may
conclude that wage differentials between men and women in
the same occupation are to be taken as *prima facie* evidence
of the existence of discriminating monopsony.

Now the price discrimination in the factor market just
discussed is a particular kind of price discrimination. Factor
markets apparently provide scope for paying a particular
provider of a factor service a different price for different

units of it. Overtime payment arrangements for workers are an example of such behaviour. We have already analysed certain aspects of such behaviour in Chapter 5. As with perfect price discrimination in the product market (see Chapter 13, pp. 191–195), the more finely can a monopsonist separate from one another the services he is buying, and pay a different price for each of them, the more closely will the quantity of the input that he buys approach the competitive solution. In terms of figure 16.4, a perfectly discriminating monopsonist would buy L_1 of labour, paying W_1 for only the last unit of it, and lower prices for each intermediate unit, always provided he was a competitor in his output market.

Bilateral Monopoly

There is one further topic that we might deal with at this juncture: *bilateral monopoly* or *monopoly–monopsony*. This situation arises whenever a single seller of a particular item finds himself faced with a single buyer. Clearly, the phenomenon is by no means confined to the factor market but obviously can arise there whenever a firm is buying an input service which is itself the output of some other single firm; moreover, it is often argued that we can get some insight into the bargaining processes that take place between large firms and trade unions if we treat the process as one of bilateral monopoly.

The interesting conclusion that the analysis of bilateral monopoly yields is that no unique price/quantity equilibrium is determined by the interaction of the purely economic forces which we build into our analysis, and which have carried us along thus far. Consider figure 16.6. The monopolist supplier of the factor service produces it along a marginal cost schedule given by the line S. Were he supplying the service under competitive conditions this would be his supply curve, but since he is a monopolist he tries instead to equate marginal cost to the marginal revenue arising from the sale of his output. The demand curve for L would of course be given by the marginal revenue product curve if it was being bought by a competitive industry. The curve marginal to this labelled M in figure 16.6, is the monopolist's marginal revenue curve;

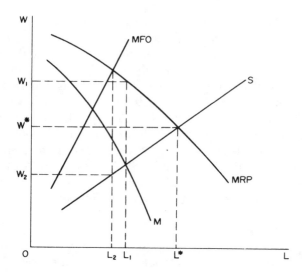

Figure 16.6 Bilateral monopoly. The monopoly seller of labour would try to sell L_1 at a wage rate of W_1 and the monopsony buyer would try to purchase L_2 at a wage of W_2. The solution for either a perfectly discriminating monopolist or monopsonist would be L^* with a wage of W^* for the marginal unit. A monopolist would try to charge more than W^* for intra-marginal units and a monopsonist to pay less than W^*. In the case of bilateral monopoly there is no determinate solution for the wage rate (or structure of wage rates), but quantity will not exceed L^*. Though the problem is here illustrated in terms of a labour market, it can obviously arise wherever a single buyer and a single seller meet each other.

profit maximising considerations suggest that he will try to sell L_1 units of the service at a price of W_1 per unit. If the structure of the market were such as to enable him to engage in anything approaching perfect price discrimination, he would supply up to L^*, with W^* being the price for the marginal unit supplied, and higher prices being charged for intra-marginal units.

However, he is selling to a monopsonist, and that monopsonist wishes to equate the marginal revenue product of L to the marginal cost of acquiring that input. A curve drawn marginal to S shows marginal factor cost to the buyer as a function of the quantity of L bought. The monopsonist would like to take L_2 units of L at a price of W_2 and would do so if buying from a competitive supplier. Of course, if the monopsonist could engage in perfect price discrimination, he would buy $L*$ with $W*$ being the price he would pay for the marginal unit, while he would pay a lower price than that for intra-marginal units. What can we say when monopolist and monopsonist meet each other? Only that it seems likely that the outcome of the bargaining between them will lead to a quantity of $L*$ being traded, for that quantity would maximise the profits of the monopolist, were he dealing with competitive buyers among whom he could discriminate, and of the monopsonist if he were dealing with competitive sellers among whom he could discriminate. Hence it is the quantity which will maximise the profits to be shared out between them, and they could presumably agree on it when they came to negotiate with one another. Price is a different matter, however, because the pattern of prices decided upon would determine how profits were divided up between buyers and sellers, and our analysis gives us no clue as to how this matter might be settled in any particular instance. It is all going to depend upon the relative bargaining skills of the two parties.

Even so, the reader will surely agree that, if it does not yield a fully determinate solution to the problem in and of itself, the foregoing analysis might be of considerable help in understanding the relationships between large firms and trade unions, to cite one possible application.

Concluding Comment

Now in this and the previous chapter we have been concerned with the demand for factors of production, and the determination of their prices. In this analysis we have simply taken supply conditions for granted. Of course we have already said something about supply side considerations in Part II. The general decision as to whether to work or not, and for how long (Chapter 5) is clearly one factor that underlies the supply of labour to a particular firm or industry. Similarly, capital equipment cannot be made available for leasing out to firms unless someone refrains from current consumption in order to acquire such equipment. Thus, the analysis of saving behaviour set out in Chapter 6 is of some relevance in dealing with the supply of capital equipment to particular firms or industries. However, when the decision to work has been taken, or the decision to acquire savings, and hence perhaps capital equipment, there still remains the issue of whom to work for, and whom to rent capital equipment to. Thus, we still need to say something about influences on the supply of factors of production to particular firms and industries. This topic provides the subject matter of the next chapter.

17
Some Aspects of the Theory of Factor Supply

Introduction

In the last two chapters we have analysed various aspects of the theory of the demand for factors of production. Of course the price of a particular productive input, just like that of any output, is determined by the interaction of both demand and supply side considerations. We have dealt with the firm's demand and the industry's demand for factors of production, very much taking the supply side of the market for granted. In this chapter we consider the supply side of the factor market in more detail.

Flows, Stocks and Their Relationship

Recall at the outset the nature of the units in which we measure factor inputs. The production function relates a flow of output to a flow of inputs. Labour is measured in units such as man-hours per week, capital in terms of machine-hours per week, and so on. The demand for factors discussed in the last two chapters has also been for inputs measured in such units. However, when we think of the level of employment of labour in a firm or industry, or the amount of capital it utilises, we usually think in terms of stocks: the number of men and women on the payroll, or the number of machines of particular types that the firm has on hand. Clearly, a given increase in inputs to production may be realised in many

245

ways: by working the existing stock, be it capital or labour, more intensively; by increasing the stock and working each unit at the same rate as before; or by some combination of the two. Similarly, the flow of inputs can be reduced by short-time working, by reduction of the number of employees and machines, or by a combination of these methods. The analysis of the last two chapters, which implicitly assumed that there was one and only one way to increase or decrease the quantity of any input, and one price – or marginal factor cost – at which this was possible, greatly simplified the nature of the problem that any firm has to solve.

There is no reason why the costs of obtaining more inputs by taking on more employees, or by buying more machines, should be the same as those involved in lengthening working hours. For example, to get more capital services by utilising a given stock of machines more intensively might involve maintenance difficulties; buying new machines might involve the firm in costs of ordering and installing them. On the labour side, the cost involved in inducing workers to put in more hours may be a higher overtime wage rate, but associated with an addition to the labour force in a firm are administrative costs having to do with each employee's tax and social security contributions etc.

We raise these problems now although we are not going to go on and analyse them. Nevertheless, the reader ought to be aware that a whole set of interesting economic problems is involved if one is to proceed carefully from an analysis of the demand for the services of factors of production to conclusions about the level of employment, in any firm or industry, of labour or of machines or indeed of any other stock that yields a flow of productive services. As before, so in this chapter we will make the simplifying assumption that there is a unique relationship between the number of employees which a firm or industry has and the man-hours of labour services which go into its production process, and we shall make a similar assumption about the relationship between capital inputs and the stock of machines. Thus, when we talk about the supply and demand for labour, we talk of both man-hours and men, and when we talk about capital we talk about machine-hours and machines. This will greatly simplify the exposition of the following analysis without, it is hoped, making it also too misleading. Nevertheless, a whole set of interesting problems is bypassed by making this assumption.

Supply to the Firm and the Industry

With this caveat in mind then, let us consider the factors that determine the nature of the supply curve of a productive input. The first question that must come to mind is surely 'supply to whom?' We must distinguish between the supply curve of an input as it appears from the point of view of a particular firm, of an industry and, indeed, of employment in general, given that not working is a viable alternative for some inputs.

The more narrowly we define the entity to which factor services are being supplied, the more alternatives there are open to their owners and hence, one would suppose, the more elastic the supply curve. Thus, if we consider by way of example the supply curve of a particular type of labour to a typical perfectly competitive firm, each worker has open to him the alternatives of working for that firm or for some other firm in the same industry at the going wage rate. If the firm is indeed 'typical' of the industry, there is no reason why any worker should have a preference for working for this firm rather than any other, and hence there is no reason why he should be willing to accept a lower wage in order to work for it. Nor, of course, is there any reason why any worker in the industry should remain with any other firm if the one whose supply curve we are studying were to be paying even slightly more than the going wage rate. In short, one would expect the supply curve of labour to this particular firm, and to every other in the industry, to be perfectly elastic at the going market wage rate.

There is nothing specific to the behaviour of labour in this analysis. One can equally well think of the owners of machines, or factory buildings, or land, or any other productive resource, deciding to whom to lease that resource and, if they have no reason to prefer one firm in the industry to another, a perfectly elastic supply curve at the going payment rate for the resource will be the result in the long run. The argument here is, as the reader will have realised, exactly parallel to the reasoning that underlies the perfect elasticity of the demand curve that faces the perfectly competitive firm in the output market. In the short run, obviously, such inputs cannot so readily be transferred from one firm to another, so that the short-run supply curve of inputs even to a single firm might have a positive slope to it (indeed, being vertical in the limit), this supply curve becoming horizontal as time passes.

When we come to look at factor supply from the point of view of the industry, matters immediately become more complex. We cannot easily ignore the possibility that the owners of a particular resource might have a personal preference for having it used in one industry rather than in another. The most obvious reasons for such preferences arise when we consider labour, for conditions of work may be more pleasant in one industry than in another; though such differences can exist between firms in the same industry, they are likely to be greater and hence more important across industrial boundaries. Moreover, what are or are not 'pleasant' working conditions is to some degree a matter of taste for the individual worker, involving preferences for the type of work, etc, and tastes are likely to differ in this respect.

Though differences of taste about employment are most obviously relevant in the case of labour, they can also affect the choices made by the owners of other factors when they decide to which industry they might be allocated. Thus, the owner of a hall (to pick a less usual example) may have a taste for the performing arts that would lead to his permitting it to be used for live performances of plays or classical music at a lower rent than he would require for it to be used as a cinema or a bingo hall.

Furthermore, differences in the alternatives available elsewhere, to what, from the point of view of one particular industry, are different units of the same input, might affect its elasticity of supply. Just because two units of a resource are equally productive in one industry does not mean that they are equally productive in alternative uses. Two halls may be equally suitable for bingo, but because of their acoustic properties only one might be a viable theatre. Two men may be equally productive as pop singers, but because of differences in education may have completely different alternative job opportunities: one might otherwise be a lawyer, and the other a lorry driver.

Transfer Price and Rent

Thus, some resources are more specific to a particular industry than others, and some will work in a particular industry at a lower rate of payment than others, either because of a subjective preference for employment in that industry on the part of their owners, or as a result of an objective inability to work more productively elsewhere. We call the price at which a particular unit of a resource will come into industry its *transfer price* or *transfer earnings* to that industry. We would expect this price to rise on the margin as more resources are brought in to any particular industry, those whose owners find it particularly congenial to be in that industry being available at a lower price than those for which there are more attractive alternatives. Now given a competitive industry demand curve, the equilibrium price of any factor in a particular use is determined. As should be apparent from figure 17.1, at this equilibrium price only the marginal unit of the resource is being paid its transfer price — indeed this statement is just a way of defining the term *marginal unit*. Every other unit is being paid more than would be necessary to keep it in this particular use. The amount by which the price it receives exceeds its transfer price is called a 'rent'. There is a close relationship between such a 'rent' and the notion of consumer's surplus which we explored earlier in this book. The consumer of a good receives a 'surplus' from being able to obtain all but the last unit of it at a price below the maximum which he would be willing to pay to obtain them; the owner of a productive resource receives a rent because he is paid more for the services of that resource than the minimum price at which he would be willing to provide them to a particular industry. Just as a discriminating monopolist appropriates some or all of the available consumer surplus to himself so clearly would a discriminating monopsonist be appropriating rents to himself.

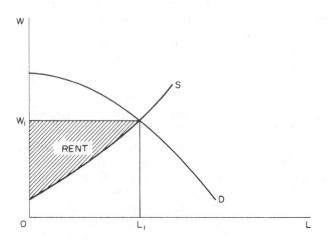

Figure 17.1 The demand for and supply of labour to a particular competitive industry. The L_1 th worker is just being paid his transfer earnings. At any wage below W_1 he would leave the industry, and is the marginal worker at that wage. The shaded area represents the total amount of payments to labour that represent rents, payments above transfer earnings.

Now how much of the payment to a particular factor of production is made up of transfer earnings and how much of rent clearly depends upon the elasticity of its supply curve. As we have seen in our analysis of the firm, a perfectly elastic supply curve involves all factor payments being transfer earnings; and at the opposite extreme, a perfectly inelastic supply curve would mean that all payments are rents, for the resource would be available in the same quantity even at zero price. These two extreme cases are depicted in figure 17.2.

Quasi-Rent

When might a resource be in completely inelastic supply to a particular industry? Only when it is specific to the technology of that industry and has no alternative use elsewhere. The reader will recall that in the short run the quantities of some productive resources available to any particular firm are

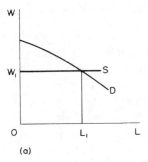
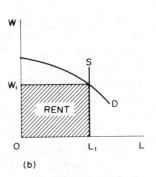

Figure 17.2 (a) When the supply of labour to an industry is perfectly elastic all wage payments are transfer earnings. (b) When the supply is perfectly inelastic all payments are rents since a perfectly inelastic supply curve implies that all workers in the industry would be there even for zero wages.

fixed. From the point of view of their owners then, they cannot be moved elsewhere and hence have no alternative use. In the short run, the income accruing to them has the character of a rent. In the long run, of course, the owners of such resources can move them in and out of particular uses and considerations of transfer earnings enter into the determination of their earnings in any use. Hence, returns to factors fixed in the short run are often referred to as *quasi-rents*. As far as capital equipment is concerned, the rental price to be paid for it is a fixed cost in the short run, and a firm whose quasi-rents are insufficient to meet this fixed cost is making a loss. To the extent that the rental price of capital equipment represents a 'normal' rate of return to the owner of the equipment, then it is apparent that 'making a loss' and 'making less than a normal rate of return' are synonymous phrases.

Though it is usual to think of such factors as machinery as being the inputs whose services yield quasi-rents in the short run, the same concept is also helpful in dealing with labour income. Labour services, after all, are not some kind of homogeneous raw input. They consist of the application of many different kinds of skills to the production process, skills that can only be acquired by the labourer making an investment of time and trouble, to say nothing in some cases of forgone income, in their acquisition.

To the extent that a worker's skills are specific to the production process of a particular firm, the return to that skill in the short run is just as much a quasi-rent as is the return to a machine; his alternative is not to utilise his skill. Thus the difference between his earnings as a skilled worker and as an unskilled worker is a quasi-rent accruing to his specific skill. If his skill is specific to a particular industry and there is short-run mobility of workers between firms then, from the point of view of any firm, his wages represent transfer earnings, though from the point of view of the industry they contain an element of a quasi-rent. Now all this amounts to saying that for some problems it is illuminating to treat the ownership of skills by a worker as analogous to the ownership of machines: to treat these skills as 'human capital' and to view their acquisition as an act of investment. A good deal of the specialised literature in the field of labour economics is concerned with this particular application of microeconomic theory.

Factor Prices and the Distribution of Income

Now, in this chapter, we have been concerned with the supply of factors of production to firms and industries. In the last two chapters we dealt with the demand for factors of production. Hence we have the ingredients of a theory of factor prices and hence of factor incomes. Is this theory sufficient to tell us about the distribution of income? The brief answer to this question is: between factors, yes, but between people, no. We have the ingredients of a theory of the 'functional' distribution of income, but not of the 'personal' distribution. Before one can say anything about the distribution of income among people on the basis of a theory of factor pricing, we must have a theory which explains how the ownership of factors of production is distributed among people.

The theory alluded to above that treats the acquisition of particular productive skills as investment in human capital tells us something about the way in which the ownership of labour services might be acquired. Moreover, the acquisition of machinery and such, as well as that of human capital, requires that current consumption be deferred. Hence the elementary analysis of saving behaviour set out in Chapter 6 is also relevant to the theory of factor ownership. Though we may have acquired some insights into some of the matters which will influence it, we are far from being able to produce a coherent overall model for the distribution of income between people. The reader should not expect too much from the analysis developed in this book as regards helping him to understand the overall distribution of income among people in any economy.

However, this is not to say that distribution is an unimportant matter for economics, just that it is not thoroughly understood. As we shall see in the final part, where we deal with the workings of the economic system as a whole, questions concerning distribution are an important element to be taken into account when we try to appraise the success or otherwise of the way in which a market economy works, and put an important limit on the amount that we can say about such matters.

Part VI
General Equilibrium and Welfare Economics

18
General Competitive Equilibrium and Pareto Optimality

Introduction

Up to now we have dealt chiefly with the behaviour of individual economic agents, the individual consumer, and the individual firm. Even when we have considered market activity, we have dealt with the market for a particular good or productive service. The rest of the economic system, the behaviour of other economic agents, the markets for other goods and services have always lain in the background. We have been concerned with what is generally called 'partial equilibrium' analysis, in which specific aspects of the economic system are picked out and studied in detail on the assumption that the relative neglect of other aspects will not lead us into serious error.

There also exists a well developed body of 'general equilibrium' analysis which deals with precisely those aspects of the interaction of individual economic agents and the interaction of the markets for particular goods and services that we have so far ignored. General equilibrium theory tries to describe how a market economy as a whole would operate. This chapter will deal with some aspects of this body of theory. First we will describe a simple economy in general equilibrium and then look at certain normative propositions that may be developed in the context of such an economy.

A Simple Exchange Economy

Consider an economic system in which there are two goods, made available to consumers at constant rates per unit of time. There is no production, the goods are simply regularly delivered from the outside. Moreover, let there be only two consumers in this economy. Certain properties of general equilibrium systems may be displayed in terms of this simple exchange economy and its essential aspects can be set out in a diagram. Let the goods with which the economy is endowed be called X and Y, and let us call the two consumers A and B.

In figure 18.1 we measure quantities of X on the horizontal axis and of Y on the vertical. There is a maximum amount of X in the economy, X_0, and a maximum amount of Y, Y_0, so let us close off the space above and to the right of the axes at these quantities, thus drawing a box. Let us measure the quantity of X available for consumer A (X_A) from left to

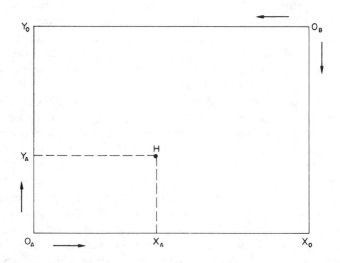

Figure 18.1 X_0 and Y_0 are the total quantities of X and Y available. Consumer A's consumption of the goods is measured from the bottom left-hand corner O_A and B's from the top right-hand corner O_B. Any point such as H represents a division of X and Y between the consumers that results in the available quantities of both goods being entirely consumed.

right along the horizontal axis and the quantity of Y available to him (Y_A) from bottom to top of the vertical axis. If we do this it is apparent that X_0 minus A's consumption of X gives us the amount left over for B to consume, while Y_0 minus A's consumption of Y gives us the amount of Y left over for B. That is, if we treat the bottom left-hand corner of our box as the origin from which A's consumption is to be measured, the top right-hand corner becomes the origin from which B's consumption can be measured. If we impose the condition that A and B between them will consume all available goods, then we may interpret any point within the box as representing a combination of X and Y consumed by A and a combination of X and Y consumed by B. Thus, if A consumes X_A of X and Y_A of Y, then B will consume $X_0 - X_A$ and $Y_0 - Y_A$, and the point labelled H represents this joint consumption pattern. Any point within the box — including those on the axes — represents a joint consumption pattern that is feasible given the quantities of X and Y available.

We may draw our two individuals' preference patterns for X and Y as figure 18.2. A's satisfaction increases as we move from bottom left to top right and B's increases as we move from top right to bottom left. If our two individuals trade X and Y on a competitive market, so that X is purchased and paid for in terms of Y, and *vice versa*, there is a little that we can say about the equilibrium solution to their trading activities. An essential characteristic of a competitive market is that every participant in it trades at the same price for each good. Equally essential as a characteristic of the behaviour of a utility maximising individual is that he equates the marginal rate of substitution between goods to the ratio of their prices. If we combine these two properties with the condition that joint consumption of X and Y must just exhaust the amounts of these goods available, we may deduce that the market for X and Y will be in equilibrium somewhere along a line which passes through all those points at which the two individuals' indifference curves are tangent to each other. This line is known as a *contract curve* and links up all those points at which A's marginal rate of substitution of X for Y is equal to B's — and hence equal to a common price ratio — and at which their joint consumption just exhausts

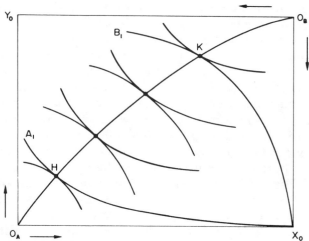

Figure 18.2 A's indifference map is drawn relative to O_A and B's relative to O_B. The contract curve $O_A O_B$ is a locus of points of tangency between the two indifference maps. At any point on it, the consumers' marginal rates of substitution between the two goods are the same. Hence, if they are both faced with the same prices for the two goods, the consumers will only be in equilibrium on this curve. If A begins with all the X and B with all the Y, voluntary trade will never move A below indifference curve A_1 or B below B_1. The equilibrium outcome of their trading would thus lie between H and K.

the amount of the goods available to be consumed.

There is nothing in the foregoing analysis that tells us whereabouts on the contract curve our consumers will end up. However, if we take into account some initial distribution of X and Y between them we may put bounds upon this because, if trade is voluntary, it is hard to imagine any individual leaving a competitive market worse off than when he entered it. Suppose, for example, that X and Y were delivered to this economy in such a way that A received all the X and B received all the Y. If neither of them traded, A would be on indifference curve A_1 and B on his indifference curve B_1. Trade between them, if it did achieve an equilibrium, would presumably leave them somewhere on the contract curve between H and K. At K, A would be better off and B no worse off than in the initial situation, at H all the gains would go to B, while between these points both A and B would be better off.

Note the qualification 'if trade did achieve an equilibrium'. The reader must be careful not to read too much into the foregoing analysis. We have shown that if a competitive equilibrium were to exist in this simple two-good/two-person/ no-production economy, then it would involve the joint consumption pattern of our individuals lying on the contract curve. We have done nothing to pinpoint any particular position on the contract curve as the solution that will in fact be achieved, nor have we given an account of any mechanism whereby the contract curve will be reached if the economy is not initially on it. We have described certain characteristics of an equilibrium that *could* exist, but have done nothing to show that it *would* be achieved.

The Production Sector

Now it is easy enough to extend our analysis to an economy with production. Let us assume that our two goods X and Y are produced by using the productive services of capital and labour. Let us also assume, as we did in our earlier analysis of the firm, that smooth production functions exist to translate input services into outputs of X and Y. Finally, to keep the analysis manageable, we will treat the quantities of factor services available to our economy as exogenously fixed. We may now use a box diagram similar to the one we used in analysing consumption.

In figure 18.3 the quantity of labour service inputs (L) available to the economy are measured horizontally and those of capital services (K) vertically. If all available factor services are utilised and are fixed in overall quantity, we may measure inputs into the X industry from an origin at the bottom left-hand corner and for the Y industry from the top right-hand corner. Any point within the box represents an allocation of factors between the two industries. We may draw the production functions for the two industries as isoquant maps — just as we draw the indifference maps of

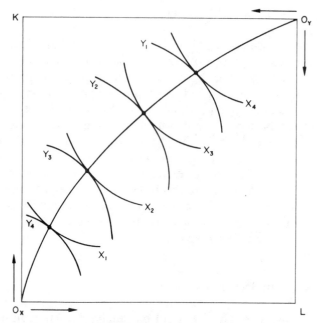

Figure 18.3 A production box diagram. The lengths of the K and L axes represent the amount of these two factor services available to the economy. Isoquants representing the output of X are drawn relative to the origin O_x and those representing the output of Y relative to the origin O_y. $O_x O_y$ is a production contract curve and the economy will be in equilibrium somewhere along it if output takes place under competitive conditions. Figure 18.4 is directly derived from figure 18.3.

our individuals — so that any point within the box is also associated with particular levels of output of X and Y. Moreover, there exists a locus of tangencies between isoquants directly analogous to the contract curve of our previous analysis. At any point on this locus, given the output of X, the output of Y is the maximum attainable, and *vice versa*. Thus, on this locus, the 'technical efficiency' of the production side of the economy is maximised.

Is there any reason to suppose that it would be a characteristic of competitive equilibrium in production that the two industries would be on the contract curve? There is indeed. A competitive factor market would have each unit of a particular factor of production being paid the same amount for its services regardless of the firm or industry employing it. Moreover, in an industry that is competitive *vis-à-vis* both output and factor markets, each factor receives a payment equal to the value of its marginal product, which is the marginal physical product of the factor multiplied by the price of the output to whose production it is contributing.

Now the slope of an isoquant at any point measures the ratio of the marginal physical products of the two factors. It tells us by how much K must be increased in order to keep production constant in the face of the withdrawal of a small (in the limit, infinitesimal) quantity of L. If each factor of production gets the same payment in each industry, the ratio of the payments going to each factor must be the same in both industries, and this ratio must be equal to the ratio of their marginal physical products in both industries, if firms are competitive profit maximisers. At the same time we have assumed that all factors are fully employed. It is only at those points at which the isoquants of figure 18.3 are tangent to each other that all these conditions are satisfied.

Again, note that we have said that a competitive equilibrium in production will involve an allocation of factors of production between industries that lie on the contract curve. We have said nothing about where it might lie, nor indeed is there anything which we can say about this on the basis of the information so far given. Moreover, we have said nothing about any mechanism that might get us a competitive equilibrium if we do not start out from one. However, we have identified particular conditions that are consistent with the existence of competitive equilibrium, as opposed to those which are not.

Production Possibilities and the Transformation Curve

The ultimate aim of our analysis is to bring the consumption and production sectors together and study the properties of their joint equilibrium. The next step towards this goal is the construction of the *transformation curve*. Consider figure 18.3 once again. Each point in the box lies on both an X-isoquant and a Y-isoquant. Competitive equilibrium involves

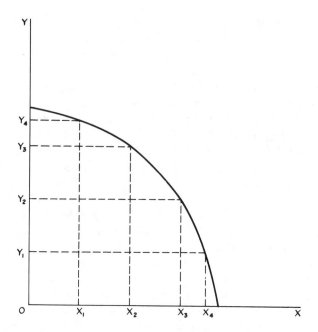

Figure 18.4 A competitive economy's transformation or production possibility curve. It shows, for given factor availability and technology, the maximum output of X attainable for a given output of Y. Its slope at any point measures the marginal cost of producing X in terms of units of Y. It is derived from figure 18.3 by reading off the values of the X and Y isoquants as the output moves along the contract curve from O_x to O_y, and plotting pairs of these, e.g. $X_1 Y_4$, as points on the transformation curve.

being on the contract curve and we may take the information implicit in that curve and display it in another way. In figure 18.4 we measure quantities of X on the horizontal axis and Y on the vertical and draw the *transformation curve* which shows how the output of X and Y vary as we move along the production contract curve, i.e. how X is 'transformed' into Y. The point at which this transformation curve cuts the Y-axis on figure 18.4 corresponds to the X-origin of the box diagram and the point at which it cuts the X-axis corresponds to the Y-origin. Because this transformation curve for a competitive economy is derived from the contract curve, along which, for any output of Y, the output of X is maximised given the resources available in the economy, and *vice versa,* it may also be referred to as a *production possibility curve,* or *production frontier.*

In general, the shape that this competitive equilibrium transformation curve will take depends upon the nature of the production function. It has been drawn concave to the origin in figure 18.4, but there is no general technical necessity for it to have this shape. Increasing returns to scale in one or both industries would lead to the curve being convex over some of its range, and if they were strong enough, over all of its range.

However, constant returns to scale will be assumed throughout the following analysis and it is easy to show that, given constant returns to scale, the production possibility curve is indeed concave to the origin. Figure 18.5 presents the relevant

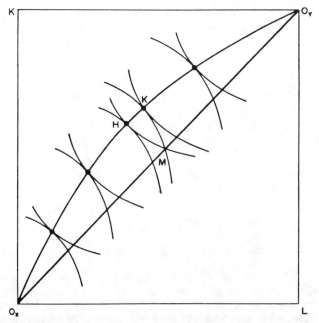

Figure 18.5 A production box diagram. With constant returns to scale, successive equidistant moves along the diagonal drawn between O_x and O_y involve equal changes in the output of X and equal changes in the output of Y. For any point on the diagonal such as M, except the two origins, a higher output of X or Y or both can be obtained by moving to the appropriate segment of the contract curve, HK in the case of point M. Figure 18.6 may be derived from figure 18.5.

box diagram. Consider the straight line drawn between the origins in this case. It is technically feasible to vary the outputs of X and Y along this line, and since each industry is characterised by constant returns to scale, the rate at which output of X would have to be sacrificed for Y, i.e. the rate at which X would be transformed into Y, would be the same at every point on it. Thus, a straight line transformation curve relating the output of X to that of Y, such as has been drawn in figure 18.6, would correspond to moving along this diagonal.

Only two points on this diagonal are also on the contract curve — the two origins. For any other point on the diagonal it is possible to move to the contract curve and increase the output of at least one good without reducing the output of the other. Thus, relative to point M on the diagonal, anywhere between H and K on the contract curve involves higher output of X (at K) or Y (at H) or both. In terms of figure 18.6, then, except at its intersection with the axes, the transformation

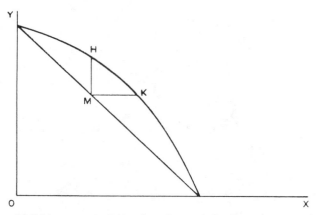

Figure 18.6 Movement along the diagonal in figure 18.5 involves a constant ratio of changes in the outputs of X and Y. Hence the straight line on which M lies is constructed by reading off the values of the isoquants as we move up this diagonal. Because M represents a combination of output of X and Y that can be exceeded by moving to the contract curve, any point on this straight line, except those at which it meets the two axes, lies inside that implied by the contract curve. Hence, the production possibility curve, given constant returns to scale, will be generally concave to the origin except in the limiting case when the contract curve itself is a diagonal.

curve derived from the contract curve lies outside the straight line derived from the diagonal, and hence must be generally concave in shape. This transformation curve is the production possibility curve, and is, as we have seen, the one that is relevant for a competitive economy. Only in the limiting case in which the contract curve itself was the diagonal would the production possibility curve be a straight line. Such a state of affairs would arise if the production functions of the two industries were such that, at a given ratio of factor prices, each one used the two factors of production in the same proportion at any level of output. If this, rather stringent, condition does not hold then, with constant returns to scale, the production frontier is concave to the origin.

Simultaneous Equilibrium in Consumption and Production

Production and consumption equilibria are brought together in figure 18.7. Here we explicitly assume constant returns to scale, competitive equilibrium, and full employment of all resources, and draw the transformation curve concave. The key to understanding figure 18.7 lies in grasping the fact that the slope of the transformation curve at any point measures the rate at which one good must be sacrificed in order to obtain more of the other. This slope then measures the marginal cost of X in terms of Y (and its inverse thus measures the marginal cost of Y in terms of X). But in perfectly competitive equilibrium the supply price of any good is equal to its long-run marginal cost of production. Therefore the slope of the transformation curve also measures the ratio of the prices at which the two goods will be supplied by competitive industries. Hence a simple competitive economy, such as the one which we are considering, will be in equilibrium when the outputs of the two goods are at levels at which the ratio of their prices, as given by the slope of the transformation curve, is such as to put our two consumers into equilibrium at a point on the consumption contract curve.

Such a situation is depicted in figure 18.7. The equilibrium level of output is given at O_B with the ratio of the supply price of X to that of Y equal to W/V. We construct a con-

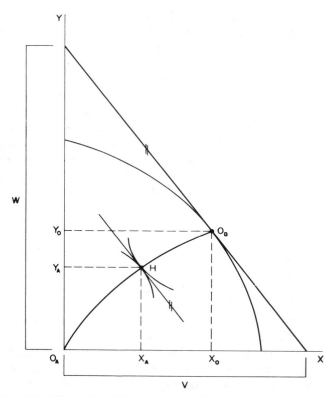

Figure 18.7 General equilibrium in the two-good/two-person/two-factor model. W/V measures the ratio of the marginal cost of and hence supply price of X to that of Y. The aggregate output mix is given at point O_B. Consumer A consumes X_A of X and Y_A of Y, while B consumes $X_0 - X_A$ of X and $Y_0 - Y_A$ of Y. Note that the slope of the indifference curves at H, which gives the ratio of the demand price of X to that of Y, must be equal to W/V.

sumption box diagram having one of its two origins at the equilibrium point on the transformation curve and the other at the origin relative to which the transformation curve is drawn. Within this box diagram the consumers' indifference curves cut the contract curve at H, their slopes at this point being equal to the slope of the transformation curve. Consumer A thus consumes X_A of X and Y_A of Y while B gets $X_0 - X_A$ and $Y_0 - Y_A$.

How does this distribution of consumption between the two consumers get settled? Consumers in this economy also own factor services and derive their incomes from selling them to firms. The point O_B of figure 18.7 corresponds to a point such as P on figure 18.8 where the slopes of the isoproduct curves tell us what the relative payment rates for capital and labour will be. Values of the isoquant tell us the levels of output. Since factor payments exhaust output where there are constant returns to scale, factor payments are fully determined at this point. Hence, our situation of general equilibrium is one in which the ownership of factor services, given exogenously, is distributed in such a way that the distribution of income corresponding to the output mix given by O_B is just such as to permit our two consumers willingly to achieve the consumption mix corresponding to point H. It is also, of course, implicit here that different distributions of resource ownership can result in different output mixes.

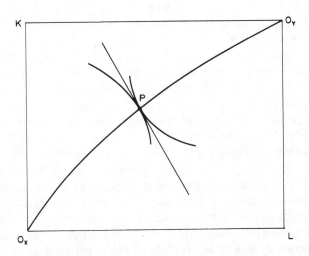

Figure 18.8 The production box diagram. Point P corresponds to O_B in figure 18.7. The slope of the isoquants at this point gives the ratio of the price of labour services to that of capital services. Since the levels of output and the prices of output are both given by the analysis set out in figure 18.7 and since factor payments exhaust output, the level of payments to factors of production is thus set. Given the ownership of factors, which is taken as exogenously determined in this analysis, the distribution of income is determined. This distribution must be such as to enable each consumer to be in equilibrium at point H in figure 18.7, if the whole economy is to be in equilibrium.

Let it be repeated yet again that there is nothing in the analysis presented here that proves that an equilibrium will exist; or that if it does exist, that there is only one equilibrium solution for the economy for each allocation of ownership of productive services; or that, if the economy is not in equilibrium, there exists a mechanism by which equilibrium will be attained. All that has been done is to describe some of the attributes of competitive equilibrium in a simple two-factor/two-good/two-person economy.

Needless to say, the attributes of so simple an economy would not be of much interest if they did not carry over to much more complex cases of many more goods, factors and persons. It would be far beyond the technical scope of this book to prove that they do so, but the reader may accept that this can be, and has been, proved. The basic implication of the analysis of competitive equilibrium which we have carried out for a special simple case is this: if consumers maximise utility in the way discussed in Parts I and II and if perfectly competitive firms maximise profits as in Parts IV and V, then there exists a set of market prices that will render all their individual plans compatible with one another and with the overall constraint imposed on the economy by available resources and technology. In short, the price mechanism operating in a market economy can, at least in principle, provide a coherent solution to the social problem of scarcity. The solution is coherent in the sense that factors are allocated, income is distributed, and consumption goods are chosen in mutually consistent patterns, but whether such a solution is desirable is another question. The mere fact that it might exist tells us nothing about this matter. Nevertheless, questions about whether monopoly or competition does more to promote economic welfare, about the consequences of various tax and subsidy schemes for economic welfare, and so forth, are surely worth asking. Once the prior question of what constitutes economic welfare is settled, economic models of the type dealt with in this chapter may be used in many attempts to get to grips with these questions, as we shall now see.

The Pareto Criterion and Pareto Optimality

There can be no completely objective basis for selecting the criteria upon which judgments about the superiority of one social situation over another may be made. Inevitably there is a normative element present in such a judgment and the discussion of normative criteria is more the business of moral philosophers than of economists. That branch of economics known as welfare economics usually bypasses detailed normative debate by taking a particular criterion as a starting point and then applying it to compare various social situations. The criterion in question is known as the *Pareto criterion*. It states that if, when the resources available to a society are reallocated among alternative uses, the 'economic welfare' of at least one member of the society is increased without that of any other member being reduced, then the 'economic welfare' of that society has increased. An increase or decrease in an individual's economic welfare simply involves his moving from a lower to a higher indifference curve or *vice versa*. A *Pareto optimal* situation is then said to exist when it is no longer possible to so reallocate resources as to increase the economic welfare of one individual except at the expense of another.

This criterion is to some extent controversial. It identifies the welfare of society solely with the welfare of the individuals that make up the society. This is a defensible position but there are ethical systems which invest society itself, or groups within society (such as social classes) with a moral importance that is distinct from that attaching to individuals. In terms of such systems the Pareto criterion is at best inadequate and at worst meaningless.

Even granted the individualist ethic, the Pareto criterion is far from providing a complete guide to economic policy. It says nothing about the extent of the superiority of one situation over another, nor does it enable us to distinguish between alternative situations, both of which may be Pareto superior to some starting situation, but which involve the welfare of different individuals being increased. A resource reallocation that makes a poor man better off by a pound a year and lowers the welfare of no other member of the community represents a movement to a Pareto superior situation, but so does a reallocation that makes a rich man better off by the same amount if no one else's welfare is altered. The Pareto criterion gives us no way of choosing between the two reallocations. Even though most of us would agree that questions about distribution are of central importance to the assessment of alternative situations, the criterion has nothing to say about the distribution of economic welfare between individuals. There are in general as many non-comparable Pareto optimal situations as there are distributions of income. In short, the Pareto criterion tries to distinguish between questions concerning what is usually termed the allocative efficiency of a particular economic situation from those dealing with the justness, or otherwise, of the income distribution ruling in that same situation. The distinction here is certainly one that can be made in principle, but, in practice, because payments to owners of factors of production are an integral part of the mechanism whereby a market economy allocates resources, questions about allocation and distribution tend to turn up together.

The Pareto Criterion and Equilibrium in Consumption and Production

Nevertheless, a standard that does not enable us to make all the judgments we might want to make may be useful for some purposes and it is worth looking at the implications of the Pareto criterion in more detail. In particular, it is worth showing that a situation of competitive equilibrium such as was described in the last chapter is Pareto optimal, and is in fact a situation in which it is impossible to make one person better off without making someone else worse off.

Consider the consumption box diagram again, drawn here as figure 18.9. Let M represent any point not on the contract curve and hence an allocation of consumption goods between individuals that is inconsistent with competitive equilibrium. By moving from M to any point on the contract curve between

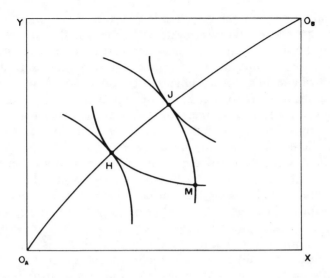

Figure 18.9 A consumption box diagram. For any point, such as M, off the contract curve, there is a segment of the contract curve (H J) a movement to which would make at least one consumer better off without making the other worse off.

H and J, it is possible to make at least one or, in all but the limiting cases at H and J, both individuals better off. Hence any such move would take us to a Pareto superior situation. Note that this does not say that a move to *any* point on the contract curve from M involves an improvement of welfare. Points to the left of H and to the right of J involve one individual being made better off and the other worse off and hence are not comparable to M.

However, it is the case that, for every point in our box diagram that is *not* on the contract curve, there is at least one point *on* the contract curve that is Pareto superior to it. Moreover, any point on the contract curve is Pareto optimal. Consider point H in figure 18.9, and let it represent any point on the contract curve. To move away from this point by leaving the contract curve will involve at least one and perhaps both individuals in a loss of economic welfare, while to move away from it up or down the contract curve involves the welfare of one individual being increased at the expense of the other.

Similar arguments may be made about the production side of the general equilibrium system. Figure 18.10 reproduces the production box diagram analysed earlier. If it is possible to increase the output of one good without decreasing the output of another, it is possible to increase economic welfare. The application to figure 18.10 of arguments analogous to those made about consumption should readily convince the reader that for any point *not* on the production contract curve there is at least one point *on* the curve at which the output of at least one of the goods is higher without that of the other being reduced. It should also be obvious that it is impossible to move along the contract curve without reducing the output of one good while that of the other is increased. Thus, as far as production is concerned, a situation of competitive equilibrium that lies on the contract curve is required for Pareto optimality. This argument, of course, amounts to a re-affirmation of a point made earlier: namely that the transformation curve for a competitive economy also represents its production frontier (see pp. 263—5).

The foregoing argument implies that the transformation curve between X and Y derived earlier (*cf.* figures 18.3, 18.4) tells us, for any level of output of Y, what is the maximum

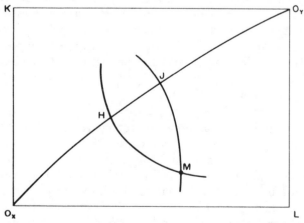

Figure 18.10 A production box diagram. For any point off the contract curve such as M, there is a segment of the curve $(H\ J)$ movement to which will permit the output of at least one good to be increased without reducing the output of the other.

output of X it is physically possible to produce, and *vice versa*. It divides the area of a figure such as 18.4 into a region below and on the curve which contains bundles of X and Y whose production is feasible with available resources and technology, and a region which contains bundles whose production is not feasible. Thus it represents the economy's *production frontier,* as we have already noted.

The Pareto Optimality of Competitive Equilibrium

Now we saw earlier that a situation of competitive equilibrium would result in each good's market price being equal to long-run marginal cost. The economy's competitive equilibrium production pattern was thus at a point on the production frontier where the ratio of the goods' marginal production costs equalled the ratio of their market prices. It remains to show that such a situation is Pareto optimal.

In terms of our simple model, this is best done by considering a situation in which the market price of one of the two goods differs from its competitive level. There are many ways in which this could happen. The output of one good could be monopolised and a monopolist, other than a perfect price discriminator, would set price above marginal cost. Or a government could impose a per-unit sales tax (subsidy) on the output of a competitive industry thus raising (lowering) its price to consumers above (below) long-run marginal cost. In analysing such matters we must assume that the recipients of monopoly profits are also consumers; or that the proceeds of a tax (costs of a subsidy) are redistributed to (collected from) consumers as lump sum additions to (deductions from) their incomes. If we did not do so we would have to deal with the complexities that arise when the income accruing to members of an economy differs from the economy's output, and the analysis of such complexities would simply distract attention from the matter now to be dealt with.

We wish to show that an equilibrium situation in which the price of one good differs from its long-run marginal production cost is not Pareto optimal. We shall explicitly deal with a situation in which the price of Y is initially above marginal cost either because its production is monopolised or taxed, but the reader should satisfy himself that consideration of a subsidy of X would produce identical analysis. Figure 18.11 shows an equilibrium situation for an economy in such a situation. The key feature of figure 18.11 as far as the current analysis is concerned is that the ratio of the market prices of X and Y differs from that which competitive equilibrium would produce. Monopoly pricing or a tax on Y raises its price above its competitive level so that the ratio of the prices of X and Y comes to fall short of the ratio of their marginal production costs. It should go without saying that when these ratios differ consumers will allocate their expenditure between the two goods in accordance with relative market

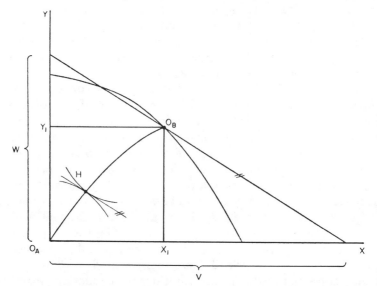

Figure 18.11 General equilibrium when the price of Y is above its competitive level, either as a result of monopoly pricing or the imposition of a tax. The ratio of the market price of X to that of Y is given by W/V and falls short of the ratio of their marginal production costs at X_1, Y_1. The consumers' marginal rate of substitution between X and Y is given at H by the ratio of their market prices. More Y is in fact being sacrificed on the margin to obtain X than consumers are willing to sacrifice. The market price of X relative to that of Y is below its marginal cost of production in terms of Y and a Pareto gain in welfare is possible by substituting Y for X in production and consumption, given the distribution of income ruling at H.

prices, and not in accordance with relative marginal costs of production.

Recall that the slope of a consumer's indifference curve measures the rate at which he is just willing to trade one good for another if he is to maintain his satisfaction — his welfare — constant; the slope of the production frontier measures the rate at which it is physically possible to substitute one good for the other. If production of Y is monopolised or taxed, this leads both of our individuals to consume Y and X in quantities such that the amount of X that they are willing to give up for extra units of Y exceeds the amount that must in fact be given up as far as the technical conditions of production are concerned. Clearly then, a substitution of Y for X in production could lead to a Pareto superior situation as long as the consequences of such substitution for the distribution of income between the two consumers were offset in some way. Whenever the marginal rate of substitution between goods in consumption differs from that in production, a Pareto gain in welfare is possible. When the two rates of substitution are equal and the other conditions already discussed are satisfied, no such gain is possible. In short, when the economy is in a competitive equilibrium, it is impossible to make anyone better off without making someone else worse off and a Pareto optimal situation therefore exists. This is a result of considerable importance, because it tells us the precise extent to which the coherent solution to the social problem of scarcity that a competitive economy generates is also desirable. A moment's reflection on the limitations of the Pareto criterion as a guide to the assessment of social welfare should convince the reader that, important though the result in question might be, it still leaves crucial aspects of this matter, notably those having to do with distributional questions, unresolved. The next chapter considers some of the issues involved here in more detail.

19
Pareto Optimality: Distribution and Externalities

Introduction

The Pareto optimal properties of a perfectly competitive equilibrium lie at the root of a great deal of work on problems of economic policy. At one time the existence of this property was widely regarded as an important argument in favour of competitive capitalism as a form of social and economic organisation. One would now be hard put to find a professional economist who would take up such a position, at least when it is put so baldly, but it is worth looking more closely both at the nature of the competitive economy, whose properties we have been studying, and at the nature of the optimum we have been considering, in order to see just why it is that this superficially appealing point of view has so little substance to it.

Achieving a Pareto Optimum and Changing the Income Distribution

The most obvious difficulty with the Pareto criterion, and one to which we have already referred, is its silence on the matter of distribution of income. It is all very well to distinguish between allocative efficiency on the one hand and distributive justice on the other, and to have a criterion that deals only with the former, but payments made to factors of production are an integral part of the allocative mechanism. A competitive equilibrium may be optimal, but the movement to an optimal situation from a non-optimal situation is not the same thing as a movement to a socially superior, or preferred, situation. Such a movement may well involve making someone worse off. Consider again the example we used in the previous chapter, in which some such distortion as monopoly pricing or a tax leads to the price of Y exceeding its competitive value. The removal of such a distortion leads to an increase in the demand for Y and hence in the demand for the factor of production that is particularly heavily used in the production of Y. The factor's price will rise and the incomes of its owners increase, perhaps, though not necessarily, at the expense of reducing the incomes of the owners of the other factor. In figure 19.1 the utility level of A, whose consumption is measured from the origin O_A, is lowered if the economy moves to the optimal situation. Is there then any way of judging whether this optimal situation is to be preferred to the non-optimal alternative? How in general does one decide between situations in which the welfare of one individual, or group, is increased at the expense of some other individual or group?

Compensation Criteria

A moment's reflection should convince the reader that the problem of making judgments about alternative situations in which the welfare of one group rises (or falls) at the same time as the welfare of others falls (or rises) commonly arises in the real world. Consider for example a country in which airline service was provided by a government regulated monopoly, which, as a condition of being allowed to maintain its monopoly power, used some of the excess profits extracted from heavily travelled routes to subsidise the provision of loss-making services to remoter areas. Suppose it was proposed that the government take steps to end the airline monopoly and open up the industry to competition. If this step was taken, one might expect users of heavily travelled routes to benefit from the fact that fares there would fall. However,

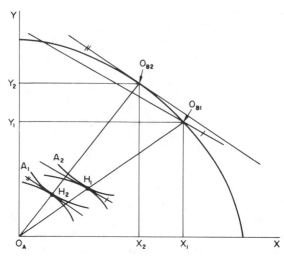

Figure 19.1 The change in the general equilibrium situation when the price of Y is restored to its competitive level. This figure depicts the *possible* outcome of such action, but not, in every detail, the *necessary* outcome. First, equality between the ratios of the goods' market prices and marginal production costs is restored in the move from $X_1 Y_1$ to $X_2 Y_2$. This must happen if the tax was the only source of discrepancy here. Figure 19.1 is drawn so that the structure of outputs shifts towards Y and the distribution of income changes in such a way as to reduce A's welfare. Point H_2 lies on a lower indifference curve for A than does point H_1. Note here that A's indifference map is drawn relative to O_A and hence does not shift between the two situations. This reduction in A's welfare is not a necessary outcome of the removal of the tax but it is a logically possible outcome. Hence, though the movement from the first situation to the second takes us from a non-Pareto optimal to a Pareto optimal situation, we cannot say that it represents a movement to a Pareto superior situation. Someone has been made worse off in the shift.

those living in more remote areas might face a sharp increase in travel costs, or even the loss of all airline service and their welfare would fall. And what judgment would one make about the fall in the income of shareholders in the monopoly airline? How would one weigh these issues in deciding whether or not to implement the proposal in question? Or consider what might be involved in a plan to flood a mountain valley in order to enhance the water supply of some distant city. To carry through the plan would make the city dwellers better off, but the welfare of people living in the valley would be reduced. Can one make a decision about cases like these without assuming from the start that the welfare of one group is to be given greater weight in the decision-making process than that of another? Economists have developed the analysis of *compensation criteria* in an attempt to avoid the necessity of making judgments about whose welfare is to be given priority in just such instances.

Two compensation criteria have been proposed in order to enable us to judge the desirability of making changes that cause some people to gain and others to lose. The first suggests that a move from one situation to another would be desirable if those who gain from the move were able to compensate those who lose and still remain better off after the move. The second criterion suggests that the same move would be undesirable if the losers were able to compensate the gainers for remaining in the initial position and still themselves be better off than they would be if the move were to be made.

Unfortunately, these criteria do not cover all possible cases, for it is easy to construct examples in which it is simultaneously possible for the gainers to compensate the losers if a move is made (indicating the move is desirable) and for the potential losers to compensate the potential gainers if the move is not made (indicating that the move is not desirable)! However, this does not always happen, and it will be convenient to discuss an unambiguous case first of all.

Consider once more the two-person, two-input, two-output, general equilibrium model developed in the previous chapter. In that model, just as the production box diagram yields a production frontier, so, once the outputs of X and Y are determined at a point such as O_B in figure 18.11, does the consumption box diagram yield an analogous relationship that might be called a utility possibility curve. Such a relationship, derived in figure 19.2, measures the maximum level of utility that A may obtain, given the level of utility made available to B and given a particular output mix of X and Y.

There exists one such utility possibility curve for every point on the production frontier. Since any reallocation of resources involves a change in the outputs of X and Y we may think of it as shifting the utility possibility curve.

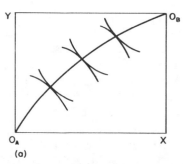
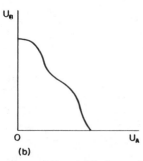

Figure 19.2 (a) shows a consumption box diagram. Panel (b) shows the utility possibility curve generated by moving along the contract curve. We can say that, as B's utility decreases, A's increases as we move along the curve. However, if we are dealing with ordinal utility functions we cannot say by how much. Thus the utility possibility curve slopes downwards, but not at any defined rate, and is drawn as a wavy line in panel (b) to remind the reader of this.

Whether we can say anything about the desirability of any reallocation depends not only upon how the utility possibility curve is shifted by it, but also upon which point on the original curve we start from and upon which point on the new curve we arrive at. Let us look at some of the possibilities, dealing with the simple example of the restoration of the price of one good to a competitive level. One logically possible consequence of the removal of monopoly or of a tax is a reallocation of resources that results in a pattern of output such that, for any given level of utility attained by A, B could attain a higher level.

Such an unambiguously outward shift of the utility frontier is shown in figure 19.3. If, beginning at D, the removal of the tax results in the economy generating a consumption pattern that puts our two individuals at a point on the new frontier between E and F, then the new situation is unambiguously Pareto superior. But what if the new consumption pattern were to lie at G? Here A would be worse off than initially with U_{A2} rather than U_{A1}. But B could cut his own utility by giving consumption goods to A until the latter was enjoying his starting level of utility while B was still better off. That is, the consumption pattern *could* move to E, and here we would have a situation in which one person (B) was better off without the other (A) being worse off. Equally, in

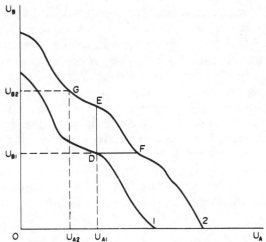

Figure 19.3 There is a different utility possibility curve for every composition of output, for every point on a given production frontier. In terms of figure 19.1, a movement from a structure of output such as X_1Y_1 to X_2Y_2 produces a new utility possibility curve. It is possible (though not necessarily the case) that the new curve lies everywhere outside the old one. If we start at D and the change in output results in a shift to some point on the segment EF of the second utility possibility curve, then the shift is unambiguously desirable from a Pareto point of view. Both consumers are made better off. However, if we go, say, to point G, A is made worse off and we cannot say that G is Pareto superior to D. However, B could bribe A and make him better off than he was at D and still leave himself with a gain. Moreover, there is no way that A could bribe B to move back to the first situation. Hence, according to the compensation criteria, the move from utility possibility curve 1 to 2 is desirable.

order for A to persuade B to remain in the initial situation he would have to be able to increase B's utility to at least U_{B2} in that starting situation while leaving himself better off than he would be at point G. This is clearly impossible. Thus, the new situation meets both compensation criteria and according to them would be judged superior to the original one.

Even in so clear-cut a case as this, though, one might have qualms about accepting that the move from D to G represented an unambiguously desirable step to take. It is *possible* to move from G to E, and hence it is *possible* to achieve a situation Pareto superior to that ruling at D. However, unless, after the move is made, the gainers are *actually* taxed and the

losers *actually* compensated so as to move to E, the achievement of a Pareto superior situation is only a possibility, not
an established fact. To accept the possibility of compensation
as a sufficient criterion for regarding a change as desirable,
rather than insisting that compensation be carried out, involves
one in making stronger judgments than strict application of
the Pareto criterion would permit. If a cost—benefit analysis
of a particular economic project finds that the benefits
outweigh the costs, but that these accrue to different people,
the decision to proceed with the project without insisting
that the losers be compensated by the gainers involves a
comparison of the economic welfare of the two groups, the
very thing that the Pareto criterion seeks to avoid.

The Compensation Criteria in an Ambiguous Case

Even so, the two compensation criteria we have been discussing
may well produce contradictory results. One example will
suffice to demonstrate this point. It hinges on the perfectly
straightforward proposition that there is no particular reason
why the removal of a tax on one good should result in an
unambiguously outward shift of the utility frontier. Hence,
what we have here is not just an analytic curiosity, but an
illustration of an extremely important limitation on the
practical usefulness of compensation criteria. Suppose consumer A found Y a relatively unappealing good. Then to
substitute Y for X in production could well result in his
maximum attainable level of utility falling. Such a situation is
depicted in figure 19.4. It is possible that the removal of
monopoly or of a tax on Y could result in a reallocation of
resources and redistribution of income between A and B such
that there was a movement from D on utility frontier 1 to G
on utility frontier 2. In this case B could certainly compensate
A for making the change with a shift to point F. However, A
could simultaneously compensate B for not making the change
by a shift to point E.

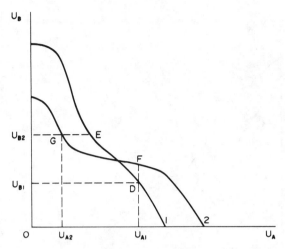

Figure 19.4 A change that involves a shift in composition of output can produce a new utility possibility curve that crosses the old one, and then the compensation criteria can prove contradictory and hence unhelpful. Suppose we start at D in the first situation and shift to G in the second. Consumer B can bribe A to accept the move by permitting a move to F, where A can enjoy U_{A1} just as he did at D, while B is left better off. However, once at G, A could bribe B to return to the original situation. In that situation point E is available and here U_{B2} is available to B, just as it is at G, while A is better off than at G where he gets U_{A2}.

The Utility Frontier and the Distribution of Welfare

We may use the utility possibility curve construction to set out more clearly the nature of the distributional problem with which we have been dealing. For every point on the production frontier, there is a utility possibility curve derived from the relevant consumption contract curve. In principle, we can derive every such curve and plot them in a figure such as figure 19.5. Some of these curves will lie entirely inside others, others will criss-cross one another, and not necessarily only once. In just the same way as, in Chapter 10, we derived the isoproduct curve as a boundary showing the *minimum* quantities of factors of production required to produce a

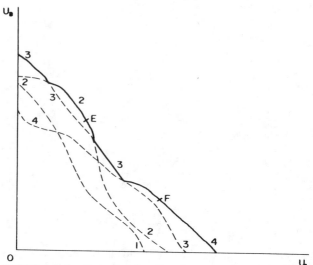

Figure 19.5 The derivation of the utility frontier. For every point on a given production possibility curve we have a different utility possibility curve. The potentially infinitely large number of such curves is reduced to four here only for the sake of geometric clarity. The utility frontier shows us the maximum amount of utility available to A given the utility available to B, and given, not a particular structure of output, but a particular set of productive resources. It is thus made up of those segments of the individual utility possibility curves that lie outside any other. This frontier is drawn here as a continuous curve and the segments of the utility possibility curves that lie inside the frontier as dotted curves.

given level of output, so in figure 19.5 we derive an overall utility frontier from all these utility possibility curves. It shows what is the maximum level of utility available for A given a certain level of utility for B, when fixed quantities of factors of production are available to be reallocated between the production of various goods. Thus, in terms of figure 19.5 the movement from E to F not only represents a reallocation of utility in favour of individual A, it also represents a re-allocation of resources such that the output mix changes from that underlying utility possibility curve 2 to that under-lying utility possibility curve 4.

The overall utility frontier of figure 19.5 shows clearly why the Pareto criterion does not permit us to make all the judgments about the performance of an economic system that we might want to make. Every point on it is Pareto optimal and, without making explicit judgments about the distribution of economic welfare between our two individuals, we cannot choose between them. But can we at least say that, since every point on the frontier is Pareto optimal, we should nevertheless aim economic policy at being somewhere on the frontier rather than inside it, and avoid discussing distribution in this way? Inspection of figure 19.6 will readily confirm that we cannot do so. It would only be possible to say this if it were the case that every point on the frontier was Pareto superior to every point within it, and this is not true. For any point within the frontier, such as D, there is certainly a segment EF of the frontier that is made up of Pareto superior points, but a point such as G is not Pareto superior to D. To move there involves making someone worse off. Depending upon the judgments that one might make

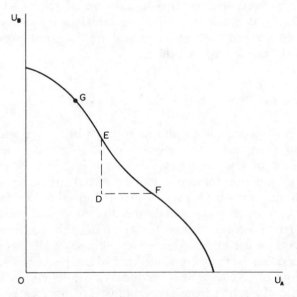

Figure 19.6 For any point inside the utility frontier, such as D, there is a segment of the frontier EF, any point on which is Pareto superior to D. However, a point such as G is not Pareto superior to D since A is worse off there. Despite the fact that G, like every point on the frontier, is a Pareto optimal point while no point within the frontier is, we cannot say that the achievement of Pareto optimality is always desirable in and of itself.

about the distribution of welfare between the two individuals whose situation is depicted in figure 19.6, one might well regard point D as superior to G even though it is non-Pareto optimal. Thus, there can be no overall implication from the foregoing analysis that the achievement of Pareto optimality can always be regarded as desirable as an end in itself!

The story which we have been telling is abstract and complex, but it has a very clearcut moral. It is, in general, impossible to make judgments about social welfare without also making judgments about the distribution of income. Allocative efficiency is not the only factor to be taken into account in judging a particular social situation or a particular form of social organisation. Its achievement puts one on the utility frontier, but the desirability of a particular distribution of utility between individuals must still be judged. Such judgments must involve the application of ethical criteria. That *does not* mean that they are arbitrary by any means, but it does mean that economics alone does not provide a sufficient basis for making them.

Taxation and Pareto Optimality

No form of economic organisation exists in a social vacuum. A competitive market economy needs, at the very least, a framework of law concerning property rights and contracts, if it is to function smoothly, and laws need enforcing. This is the minimal necessity for its operation, but even the provision of this bare necessity would require the use of real resources: policemen and court officials must be fed, clothed and housed. Thus taxes must be levied in order to provide the necessary resources. Far from being some kind of interference with the operation of a competitive economy, the levying of taxes must, therefore, be a necessary condition for its existence.

As we have already seen, to levy a tax on sales of one good leads the ratio of the market prices of goods to depart from the ratio of their marginal costs of production, and hence to a less than Pareto optimal allocation of resources. In terms of the analysis presented in the last chapter, the solution to the problem might appear to be simple: levy a sales tax at the same rate on each good, or, what apparently amounts to the same thing, levy an income tax.

There are two objections to this. First, if taxes are not the only potential source of distortion in the economy then, in addition to raising revenue, they may be used to offset other distortions. If the price of X is already too high relative to its long-run marginal cost of production because the output of that good is monopolised, then to tax each good equally will leave resources misallocated. It would be appropriate to levy taxes on Y at a higher rate in order to offset the effect of the initial monopoly. What is an appropriate pattern of taxes is dependent upon the initial pattern of resource allocation in an economy and there are no general rules to be laid down. There can, then, be no general presumption in favour of an income tax over sales on specific goods as means of raising revenue.

In any event, the initial impression of an income tax as a non-distorting tax arises from a rather special property of our model. The model assumes that the supply of productive resources to the economy is given. In general we would not expect this to be the case. We would expect the supply of labour to vary with the wage rate received; indeed we have analysed some of the factors underlying this phenomenon in Chapter 5.

Once we permit the owners of labour services to choose between work and leisure, we open up another area of choice where a tax can be distorting. An income tax ensures that a worker will receive less for his marginal hour of work than those who purchase his output would be willing to pay for it. It is equivalent to levying a tax on every good in the economy except leisure, and hence leads to a misallocation of resources just like any other specific tax.

The only tax that will not involve some such distortion is a tax which does not affect any choice about resource allocation. It must be independent of any consumption pattern or work pattern. The only such tax appears to be a poll tax, and even that is suspect if one takes the view that family size, and hence the future supply of labour, is partly the result of choices based on economic factors! Besides, it would be hard to find anyone willing seriously to defend a poll tax from the point of view of distributional equity. In short, even in the most competitive economy conceivable, taxes have to be levied, and they are going to affect both allocation and distribution. The problem is not, then, to achieve allocative efficiency by making sure that the economy works competitively and then to discuss income distribution as a separate problem. It is to pick a pattern of taxation that will, given the framework of the economy, get the economy as close as it can to the desired point on the utility frontier. No matter how hard we try to keep them separate in principle, the problems of allocation and distribution are interdependent in practice.

Externalities and Absence of Markets

Allocative and distributive problems also arise when so-called *externalities* are under analysis. Such effects can involve both costs and benefits and arise whenever an important, but nevertheless so far implicit, assumption of our analysis of competitive equilibrium is violated. In analysing the competitive equilibrium model we assumed that there were two, and only two, scarce resources; and in identifying its equilibrium properties with a Pareto optimal allocation of resources we took it for granted that there was a perfect market for every scarce resource available to the economy. Externalities arise whenever there is a scarce resource for which there is no such perfect market, and this is quite a common phenomenon in any actual economy.

A simple example will illustrate the nature of the problem. Consider a river which is utilised by two groups of economic agents: fishermen for fishing and manufacturers for discharging waste materials. The river is clearly a productive resource, but not necessarily scarce. It is a property of rivers that they can absorb a certain amount of waste material without their capacity to support life in their waters being affected, and as long as the amount of waste disposal undertaken is below this limit, the river, though productive, is nevertheless free. By free, we mean that there is enough of it to meet all demands being put upon it without any need to choose between alternative uses.

But now suppose that for some reason the manufacturers along the river expand their output and with it the volume of their waste disposal up to a level at which it affects fishing prospects. Part of the cost of the new higher level of manufactured output is clearly the fish lost to fishermen. However, this is not captured in the private costs of production facing manufacturers and, if they are profit maximisers (and are not fishermen), will be ignored by them. What has happened is that a resource that once was free has become scarce as the demand for its services has increased, but has not had a market price attached to it.

From the point of view of allocative efficiency, the marginal *private* cost facing manufacturers, upon which the pricing of their output is based, falls short of the marginal *social* cost upon which price ought to be based if an optimal allocation of resources in the Pareto sense is to be achieved. The output of manufacturers is thus too high, and the costs involved in lost fish are borne by fishermen instead of by the consumers and producers of manufactures. These costs are *external* to the market for the goods in whose production they are actually incurred.

Now one can have external benefits as well. Suppose the activities of manufacturers enhanced the fish bearing capacity of our river in such a way that when manufacturing expanded so did the output of fish. In this case the private benefits of expanding manufactured output would fall short of the social benefits, since the greater yield in fish would not enter into the cost calculations of the manufacturers (unless they were fishermen). Their output would fall short of a Pareto optimal level. Indeed, everything in the foregoing analysis — and that which is to follow — is simply reversed in the case of external benefits and so there is no need to deal with the latter as a different case.

How should an external dis-economy be dealt with? The answer obviously is to internalise the external cost so as to ensure that it is taken into account by the producers and consumers of manufactures. What may not be quite so obvious in the above example is that there is more than one way to accomplish this, each of which has different distributional implications. The most obvious solution would be to charge the manufacturers for discharging waste into the river in such a way that their outlay on waste disposal expenses reflected the costs imposed upon the fishermen who could then be compensated for their losses. Alternatively, one could think of instituting a scheme whereby fishermen paid the manufacturer a certain sum for each fish taken from the river, thereby compensating the manufacturer for not polluting the water. The more waste disposal undertaken, the less revenue from fishermen and hence the costs of waste disposal would again come to be included in the manufacturers' cost and revenue calculations.

The second of these two solutions sounds unfair to fishermen, but that is because we have constructed our example in a particular way. We have had manufacturing expand to cause the externality problem; but suppose manufacturers had always maintained a given level of waste disposal and it was fishermen who found this level of disposal a hindrance to expanding their activities? It would seem more reasonable then for fishermen to pay the manufacturer to reduce his activities rather than to ask the manufacturer to compensate the fishermen.

The point here is that, as long as the cost of manufacturing operations, in terms of fish, or the cost of fish, and in terms of manufactured goods, are reflected in the cash revenues and outlays of firms involved in these activities, then correct (from a Pareto point of view) decisions about resource allocation will be made. It is the distributional consequences of the above two solutions that differ. In the first case we are essentially suggesting that the fishermen become owners of the river and rent out its waste disposal services to manufacturers, while in the second case that manufacturers become the owners of the river who may then sell fishing rights.

Now in the foregoing example it is indeed feasible to think of solving the 'externality' problem by vesting in someone or other property rights in the resource that has become scarce, that is the river, and then allowing for market transactions among the parties involved, the manufacturers and the fishermen (and the owner of the river if he is not a member of one of the other groups), to solve the problem of allocating the resource. However, such a solution is not always feasible.

Consider instead the case of a group of householders who have been using the airspace around their homes to provide themselves with fresh air and peace and quiet, but who now find that an airport is to be set up in the vicinity. In this case, the airlines operating from the airport would use that same airspace for absorbing the kerosene fumes and the noise emitted by their aircraft, thus reducing its capacity to provide fresh air and peace and quiet. The problem here is formally similar to the one considered earlier, but problems of allocating property rights in airspace, and of monitoring its use so that it can be charged for, are altogether more difficult. In this case, the problem might have to be dealt with by some direct form of government intervention, perhaps by levying taxes on aircraft movements, or by enforcing regulations concerning permissible noise levels and such.

Concluding Comment

Now if there existed a market for every scarce resource; if all the costs and benefits of every aspect of productive activity were reflected in market transactions; and if there were no need to provide a background of enforceable legal arrangements, then one could talk about the Pareto optimal properties of competitive equilibrium without qualification, though all the ethical problems concerning the distribution that were raised earlier would remain to qualify one's judgments about the desirability of one such equilibrium relative to another. However, as soon as one considers the desirability, indeed, in some cases the necessity, of providing public goods, and as soon as one recognises the many ways in which the costs and benefits of various aspects of economic activity can escape the market and appear as 'externalities', then it becomes apparent that the solutions to such problems have both allocative and distributional consequences that require analysing together, and that the inter-connectedness of these problems is, as we stressed in the last chapter, inherent in the operation of a market economy.

These matters are of fundamental importance. They mean that, as a practical matter, even if we ignore the question of distribution, we can still not rely on the operation of competitive markets to provide a *first best* solution to the problem of allocating resources. Because externalities exist, and because some taxes have to be levied, the maximum feasible degree of competitiveness in the economy will in general provide an allocation of resources that is Pareto inferior to some *second best* solution that could be achieved with some extra intervention on the part of government.

Thus the analysis that we have been pursuing in the last two chapters of this book in no way implies that a competitive economy free of any government intervention is in any sense the 'best' economy. Nor does that analysis provide any blanket justification for all the many different sorts of government intervention in economic life that one might encounter in practice. Rather it provides a set of analytic principles that enable coherent judgments to be made about the allocative, but *not the distributive*, aspects of such intervention, or absence thereof. It does not provide all the answers to all the questions one might raise about these issues, but that does not mean it is useless. The very fact that it helps us to think coherently about the type of issues we have discussed above surely means that it is a great deal better than nothing.

Questions for Study and Discussion

1. Draw the budget constraint implied by the following information.

Consumer's income	£500 per week
Price of X	£1 per unit
Price of Y	£2 per unit

Would the consumer be able to attain any of the following consumption patterns?

100 Y and	200 X	per week
100 Y and	20 X	per week
200 Y and	100 X	per week
200 Y and	1600 X	per month
300 Y and	1200 X	per month

How much would he have left over per week from purchasing those bundles within his reach?

Suppose that the budget constraint instead were given by:

Consumer's income	£500 per week
Price of X	£1 per unit for the first 150 per week, thereafter £2 per unit
Price of Y	£2 per unit

How would this affect your answers to the above questions?

295

2. Draw the indifference curves between X and Y where:

   (a) An extra unit of X adds nothing to a consumer's satisfaction unless accompanied by an extra unit of Y.

   (b) The consumer may always be compensated for the loss of one unit of X by being given two units of Y, regardless of the proportions in which he is originally consuming them.

   (c) The consumer must be compensated for consuming extra units of X by being given extra units of Y, the amount of Y needed to compensate for consuming one unit of X increasing as the level of consumption of X increases.

3. Derive the relationship between the quantity of X demanded and the price of X if the consumer's indifference map vis-à-vis X and Y has curves concave to the origin.

   Let X be games of golf per annum and Y all other goods. Draw the indifference map and budget constraint of:

   (a) an amateur who pays to play golf; and
   (b) a professional who is paid to play golf.

   May we conclude that golfers turn professional because they dislike the game?

4. Draw the budget constraints and indifference map implicit in the following observations made in two different weeks on two different consumers. Assume in each case that all income has been spent on X and Y.

Consumer A week 1	Price of X	$2
	Price of Y	$1
	Income	$500 per week
	Quantity of X bought	100 units per week
week 2	Price of X	$2
	Price of Y	$1
	Income	$600 per week
	Quantity of X bought	80 units per week
Consumer B	Price of X	$2

week 1   Price of Y $1
                   Income $300 per week
                   Quantity of X bought   110 units per week

week 2   Price of X $2
                   Price of Y $1
                   Income $250 per week
                   Quantity of X bought   110 units per week

Is X an inferior good for consumer A or B? If someone told you that consumers A and B had identical tastes vis-à-vis X and Y would you be able to contradict him on the basis of the above information?

5. We observe the same consumer in two successive weeks.

week 1   Price of X   £10
                   Price of Y   £10
                   Quantity of X bought   10 units per week
                   Quantity of Y bought   10 units per week

week 2   Price of X   £5
                   Price of Y   £15
                   Quantity of X bought   7 units per week
                   Quantity of Y bought   11 units per week

Calculate his income in the two weeks on the assumption that he spends it all on goods X and Y. Do the above observations enable you to conclude that his tastes have changed between the two weeks?

6. Is it possible when there are only two goods, X and Y, (a) for Y to be both a substitute for X and a normal good, (b) for Y to be both a complement to X and an inferior good?

7. (With thanks to Mr. Leslie Rosenthal.) An individual is faced with a choice of buying housing in one of two markets: the private market where he may buy any amount of housing he pleases at the going price, and the public housing market where he will be offered, on a take

it or leave it basis, a particular amount of housing at a price lower than that which he would pay for it on the private market. Will he necessary choose the public housing? If he does, may we conclude that he will consume more housing than he would have purchased had he been forced to buy it on the private market?

8. The following observations are taken on a consumer's behaviour on two successive weeks.

week 1	Price of X	$10	
	Price of Y	$10	
	Quantity of X bought	10 units per week
	Quantity of Y bought	10 units per week
week 2	Price of X	$5	
	Price of Y	$20	
	Quantity of X bought	20 units per week
	Quantity of Y bought	5 units per week

Has the consumer's money income changed between the two weeks?

Calculate the Laspèyres Price Index for week 2 taking its value in week 1 to be 100.

Calculate the Paasche Price Index for week 2 taking its value in week 1 to be 100.

Has the 'cost of living' risen between week 1 and week 2?

9. Suppose that it costs 12 cents a mile in *direct* operating costs to run an automobile.

Let X be miles per week and P be measured in cents, and an individual's demand curve for automobile transport be given by

$P = 400 - 4Q$

(a) How many miles per week will he drive?

(b) How much consumer's surplus will he gain from operating his automobile?

(c) Would he be willing to pay a fixed cost, over and above variable costs, of $60 per week to operate his car?

(d) Suppose the direct cost of operating a car rose to $2 a mile because of an increase in the price of petrol. How would your answers to questions (a), (b) and (c) change?

Use the Marshallian demand curve assumptions in answering this question.

10. Starting with an individual's Marshallian demand curve for hours of television watching and the knowledge that each hour's watching uses a given amount of electricity, show how a fall in the price of electricity will affect:

(a) the amount an individual is willing to pay to rent a television; and
(b) the market demand curve for rented television.

11. Draw the two-period budget constraints implied by the following information.

(a) Income this period	$50	
Income next period	$50	
rate of interest	10%	
(b) Income this period	$50	
Income next period	$50	
rate of interest	5%	
(c) Income this period	$0	
Income next period	$105	
rate of interest	10%	
(d) Income this period	$0	
Income next period	$105	
rate of interest	5%	
(e) Income this period	$100	
Income next period	$100	
rate of interest	10%	
(f) Income this period	$100	
Income next period	$100	
rate of interest	5%	
(g) Income this period	$50	
Income next period	$165	
rate of interest	10%	
(h) Income this period	$50	

Income next period $165
rate of interest   5%

12. Show (a) that if an individual borrows by selling bonds at a particular value of the rate of interest, a fall in the rate of interest will make him borrow more; (b) that if current and future consumption are both normal goods, then if he borrows by taking out a fixed capital value loan, a fall in the rate of interest will also make him borrow more.

13. It is known that, were his current period's income increased by £100, an individual would increase his current consumption by £80. If the rate of interest is 10% what will be the effect on the same individual's current consumption of a guaranteed increase in his next period's income of £110?

14. Two individuals have the same tastes vis-à-vis consumption now and in the future and the same endowment of resources. One of them can engage in home production at a constant rate of return of 5%, but is excluded from the capital market to which the other has access and where the rate of interest is 6%. Can we predict which one will enjoy the higher level of consumption in the initial period?

15. Draw the budget constraints on the work/leisure choice implied by the following information.

(a) Non-wage income $100 per week
    wage rate $4 per hour
(b) Non-wage income $200 per week
    wage rate $2 per hour
(c) Non-wage income $200 per week
    wage rate for first 40 hours $2 per hour
    wage rate for hours above 40 $4 per hour
(d) Non-wage income   0
    wage for 40-hour week with no
    hours less than 40 permitted $120 per week
    overtime rate $5 per hour

16. An individual is known to increase the hours per week he works when his non-wage income is decreased. What will happen to the hours he works if (a) a proportional income tax is levied on his wage income; (b) a proportional income tax is levied on his total income; and (c) a proportional tax on his wage income is used solely to finance an increase in his non-wage income?

Would any of your answers differ if he was known to decrease his working hours when his non-wage income decreased?

17. An individual faces, and knows that he faces, a one in ten chance that his house, worth £60,000, will be completely destroyed by fire in the next year.

(a) He is offered an insurance policy against this risk at a premium of £6,000. Knowing that he experiences diminishing marginal utility of wealth, can we predict whether or not he will buy the insurance policy?
(b) Suppose the premium was £7,200. Could we then predict whether or not he would buy it?
(c) Suppose instead that he experienced constant marginal utility of wealth. Could we then predict whether or not he would buy insurance at either price?
(d) If the same individual thought that the chances of losing his house by fire were one in eight, would any of your answers differ?

18. It was asserted in Chapter 8 that a fall in the price of a particular brand of a good could lead to less of it being demanded. Where the good in question has but two attributes, L and M, (a) could this happen if L and M were substitutes for each other; and (b) must it happen if they are complements?

19. With price measured in $ per thousand units, and X being measured as thousands of units per week, a perfectly competitive industry faces a demand curve given by

$$P = 20 - 2X$$

and produces output at constant supply price of

$1 per thousand units

(a) Find (i) its output;
(ii) on the assumption that the area under the demand curve measures the total benefit accruing to consumers of X, the consumers' surplus accruing to purchasers of X.

(b) Now suppose that a single firm takes over the whole industry, and that $1 per thousand units now represents its long-run marginal and average cost of producing X.

Find (i) its output;
(ii) the price of that output;
(iii) the firm's profits; and
(iv) the consumer's surplus accruing to purchasers of X.

(c) Suppose a sales tax of 10 cents per thousand units is levied on X. Recompute your answers to parts (a) and (b).

(d) Suppose a maximum price of $1.20 per thousand units is imposed by government decree. Recompute your answers to part (b).

20. How will the imposition on firms of a fixed charge per annum for the privilege of operating affect (a) the price and output set by a monopolist, (b) the price and output of a competitive industry where all firms are equally efficient, (c) the price and output of a typical firm in that industry, (d) the price and output of an intra-marginal firm in a competitive industry in which some firms are more efficient than others? In each case analyse short- and long-run responses.

21. A law is passed fixing, below the level currently prevailing, the maximum price that can be charged by a monopolist who produces good X. He responds by increasing his output. Is this behaviour compatible with profit maximisation?

22. With price measured in £ per thousand units and X being measured in thousands of units per week, consider a monopolist producing X at a constant long-run marginal and average cost of £2 per thousand units, and selling to two groups of consumers whose demand curves are given by:

Group 1 P = 40 − 2X
Group 2 P = 20 − 2X

On the assumption that the monopolist cannot discriminate between the two groups find:

(a) his overall output;
(b) the price of his output;
(c) the amount he sells to each group of consumer; and
(d) his profits.

Calculate all outputs to the nearest 10 units and prices and profits to the nearest penny. On the assumption that he can discriminate between the two groups, recompute your answers to (a), (c) and (d), and also find the prices at which he sells to the two samples of consumers.

23. Suppose a firm had a natural monopoly in the production of electricity and could impose an annual rental charge at a rate chosen by itself for the use of a meter without which no electricity could be used. (a) If the firm wished to maximise profits should it set the price of electricity at marginal cost? (b) Suppose the firm was prevented by law from charging a meter rental charge. Should this affect the profit maximising price and output of electricity?

24. Consider a firm that sells as a monopolist in its home market and as a perfect competitor in export markets. Show (a) how its price and output will be determined in each market; and (b) how they will change if the currency of the home country is devalued.

25. With P measured as $ per thousand units and X measured as thousands of units per week, the market demand for X is given by

$P = 20 - X$

A group of small firms are able to provide X along a supply curve given by

$P = 2 + 2X$

(a) Find:
   (i)   the price of X; and
   (ii) the quantity of X.

(b) A large firm appears on the market which can produce X at a constant long-run marginal and average cost of $8 per thousand units.

   Find:
   (i)   the demand curve facing that firm;
   (ii)   the price and output of the firm;
   (iii) the firm's profit;
   (iv)   the overall output of X; and
   (v)   the quantity of X produced by the small competitive firms.

26. Consider a situation in which only one firm in a country produces a good X but in which foreign firms also provide X to the market under perfectly competitive conditions. How will the imposition of (a) a flat rate tariff, and (b) a ban on imports, affect the price, output and profits of the domestic firm?

27. Consider the industry described in question 19. Suppose that the monopolist who takes it over is a revenue maximiser instead of a profit maximiser. Recompute your answers to parts (b) and (c) of question 19.

28. What will be the effect on the following of fixing a minimum wage above the market equilibrium level: (a) employment in a perfectly competitive industry in which all firms are equally efficient; (b) the number of firms operating in that industry; (c) employment in a particular firm in that industry; and (d) employment in a firm that, prior to the fixing of the minimum wage, faced an upward sloping supply curve of labour?

29. A monopsonist in the labour market faces a relatively inelastic supply of female labour and hence pays its female employees a lower wage than its male employees even though the two groups are equally productive. What will be the effect on (a) the wage level paid to women; (b) the number of women employed; (c) the wage level of men; and (d) the number of men employed, of legislation forcing the firm to pay the same wage to all employees?

30. Suppose, at a given wage rate, there is unemployment in a particular competitive industry of a certain type of labour. Will government policies of (a) subsidising its wage, and (b) subsidising the rental price of capital equipment, result in an increase in the employment of that labour?

31. In a two-good, two-factor economy with a fixed quantity of factors, what happens to the transformation curve between the goods if a tax is imposed on the use of one factor in the production of one good (a) in a situation of perfectly competitive equilibrium in all markets in which there are no monopolies and no other taxes, (b) in a situation in which the use of the other factor in the production of the same good is already taxed?

32. (a) What assumptions must you make about the demand curve facing a monopolist in order to interpret the area under it as measuring the total gross benefit accruing to consumers from consuming his output?

(b) What assumptions must you make in order to interpret the area under his long-run marginal cost curve as measuring the total cost to society of having his output produced?

(c) If the area under a monopolist's demand curve did measure the total benefit to society of consuming his output and the area under his long-run marginal cost curve did measure the total cost to society of producing his output, would his profit maximising price and output decision result in the net benefit to society of his activities being maximised? Would your answer change if he were able to indulge in perfect price discrimination?

33. In an otherwise distortion-free, perfectly competitive economy, the production of X is monopolised and the firm producing X makes positive profits for its owners. Consider the effects on the distribution of income and allocation of resources of the following suggested actions: (a) taxing the profits made in the production of X and distributing them to the rest of the community; (b) subsidising the production of X so that the firm produces the level of output that would be produced by a competitive industry; (c) a combination of (a) and (b). Which action would you prefer to see taken? Would your preference be influenced by the knowledge that the owners of the firm in question were the otherwise penniless inhabitants of an orphanage?

34. Should airline operators be surcharged on their landing and take-off fees at airports, the proceeds being redistributed to the inhabitants of nearby houses as compensation for their being disturbed by aircraft noise? If aircraft are forbidden to operate from a particular airport at night, should airline operators be compensated for the resulting losses by a tax levied on the inhabitants of nearby houses whose amenities are thereby improved?

Supplementary Reading

References marked with an asterisk either deal with matters not fully covered in the text or are technically relatively difficult.

Chapter 1
Knight, F.H., Social and Economic Organisation, Ch. 1 of Breit, W. and Hochman, H.M. (eds), *Readings in Microeconomics*, New York (Holt Rinehart and Winston) 1968.

Part I
Hicks, J.R., *Value and Capital* (2nd edition), New York (Oxford University Press) 1946, Chs 1—3.

*Bailey, M.J., The Marshallian Demand Curve, *Journal of Political Economy*, 1954, reprinted in Breit and Hochman (*op. cit*).

Friedman, M., The Marshallian Demand Curve, *Journal of Political Economy*, 1949, reprinted in Breit and Hochman (*op. cit*).

Currie, J.M., Murphy, J.A. and Schmitz, A., The Concept of Economic Surplus and its Use in Economic Analysis, *Economic Journal*, 1971.

*Hicks, J.R., The Rehabilitation of Consumer's Surplus, *Review of Economic Studies*, 1941, reprinted in Arrow, K.J. and Scitovsky, T. (eds, on behalf of the American Economic Association), *Readings in Welfare Economics*, Homewood, Ill. (Irwin) 1969.

Marshall, A., *Principles of Economics* (8th edition), London (Macmillan) 1936, Book 3.

Part II
Robbins, L.C., On the Elasticity of Demand for Income in Terms of Effort, *Economica*, 1930, reprinted in Fellner, W. and Haley B.F. (eds, on behalf of the American Economic Association), *Readings in the Theory of Income Distribution*, Philadelphia (Blakiston) 1946.

Friedman, M., *A Theory of the Consumption Function*, Princeton, N.J. (Princeton University Press for the NBER), 1957, Chs 1—3.

Hirshleifer, J., On the theory of optimal investment decision, *Journal of Political Economy*, 1958.

Alchian, A., The Meaning of Utility Measurement, *American Economic*

Review, 1953, reprinted in Breit and Hochman (*op. cit*).

Friedman, M. and Savage L.J., The Utility Analysis of Choices Involving Risks, *Journal of Political Economy*, 1948, reprinted in Stigler, G.J. and Boulding, K.E. (eds, on behalf of the American Economic Association), *Readings in Price Theory*, London (George Allen and Unwin) 1953.

*Tobin, J., Liquidity Preference as Behaviour Towards Risk, *Review of Economic Studies*, 1958, reprinted in Mueller, M.J. (ed), *Readings in Macroeconomics*, New York (Holt Rinehart and Winston) 1965.

Auld, D., Imperfect Knowledge and the New Theory of Demand, *Journal of Political Economy*, 1972.

*Lancaster, K., A New Approach to Consumer Theory, *Journal of Political Economy*, 1960.

Part III

Coase, R.H., The Nature of the Firm, *Economica*, 1937, reprinted in Stigler and Boulding (eds) (*op. cit*).

*Heathfield, D.F., *Production Functions*, London (Macmillan) 1971.

Robinson, Joan, Rising Supply Price, *Economica*, 1941, reprinted in Stigler and Boulding (eds) (*op. cit*).

Viner, J., Cost Curves and Supply Curves, *Zeitschrift für Nationalökonomie*, 1931, reprinted in Stigler and Boulding (eds) (*op. cit*).

Part IV

Friedman M., The Methodology of Positive Economics in *Essays in Positive Economics*, Chicago (University of Chicago Press) 1953.

Cohen, K.J. and Cyert, R.M., *Theory of the Firm*, Englewood Cliffs, N.J. (Prentice-Hall) 1965, Chs 4–6, 10–12, *15–17.

*Heidensohn, K. and Robinson, J.N., *Business Behaviour*, Deddington, Oxon. (Philip Allan), 1974.

*Stigler, G.J., The Kinky Oligopoly Demand Curve and Rigid Prices, *Journal of Political Economy*, 1974, reprinted in Stigler and Boulding (eds) (*op. cit*).

Sweezy, F.M., Demand Under Conditions of Oligopoly, *Journal of Political Economy*, 1939, reprinted in Stigler and Boulding (eds) (*op. cit*).

*Baumol, W.J., *Business Behaviour, Value and Growth*, New York (Harcourt Brace Jovanovich) 1967.

Part V

Hicks, J.R., *The Theory of Wages* (2nd edition), New York (St Martin's Press) 1963.

Robinson, Joan, Euler's Theorem and the Problem of Distribution, *Economic Journal*, 1934, reprinted in Breit and Hochman (eds) (*op. cit*).

*Schultz, T.W., Human Capital, *American Economic Review* 1961, reprinted in Blaug, M. (ed.), *Economics of Education* (vol. 1), London (Penguin) 1968.

*Becker, G.S., Investment in On the Job Training, in Blaug, M. (ed.) (*op. cit*).

Part VI

*Johnson, H.G., *The Two Sector Model of General Equilibrium* (The Yrjö Jahnsson lectures), London (George Allen & Unwin) 1971, Chs 1 & 2.

Bator, F., The Simple Analytics of Welfare Maximisation, *American Economic Review*, 1957, reprinted in Breit and Hochman (eds) (*op. cit*).

*Bailey, M.J., The Welfare Cost of Inflationary Finance, *Journal of Political Economy*, 1956, reprinted in Arrow and Scitovsky (eds) (*op. cit*).

*Coase, R., The Problem of Social Cost, *Journal of Law and Economics*, 1960, reprinted in Breit and Hochman (eds) (*op. cit*).

*Henderson, A.M., The Pricing of Public Utility Undertakings, *The Manchester School*, 1947, reprinted in Arrow and Scitovsky (eds) (*op. cit*).

*Lancaster, K., and Lipsey, R.G., The General Theory of the Second Best, *Review of Economic Studies*, 1956.

Index